BASALT REGIONAL LIBRARY DISTRICT

99 Midland Avenue
Basalt CO 81621
927-4311

DATE DUE

MY 30 00			
AUG 1 9 '00			
DE 17 01			
FE 28 03			
JUN 2 3 2009			
GAYLORD			PRINTED IN U.S.A.

D0387908

The
Science
of
Happiness

UNLOCKING THE MYSTERIES
OF MOOD

Stephen Braun

John Wiley & Sons, Inc.

New York • Chichester • Weinheim • Brisbane • Singapore • Toronto

Published by John Wiley & Sons, Inc.

Published simultaneously in Canada

This publication is designed to provide accurate and authoritative information in regard to the subject matter covered. It is sold with the understanding that the publisher is not engaged in rendering professional services. If professional advice or other expert assistance is required, the services of a competent professional person should be sought.

Library of Congress Cataloging-in-Publication Data:

Braun, Stephen
    The science of happiness : unlocking the mysteries of mood / Stephen Braun.
       p.   cm.
    ISBN 0-471-24377-9 (alk. paper)
    1. Antidepressants.   2. Depression, Mental.   3. Happiness—Physiological aspects. I. Title.
    RM332.B73   2000
    616.85'27061—dc21   99-36213

Printed in the United States of America
10 9 8 7 6 5 4 3 2 1

To Susan

It is not for man to rest in absolute contentment . . .
He is born to hopes and aspirations as the sparks fly
upward, unless he has brutified his nature and quenched
the spirit of immortality which is his portion.

—Robert Southey, 1774–1843
Poet Laureate of England

Contents

—⁓—

Preface

I T WAS A LONG FLIGHT, AND I WAS IDLY FLIPPING
through an airline magazine to pass the time. My attention was arrested by the following headline: "Forget
Money; Nothing Can Buy Happiness." The short article
that followed said that although happiness has been
ignored by scientists for centuries in favor of its evil twin,
depression, it is now a hot topic of investigation. And the
current research strongly suggests that how happy we are
has more to do with our genes and our biology than with
such classic wellsprings as beauty, wealth, education,
health, and marriage.

The article pretty much left it at that—a brief, almost
lighthearted look at how science is corroborating the age-
old wisdom that "you can't buy happiness."

I put the magazine down and stared out the window.
Like a kind of intellectual lens, the short article snapped
into focus a set of questions that had been nagging me for
years. And as the implications of the article started to
seep in, I felt my pulse begin to quicken. Far from being
quasi-humorous fodder for bored airline passengers, the
idea that happiness has strong biological roots struck me

as being one of the most important and profound subjects imaginable.

Every human being, no matter what culture, age, educational attainment, or degree of physical and mental development, wants to be happy. It is the common end to which all humans strive—though the means we use to achieve that goal vary tremendously.

Our desire for happiness is profoundly powerful. It is composed of braided desires, hopes, and dreams that, themselves, can be overpowering. Our emotional cravings to love and be loved, our physical drives for sex, food, and drink, our urgings for artistic or scientific expression, and our spiritual hunger for meaning and comfort in a confusing universe all mix and mingle to produce a global and irresistible desire to be happy.

What, therefore, does it mean if this ultimate goal is the product not of our many vaunted efforts but of the architecture of our brains, the ebb and flow of our neurotransmitters, and the unique constellation of our genes? Are our choices in life, our efforts, and our experiences irrelevant to our happiness, or do they count for something? If so, what? If happiness is even only partially related to neurology, can we control our brains, adjust our neurotransmitters, and tinker with our wiring so that we might be happier than we are now?

I'm a medical writer with a particular interest in neuroscience—the study of the brain and how it works. In addition to covering the subject professionally, I've had the good fortune to actually work in a neuroscience lab. I've tinkered directly with living brain cells and with the incredibly sophisticated molecular machines that allow those cells to fire off the electrical and chemical signals from which human consciousness is woven.

From this somewhat unique vantage point, I have been watching for the past decade as two related branches of neuroscience blossom: neurophysiology and neuropharmacology. The one science is mapping and understanding how the brain works in all its phenomenal complexity, from the behavior of genes to the activity of brain modules that control such abilities as vision, language, memory, and emotion. The other science, fueled by the vast profits of the drug industry, is allowing scientists to construct new drug molecules with the ease and precision of engine parts. Using molecular blueprints from neurophysiology, drugmakers can now discover and bring to market molecules tailored to those blueprints like keys to specific locks, thus bringing an unprecedented rationality and precision to the business of making and selling mind-altering drugs.

The science of happiness connects these two powerful, epochmaking trends at the most personal level possible: at the level of everyone's own unique capacity for well-being and life satisfaction.

If it is true that happiness—like memory, emotion, or the capacity for abstract thought—can be located in some specific brain circuit or module, then it is only a matter of time before we understand that neural machinery in enough detail to craft molecules with which to control it. And then what? Will happy pills—true happy pills that are safe and effective—make the transition from science fiction to science fact the way submarines, spaceships, and wristwatch televisions have made the same leap? Will we soon be able to dial our happiness level the way we adjust a thermostat? What would that mean? What would life look like under those circumstances? Would it be a nightmare or a paradise?

These are the questions that set my heart beating that day in the airplane several years ago. And because of my background, I realized these were no mere academic questions. I knew it was not a question of *if* we will acquire a detailed knowledge of our happiness circuits, but *when*. And it is not a question of *if* new happiness-enhancing drugs will be found and sold. Such drugs are *now available,* and better, safer, more effective ones are being tested right now in drug-company laboratories around the world.

In short, we are not on the cusp of a revolutionary new age of pharmacology—we are *in* a revolutionary new age of pharmacology. And, for the most part, we are massively ill-equipped to make the decisions facing us. Despite many books about antidepressants such as Prozac, and an avalanche of media attention to questions of "cosmetic pharmacology" and "designer drugs," there is an almost complete lack of careful attention being paid to the issues at the bottom of those topics: the nature of the biological underpinnings of happiness, and the degree to which happiness can, or cannot, be found in a pill.

These are the issues that I explore in *The Science of Happiness*.

For the millions of people who are either using one of the new drugs or are contemplating such use, these issues have a particular urgency. Do these drugs really work? If so, *how* do they work? Is using drugs to enhance happiness unnatural? Is it really possible? Isn't it good to feel bad sometimes?

These are good, honest questions—and they are squarely addressed here with some perhaps surprising answers.

But I contend that *everyone*—not just those who have "mood disorders"—should consider such questions, because I believe that drugs are now available with the potential for use by "normal" people to subtly sculpt their mood and personality and enhance their overall capacity for happiness. "Normal" happiness is being redefined before our very eyes. And just as many people didn't realize they had eyesight problems prior to the invention of eyeglasses, so many people today don't realize they have mood irregularities that erode their happiness because they've never tried on the "glasses" of the new pharmacology.

I explore the science of happiness through the stories of real people—the story of a lottery winner, of a woman who could feel no pain, of a Zen Buddhist on Prozac, of a drug company's efforts to squelch a scientific report that would hurt its sales. I've used these true stories to put human flesh on the bones of the science.

The techniques with which I have reported and written these stories are old-fashioned: all names are real, unless otherwise mentioned; if I describe something, I either saw it myself, or it was described to me in a recorded interview; no people depicted are "composite" characters; no dialogue has been taken out of context or "telescoped" from separate interviews; and all of the science reported here was reviewed prior to publication for accuracy by the scientists I interviewed. I've provided a great deal of source information for those interested in pursuing these issues further.

Our increasingly sophisticated ability to control our moods more precisely, to shape our personalities, and to avoid unnecessary mental pain has the potential—as any technology does—for significant improvement in the world's health and well-being, or for a frightening loss of human dignity, freedom, and meaning. The key, as always, is learning to use the technology wisely. It is to that end that I have written this book.

— ∿ —

Acknowledgments

M<small>ANY SCIENTISTS AND MENTAL HEALTH PROFES-</small>
sionals took time from busy schedules to talk with me, often at length, about the ideas central to this book. I couldn't have written the book without their help. My thanks to: Sam Barondes; Jonathan Cole; Richard Davidson; Ed Diener; David Healy; Steve Hyman; George Koob; David Lykken; Robert McCrae; David Myers; Randy Nesse; Stephen Paul; Bob Postlewaite; G. Campbell Teskey; Robert Thayer; Gary Tollefson; Steve Triestman; Elliot Valenstein, and Mark Weber.

Gordon Russ and Lou Anne Jaeger were both most generous with their time, and I deeply appreciate their honesty and courage in sharing intimate aspects of their lives with a wide audience.

Ellie Baker, Tim Braun, Richard Brown, and Ann Jeffers read a rough draft of the manuscript and provided many extremely helpful comments and corrections.

I'm grateful to my agent, Gail Ross, for connecting me with an editor of uncommon insight and intelligence, Emily Loose of Wiley. It has been a pleasure working with her and the rest of the Wiley editorial and production team.

The Science of Happiness was written over a two-year period in the middle of which my second daughter, Aurora, was born. I would never have finished were it not for the unflagging support of my wife, Susan Redditt. My most profound thanks go to her.

CHAPTER I

Prozac: The Next Generation

ANYONE WHO DOUBTS THE POWER OF MOLECULES should visit Eli Lilly & Co. in Indianapolis, Indiana. Just south of the squeaky-clean city center sprawls Lilly's world headquarters—a complex of buildings dominated by a new administration building from whose apex snaps a white flag emblazoned with the red Lilly logo. The doors of the administration building are tall, and they swing heavily when you pull on their granite handles. Inside, a large art deco-style chandelier hangs over the circular reception desk, the light gleaming off the polished marble floors of the lobby.

The marble, the chandelier, the new state-of-the-art drug research facility behind the administration building—even the two-story brick replica of the building that Colonel Eli Lilly used when he founded the company back in 1876—all have been financed largely from the roughly $25 billion that has poured in from the sale of a single molecule. When it was first discovered, that molecule was dubbed compound 82816. Later it was given the generic scientific name fluoxetine, and still later the zippy commercial name Prozac.

Since going on sale in the United States in January 1988, Prozac has withstood blistering competition to remain the world's most-prescribed antidepressant. In 1997 it was the second highest-selling drug of any kind in the United States, and sales of this single molecular entity have accounted for 30 percent of Lilly's net sales in recent years.[1]

Unfortunately for Lilly, this goose that has been laying fabulously golden eggs is about to die.

Like all modern drugs, Prozac is patented. Drugmakers such as Lilly typically get exclusive rights to a molecule for twenty years—compensation for the enormous investment required to bring a drug to market. These days it commonly takes at least a decade and from $200 million to $500 million to discover a drug, test it in animals, test it in people, get it approved by the Food and Drug Administration, and ramp up the industrial production required to make it available at your corner pharmacy. And for every drug molecule that makes it to market, more than ten thousand are discarded along the development pipeline as unsafe, ineffective, or too laden with side effects.

The major U.S. patent on Prozac expires on December 2, 2003. At that point, generic fluoxetine will flood the market at a fraction of Prozac's current cost of about $2 a pill.[2] If the experience of other modern postpatent drugs is any indication, Prozac sales will then plummet. For example, sales of Zantac, once the reigning antiulcer drug, sank 37 percent in the year after its patent expired.

With the patent expiration clock ticking, Lilly is spending hundreds of millions of dollars in a furious quest to find another goose—a molecule more perfect than Prozac, more perfect at raising depressed spirits, reducing anxiety, promoting happiness, and more perfectly free of unwanted side effects.

Lilly scientists sound upbeat when discussing their new leads, their new discoveries about how antidepressant molecules work, and their candidate drugs now in testing. But they are nervous. Despite decades of effort by hundreds of scientists, they have not yet found the Holy Grail molecule that will supersede Prozac. And meanwhile other equally rabid drug companies are nipping at Lilly's heels, eager to bring down the current market leader with their own more perfect molecules.

More than a century ago, the great American philosopher and psychologist William James got right down to it: "How to gain, how to keep, and how to recover happiness is in fact for most men at all times the secret motive of all they do."

In James's day, happiness was seen as the fruit of a life well lived. The gaining, keeping, and recovery of happiness were viewed as direct results of effort: hard work, good decisions, sound education, moderate living, and a host of other activities under an individual's control. Happy people had earned their happiness. Sad, depressed, and demoralized people were likewise seen as having brought on their plight themselves. In this climate, if you suggested that happiness was, in fact, largely the fruit of genetic or biological factors or, even more radically, that drugs could facilitate the pursuit of happiness, you would have been branded an idiot at best, an immoral scoundrel at worst. The general distrust of drugs used for attaining pleasure or happiness has been called pharmacological Calvinism. Like Calvinism itself, pharmacological Calvinism is an ideology honored more in the breach than in the observance. Most people use drugs—alcohol, caffeine, and nicotine chief among them—to induce pleasure, ease pain, and modify their mood to fit their circumstances, all with the Jamesian goal of enhancing their happiness. And yet pharmacological Calvinism is deeply rooted in popular consciousness, and many people remain skeptical of using drugs to enhance or facilitate happiness, even while using such drugs on a daily basis.

One of the most powerful and memorable articulations of pharmacological Calvinism was delivered in 1931 by a sharp-witted young writer named Aldous Huxley. Imagining a world some six hundred years in the future, Huxley foresaw many problems, one of which was a side-effect-free drug he called soma. Soma provided a safe and welcome escape from the stress, pain, and emptiness of life in an overly technological, spiritually bankrupt, class-stratified society.

"Two thousand pharmacologists and bio-chemists were subsidized," Huxley wrote in *Brave New World*. "Six years later it was being produced commercially. The perfect drug. Euphoric, narcotic, pleasantly hallucinant. All the advantages of Christianity and alcohol; none of their defects. Take a holiday from reality whenever you like, and come back without so much as a headache or a mythology. Stability was practically assured."

Huxley's moral stance was obvious: soma was evil. By shielding people from uncomfortable truths, by numbing them to mental anguish, and by replacing "real" pleasures with artificial euphoria, soma robbed people of their human potential, encouraged passive acceptance of repressive rule, and created a fluffy, twinkling society full of smiles and lights and music but as insubstantial as cotton candy. In short, soma was the ultimate "happy pill," and Huxley saw nothing good in it.

In the years following the publication of *Brave New World,* Huxley became increasingly concerned that what he had envisioned happening six hundred years in the future was, in fact, coming to pass in his own lifetime.[3]

Although the world's attention in the 1940s was riveted by the blatant threats of totalitarianism and nuclear obliteration, Huxley foresaw a more subtle danger. In the foreword to a 1946 reprint of *Brave New World* he wrote: "The release of atomic energy marks a great revolution in human history, but not (unless we blow ourselves to bits and so put an end to history) the final and most searching revolution. This really revolutionary revolution is to be achieved not in the external world, but in the souls and flesh of human beings."

Huxley was referring to the fetal stirrings of two new sciences: genetics and pharmacology. A decade before James Watson and Francis Crick cracked the structure of

DNA, Huxley realized that an expanding understanding of genetics would confer the power to change human nature before birth by altering the genes from which we spring. His descriptions of deliberate human cloning in *Brave New World* were both prescient and chilling. And, with equal insight, Huxley saw that a similar explosion of knowledge about how the brain works would eventually grant us the power to change human nature *after* birth by creating drugs that precisely tinker with the brain's enormously subtle machinery.

An avid reader of scientific literature, Huxley followed the development in the early 1950s of the first antidepressant, a drug called Iproniazid. A chemical relative of antihistamine, Iproniazid was originally developed to combat tuberculosis. It was moderately successful in killing tubercle bacteria, but it was one of the drug's side effects that captured the attention of clinicians. A famous Associated Press photograph snapped at the Sea View Sanatorium on Staten Island, New York, in 1953 shows a group of tuberculosis patients clapping in a semicircle around two dancing residents. The residents were happy not just because their tuberculosis symptoms had abated, but also because of a direct energizing action of Iproniazid. Soon Iproniazid was tried on depressed patients— and some responded dramatically. Word got out of the new discovery, and Huxley was among the early people to understand its true import.

In 1958 he wrote a book called *Brave New World Revisited.* In it he said he was wrong about soma coming six hundred years in the future. In fact, he wrote, soma was already close at hand.

"The ideal stimulant—powerful but innocuous—still awaits discovery," he wrote. "Amphetamine, as we have seen, was far from satisfactory; it exacted too high a price for what it gave. A more promising candidate for the role of soma . . . is Iproniazid, which is now being used to lift depressed patients out of their misery, to enliven the apathetic and in general to increase the amount of available psychic energy. . . . The man who takes the new pill needs less sleep, feels more alert and cheerful, thinks faster and better—and all at next to no organic cost, at any rate in the short run."[4]

Huxley—and many doctors—were wrong about the lack of "organic cost" with Iproniazid. In fact, this antidepressant and the dozens of others that followed it had many side effects, some of which were occasionally lethal. But Huxley's description of Iproniazid matches well the image most people now have of Prozac and the host of Prozac-wannabes, drugs such as Paxil, Zoloft, Remeron, Celexa, and Serzone. All of these drugs lift some patients from misery and make them more cheerful, alert, and quick thinking. And, though their use is hardly universal the way Huxley imagined soma to be, these drugs *are* used in massive quantities. In 1997 antidepressants, led by Prozac, held three spots in the top-ten best-selling U.S. drugs list.[5] Prozac alone has been prescribed to more than 34.5 million people. Tens of millions of others use one of the other antidepressants. Children now account for a significant fraction of antidepressant users. In 1997, for instance, nearly 600,000 children and teens were prescribed Prozac, Paxil, or Zoloft—and the numbers of young people getting prescriptions are rising rapidly.[6]

Still, many experts argue that depression remains both underdiagnosed and undertreated.[7] Another aspect of twenty-first-century antidepressant use that reminds some people of *Brave New World* is that today's antidepressants are often used by people who would never in the past have been diagnosed with a disorder. Today the line between mental illness and normalcy has become blurred to the point that a fully functioning, relatively happy person can walk into a doctor's office, complain vaguely of periodic low mood or low energy, and walk out with a prescription for Prozac, or Xanax, or Ritalin. I know this not only from extensive interviewing, but also because I did exactly this during the writing of this book. (I describe this experience in the epilogue.)

Formally approved "subsyndromal" or "subclinical" states such as dysthymia—a prolonged period of low mood that doesn't reach the level of "true" depression—provide medical labels for shadings of personality that an earlier generation considered within the spectrum of normal human personality. Today that spectrum has narrowed, and the way that unhappiness fits into that spectrum is shifting. Unhappiness is being redefined from a normal pole of human mood to a distinct disease state. Sometimes the message from drug companies or popular advertising seems to be that *no* unhappiness is normal—that unhappiness, as well as true depression, is, like diabetes, a biological dysfunction correctable with drugs.

"We're being led to believe that you're never supposed to feel down or unhappy," says Steven Treistman, a psychopharmacologist at the University of Massachusetts

Medical Center who specializes in the neural mechanisms of mood-altering drugs. "I see it in the media. The other day, in fact, it seemed like every other ad had people dancing crazily, as though that's the way people normally live. It's amazing when you start to pay attention to it . . . happy dance, happy dance everyplace. Which would certainly make you think that if you weren't feeling that way, something's wrong with you. So I think the concept that you're supposed to be happy all the time is a shift."

As the line between clinically sanctioned unhappiness (in the form of mild dysthymia, for instance) and "normal" unhappiness becomes ever murkier, it becomes easier to view the use of drugs to enhance happiness as legitimate, rational, and moral—the exact antithesis of pharmacological Calvinism. This cultural shift, along with stunning advances in the twin fields of brain research and pharmacology, mean that Huxley's "really revolutionary revolution" is upon us. The "souls" of human beings truly are being changed by drugs. The great question is whether there's anything wrong with this.

Pharmacological Calvinism is, indeed, crumbling— but for a very good reason, namely that people are discovering for themselves that Huxley was wrong about soma. Iproniazid wasn't really soma. Prozac isn't soma. In fact, even if it were available, it's doubtful that many people would even *want* soma.

Huxley's soma was like heroin or cocaine without side effects or addictive potential. Huxley thought that eliminating these negative aspects would cause people to flock to the "improved" drugs. The end result, he feared, would be a facade of happiness rather than the real thing: the smile without the soul, the weather without the clouds, the pie without the filling. It's undoubtedly true that a safe heroin would prove popular with people looking to escape pain, oppression, boredom, or a host of other negative life situations. But there are many reasons to think that such a drug would *not* be widely used and would *not* result in the zombie society of *Brave New World*.

Why? Because from a purely pragmatic standpoint, uninterrupted bliss simply doesn't work. It's not sustainable, it doesn't facilitate health or well-being, and it results in a profound schism between self and reality. What Huxley missed was a Darwinian perspective on emotions and on happiness itself. He didn't appreciate that happiness and unhappiness have adaptive value.

Natural selection has forged in the human brain a complex set of finely honed emotional responses that guide behavior toward survival and reproduction and away from pain, death, and a lack of progeny. Happiness and unhappiness act as internal barometers of our overall Darwinian fitness level—they are vital capacities that must sensitively respond to our environment if they are to function correctly.

Artificially induced happiness unrelated to one's life situation, therefore, is inherently maladaptive. Such a state inevitably degenerates because it cuts off contact with the many societal, relational, and motivational cues a person needs to adjust his or her behavior to achieve sustained periods of true well-being.

Nature provides a fascinating real-life example of this basic dynamic in the form of a particular dysfunction of mood called manic-depression, or bipolar disorder. People with this condition repeatedly cycle between periods of intense exuberance in which they feel supremely confident, cheerful, optimistic, and energetic to equally intense periods of brooding self-loathing, pessimism, cynicism, and lethargy. Manic periods, although they occasionally produce creative brilliance such as the paintings of Van Gogh, the music of Beethoven, or the poetry of Byron, are most often unproductive and self-destructive. The soaring high always crashes, not only because of the internal malfunction in the neural machinery of mood regulation but also because of an accretion of ill effects caused by behavior that is radically decoupled from reality. Passionate affairs ruin marriages, savings are drained, debts soar, employers are insulted, friends are snubbed. In short, the manic person, although perhaps feeling supremely happy for a while, becomes less and less capable of sustaining a balanced well-being.[8]

The danger of classic happy pills has thus been overrated—by Huxley and by many people today. Happy pills—even theoretical pills free of side effects—are self-defeating and ultimately extinguish their own use.

Society's current love affair with antidepressants such as Prozac suggests a much more interesting and complicated possibility than the one Huxley envisioned. Drugs such as Prozac have been telling us for the past twenty years that happiness—not the canned happiness of cocaine or heroin or soma but *true* happiness—*can* be delivered in little cream-and-green capsules, at least for some people, some of the time. Taking an antidepressant such as Prozac gives some people access, for the first time in their lives, to the full spectrum of human emotions.

Rather than decoupling them from reality, the restoration of emotional functions allow for a much tighter and satisfying contact with the environment.

Unshackled from their neurological manacles, "good responders" to antidepressants can appreciate the scent of a rose for the first time. They fall in love, engage in creative work, raise children, and find spiritual connection. Such people—and they are as yet a minority of those who try antidepressants—would laugh at Huxley's fear.

Unlike the fast-acting soma, antidepressants work slowly—usually taking from a week to a month to "kick in"—and they produce little or no euphoria.[9] The change wrought by Prozac and other antidepressants is a shift in consciousness that varies from user to user but that typically includes a shift away from depressive thoughts and toward increased emotional stability and resilience, and a general increase in a sense of zest or vitality. Most important—and most unlike soma—Prozac and other antidepressants are not wholesale erasers of negative emotions such as anger, sadness, fear, and anxiety. Indeed, one of the deep ironies of antidepressant drug therapy is that to be fully effective the drugs must not *eliminate* depressive feelings; they must restore some functional balance to one's emotional repertoire and provide the user with enough capacity for negative emotion to ensure that they don't crash and burn after a blaze of unchecked manic glory.

When they work well antidepressants do not provoke mania, they restore emotional stability and, in a very real sense, make people happier—truly happier. And yet as miraculous as antidepressants can occasionally be for people suffering from depression, obsessive-compulsive disorder, and a host of other mental maladies, they are still relatively crude drugs compared to the drugs to come. The real story, therefore, isn't that we're drugging ourselves into happy zombies with somalike drugs but that we're using more subtle and interesting drugs in the pursuit of *real* happiness. These drugs are rapidly becoming safer, more effective, more perfect. And their easy availability will accelerate the redefinition of "normal" happiness and unhappiness, much as the discovery and widespread use of eyeglasses in the seventeenth century redefined "normal" vision as 20/20 rather than the previously wide range of visual acuities.

Are there any dangers to such mass tinkering with the machinery of our minds? What is the ultimate goal of this vast, unplanned experiment in pharmacology? Most fundamentally, what is this perfect drug that everybody—citizens and drug companies alike—so avidly seek?

Well before Prozac hit the market in 1988, Eli Lilly knew their drug had problems. Not lethal problems. Not the alleged problems of increased risk for suicide and violence that Prozac has been falsely accused of over the years. Just the normal, frustratingly familiar problems that plague all antidepressants to one degree or another: a long lag time before the drug "kicks in"; low efficacy; and an array of side effects that, while much less dangerous and troubling than previous generations of antidepressants, are still significant. (The chief selling point of Prozac wasn't that it lifted spirits faster or for more of the people who tried it, but that it was safe in overdose and had fewer side effects than previous antidepressants.)

But even as clinicians were switching patients to Prozac by the hundreds of thousands, Lilly was looking for ways to improve on their molecule—in particular, looking for ways to avoid the jitteriness, stomach upset, insomnia, and sexual problems that many users complained about.[10]

These problems remain unsolved by Lilly pharmacologists.

"We'd like an antidepressant that a larger percentage of patients achieve a response to," says Gary Tollefson, the Lilly scientist most directly in charge of leading the high-stakes search for a successor to Prozac. "We'd also like to see that response be more robust. Also, we'd like to see a greater ability to improve sleep hygiene and have a more rapid or robust anti-anxiety effect. And if we could reduce the incidence of adverse gastrointestinal and sexual dysfunction effects, that would be a plus as well. I think we have leads on at least two or three of these key areas, leads where we think we have a substantive advance so that we can have a credible story in the marketplace about an upgrade from the fluoxetine molecule."

Tollefson and other Lilly scientists don't reveal specifics when they talk about their leads. Security in the drug industry is tight, and scientific information is zealously guarded. An information leak about the structure or function of a candidate molecule could cost a company hundreds of millions of dollars. A case in point: Only two weeks after I visited the Lilly labs and extensively interviewed several scientists about the direction of drug research, Lilly announced the development of a new form of Prozac that the company hopes will take the sting out of Prozac's patent expiration—a development nobody so much as hinted at during my visit.

This new strategy is, at best, a stopgap measure to buy time while the company continues the quest for a truly better Prozac. Lilly has teamed up with a small Massachusetts company called Sepracor to develop a "purer" form of Prozac. Many molecules in nature come in two mirror-image varieties called isomers. Although chemically identical, isomers are structurally different in the same way that a right hand is different from a left. Often this difference changes the way in which the molecules behave in the body. For example, amphetamine comes in two isomers, one of which (the "dextro" form) is a potent stimulant (hence the derivation of the brand name "Dexedrine"). Lilly hopes that the "R-fluoxetine" will better reduce anxiety than the mixed-form fluoxetine now sold as Prozac, or that it will have fewer side effects. The definitive study of these points—a phase III clinical trial involving hundreds of participants—is now under way.

Lilly desperately needs a short-term Prozac "upgrade" because it has taken longer than anyone imagined to find the drug that will be a quantum jump improvement on Prozac. Creating this drug has turned out to be a scientific challenge on a par with solving the genetic code, putting a human on the moon, or creating an AIDS vaccine. Finding a molecule that works better, faster, and with fewer side effects than Prozac is simply one hell of a challenge.

First of all, Lilly scientists cannot perform experiments

on human beings. If it were possible to give trial drugs to humans, then remove their brains and study them with extensive chemical analyses, drug discovery would be vastly accelerated. Since people tend to want their brains left intact, Lilly scientists, like all psychopharmacologists, must use animals.

But animals—even very intelligent animals such as monkeys—make poor models for human mood disorders. Even if animals do experience a mood state analogous to human depression (a reasonable but hard-to-prove assumption) it is not clear how you can induce this negative mood at will, which you must do repeatedly and reliably if you want to test candidate drugs for alleviating the bad mood. How can you tell if a monkey (much less a rat, a mouse, or a pigeon) is depressed? How can you then tell if a drug has eased that depression?

"It's a huge challenge," says Christian Fibiger, the Lilly vice president in charge of its formidable research labs. Talking to me from across his tidy desk, Fibiger looks calm. His eyes twinkle from time to time behind his glasses, particularly when he says—which he often does—that he can't tell me about this or that because it is a competitive secret. At these times he smiles like a poker player with an ace up his sleeve. And yet he has no illusions about the difficulties he faces . . . and the lack of a good animal model is chief among those.

"How are we going to know that a particular molecule may not be the next great breakthrough in the treatment of depression?" Fibiger asks. "It would be easy if we had a good animal model for depression. We'd use it and find a molecule that works and then we're off to the races. But we don't have that. I think whoever can figure this out is going to have a huge competitive advantage."

Another major hurdle to progress in perfecting antidepressants is that the target of mood-altering drug molecules—the human brain—is the most complicated thing in the known universe. The organ that generates mood, perception, memory, self-awareness, and consciousness itself is a biological machine comprised of at least one hundred trillion information-processing units—neuronal synapses—and these units are wired up into circuits of enormous complexity that involve feedback, inhibition, stimulation, and delayed reactivity. Despite the enormous strides made in the past decade of neuroscientific research, many mysteries remain about brain function.

But the most fundamental obstacle to building a better Prozac is the relatively recent appreciation among pharmacologists that the disorder they are trying to cure—depression—is not a single entity at all. Instead, "depression," like "cancer," is a single word describing a variety of different disorders with fundamentally different roots. Depression comes in many forms: some depressed people overeat, can't sleep, and feel anxious. Other depressed people lose their appetites, sleep too much, and feel dismally calm. The various forms of depression undoubtedly arise from different causes, some primarily biological, some primarily psychological, and most from a mixture of the two. In short, depression has turned out to be a Hydra-headed beast, and the continued use of a single diagnostic label for this beast frustrates people such as Fibiger no end.

"The current approach to the diagnosis of depression is what somebody called a Chinese menu approach," he says. "You know, if you have one symptom from column A and one more from column B and one more from column C, then you end up with a diagnosis of depression. It is quite possible, given the current way of doing psychiatric diagnosis, for two depressed patients to not share a single symptom. That's remarkable to me. And if they don't share a single symptom, my question to the clinicians is why in God's name would you think they share any common biology?"

Given these barriers and the fact that to this day nobody really knows how antidepressants work, it is nothing short of miraculous that drugs such as Prozac work as well as they do. It is equally remarkable that Lilly scientists, and others outside of the drug industry, are optimistic that the various obstacles will be overcome and that more perfect antidepressants will, indeed, be found.

"It's a first-class and very difficult biological problem," says Steven Hyman, a Harvard neuroscientist who now heads the National Institute of Mental Health. "But the drugs are going to get better with fewer side effects, absolutely."

Despite the cloak-and-dagger secrecy of the drug industry, hints are everywhere that progress is being made in understanding the neurobiology of depression—and its flip side, happiness.

For instance, in a classic example of scientific serendipity, Lilly researchers accidentally discovered that if they gave a seriously depressed person both Prozac and Lilly's antischizophrenic medicine Zyprexa, the person starts feeling better within a week—much faster than he or she responds with either Prozac or Zyprexa alone.[11]

"In treatment-resistant disease, where you would think you would be the least likely to see a rapid onset of action, there was a very clear early onset of mood improvement," Tollefson says. "This is a case where we're retro-engineering from clinical observations back to the lab bench to try to understand what is unique about that combination and to set the stage for new drug molecules to be developed."

Another example of surprising progress in finding better antidepressants comes not from Lilly but from the labs of one of its corporate archrivals: Merck. In 1998 Merck published a technical paper in the journal *Science* announcing the discovery of a molecule that raises mood in an entirely different manner from any other drug on the market.[12] The molecule works by blocking a compound called "substance P." Although it was known for years as a chemical messenger of pain impulses throughout the body, nobody thought substance P had anything to do with mood. But it does, and Merck's preliminary data suggest that its drug may raise mood with fewer side effects— particularly sexual side effects—than the current generation of antidepressants. Merck's announcement shows that surprises remain in store for neuroscientists and that new knowledge can lead to better happiness-enhancing drugs.

Merck, Lilly, and a dozen other drug companies are locked in a furious race to find and market such improved drugs. The company that best plumbs the neurobiological machinery of happiness and can craft molecules that tweak this machinery in the right direction stands to reap huge profits. The discovery of a more perfect antidepressant may also free millions of people from dysfunctional and painful mood states. This altruistic side of the picture is real, and it motivates many drug industry workers. But the inevitable development of a more perfect happiness-enhancing drug raises a host of serious questions, and answering them requires a healthy skepticism toward the purely biological disease model of mental health and mental illness promulgated by the drug industry. Despite a genuine commitment to ease human suffering among many people in the drug industry, and despite the positive potential of future drugs, the fundamental engine driving the rapidly expanding field of mood pharmacology is fiscal, not philosophical.

As I write this, it isn't clear which company will win the race to the next Prozac—or even whether such a drug is possible. Lilly has at least four molecules in late-stage clinical trials. Other companies have their own candidates. The only certainties are that the race is on and that the contestants are making progress in their effort to win the grand prize: the fortune that will come from a more perfect happiness-enhancing drug.

Society has not yet come to grips with the current age of pharmacology. The technology of drug-making carries as much potential and as much peril as other epoch-making technologies such as atomic energy, computer science, or genetic engineering.

In 1946 Albert Einstein said, "The unleashed power of the atom has changed everything save our modes of thinking."[13] The same thing could be said today of the unleashed power of psychopharmaceuticals.

Set against the very real advantages of newer, better drugs for reducing anxiety, lifting mood, and stabilizing emotion are the very real dangers that such drugs will be used unwisely, inappropriately, and for the wrong ends. Similar hazards exist for other types of drugs, such as cholesterol-lowering agents, antiulcer drugs, and medications that lower blood pressure. These drugs, too, can be abused or simply used unwisely. Many people understandably want a quick, easy way to address a particular medical challenge such as high cholesterol. Also understandably, they would rather pop pills for the rest of their lives than alter their diet or exercise more to lower their cholesterol and blood pressure. Nothing is easier than swallowing a pill, nothing harder than changing a lifestyle.

Viewing conditions such as high cholesterol and high blood pressure as medical illnesses with strictly biological causes and pharmacological cures is a comforting perspective for those who would like to avoid changing their eating habits, exercise, or work patterns, and it rationalizes the use of pills as solitary treatments. In reality, of course, these disorders and other "diseases" such as diabetes, osteoporosis, and even cancer usually arise from a combination of genetic, biological, and lifestyle factors.

But no company stands to make billions of dollars when people make healthy choices in their lives, so there are few massive, sustained advertising campaigns mounted to promote these ideas. Instead, people are "educated" about the real but limited biological factors in such conditions, while little attention is given to lifestyle factors. Such advertising or drug-industry promotion efforts may state the truth, but it is seldom the whole truth.

This active and often insidious dynamic applies equally to the field of psychopharmacology, but an added dimension here makes this issue far more compelling, complicated, and hazardous than the usual issue of wise use of medications.

Like drugs to lower blood pressure or cholesterol or to soothe ulcers, antidepressants are marketed using a disease model. Unhappiness—ranging from the fuzzy border with normal sadness to the absolute desperation of clinical depression—is routinely described as an illness caused by an imbalance in brain chemicals called neurotransmitters. Antidepressants are described as cures for this illness because their immediate effects are to alter the levels of neurotransmitters. This is a cartoon of reality simplified to the point of absurdity, as even drug company scientists will admit. Depression actually *isn't* caused merely by low levels of neurotransmitters, a fact examined in more detail in chapter 3.

This type of factual distortion in the course of drug marketing is a problem, but not really a problem qualitatively different from that posed by the unbalanced characterization of other diseases as purely biological problems or the promotion of other drugs using oversimplified ideas.

What sets antidepressant drugs apart and makes an inquiry into drug company assertions about their value and effectiveness so vital is that these drugs act directly on the very organ we use to decide whether to take drugs. Unlike antihypertensives, antiulcer drugs, and all other types of drugs, antidepressants have the unique power to change our *attitude* toward things. They can change the degree to which we *care* about issues—issues such as the appropriate use of new drug technologies. It is not that antidepressants turn people into passive idiots. They don't. In fact, sometimes antidepressants can clarify thinking, improve perception, and enhance powers of discrimination.

But the drugs can also induce a subtle insensitivity that may, or may not, be helpful. If a drug lessens sensitivity to rejection or to emotional manipulation, all for the better. But if the same drug reduces concern about personal cleanliness or the feelings of others, problems can arise. Both of these types of insensitivities have been reported by people using Prozac and other antidepressants.

The point is that drugs that tinker with the machinery of the mind invite a higher level of scrutiny than drugs that tinker, say, with the machinery that regulates cholesterol level, blood sugar, or immune response. Other drugs may indirectly or transiently affect mood, but mind-altering, or psychotropic, drugs directly change mood, outlook, cognition, and other ingredients of personality over long periods of time.

What if using atomic energy somehow altered how concerned we were with nuclear energy production and nuclear weapons? What if using the products of the chemical industry changed our ability to rationally and objectively evaluate the use of pesticides and carcinogenic chemicals? Suddenly fields already fraught with difficult, confusing issues would become much more complicated, sensitive, and unstable.

Will the large-scale use of antidepressants make society more or less willing to use such drugs? Will it make us more or less willing to look critically at the potential hazards of the technology? Will it impair or improve our ability to accurately judge the effects of such use?

We have not yet considered carefully enough the nature of these drugs, the reality of their powers, and the potent forces shaping our attitudes toward them. For millennia, humans have used drugs such as alcohol and caffeine to tinker with their moods. Now the science of pharmacology is delivering drugs with much more power and precision. What will we do with them? Granted that Huxley's soma is *not* the perfect drug. Then what is? Most fundamentally, to what degree is happiness really a matter of brain chemicals, genes, neurotransmitters, and drugs? Can newer, more perfect drugs really enhance happiness and enhance human potential without ensnaring us in chemical traps of our own creation?

To ask such questions is not to be antidrug, and this book is by no means a diatribe against drugs or the drug industry. As readers of my first book, *Buzz: The Science and Lore of Alcohol and Caffeine,* know, I use and enjoy the traditional drugs of alcohol and caffeine. I believe that there are many times when we should say "yes" to mind-altering drugs. Drugs are tools that can be used well or badly, and I've seen examples of both uses among people I care about.

But I also believe that mind-altering drugs deserve special consideration among the many new technologies facing us. The capacity of such drugs to alter our percep-tion of the drugs themselves, coupled with the unprecedented power of multinational drug companies to frame the debate about drugs via their advertising and marketing efforts warrant unusual scrutiny, unusual skepticism, and unusually tough-minded interrogation.

With *The Science of Happiness* I want to pick up this interrogation and explain what is known about the new pharmacology of happiness, because I believe such an examination is a vital first step toward wise use of the coming generation of drugs.

I did not fully appreciate the seriousness of these questions when I began this book. A book about future mood drugs was a logical next step from my first book— a look at the science and lore of our two most ancient (and still most popular) drugs.[14] But the more I dug into this issue, and the more scientists I interviewed, the more I realized how underreported and misunderstood these issues are. For example, one of the people I met early in the project was Randolph Nesse. As a practicing psychiatrist who must decide daily whether to prescribe antidepressants and other mood-altering drugs, he has had firsthand experience with the complexities of the new pharmacology. And as a professor at the University of Michigan at Ann Arbor, he has spent decades thinking hard about the evolutionary roots of mental illness and the subtle ways in which nature has designed human emotion, human mood, and happiness itself. He is among many who view the advent of the new pharmacology of happiness as one of the most pivotal issues of our time.

"One scenario I can envision is the world being a happier place," he says. "I think that's one possible outcome.

But turn me around and ask me to look in the other direction and I can see the whole world's population having human nature changed artificially by drugs in ways that leave us all completely confused about what happiness even is anymore. I really think this may be one of the biggest issues facing the world. Even what's happening with computers and information technology over the next couple hundred years may not have as much of an impact on us. And nobody seems to get it. I mean this is one of the hottest things happening in the culture today."

The story of mankind's coming ability to manipulate happiness with drugs must necessarily begin with a look at happiness itself and the degree to which it is a function of biology. And that story begins with a lottery ticket.

CHAPTER 2

Set Point

T HE LEAVES OF THE SUGAR MAPLES AND THE BIRCH and the ash growing on the edge of the Buckland town dump flamed with mid-October color. The dump was an old gravel pit carved from the side of a hill that sloped down into a swamp. Gordon Russ, a muscular man with quick blue eyes and a Butch Cassidy mustache, heaved his bags of garbage into the pit. "Ridiculous," he thought. Ridiculous that this dump is so primitive . . . the rainwater soaking through the accumulated garbage, seeping into the swamp, and then lacing one of the finest trout streams in Massachusetts with God knows what. The town had no recycling plan—unless you counted the beer and soda bottles people returned for a nickel each.

But what could he do about it? He flung the last of the bags. Nothing. He was busy. It was 1990. He was thirty-eight and second in command of a nearby factory that kept about 150 people employed making bleached cotton for products such as cotton balls, sterile gauze dressings, and tampons. The job often kept him working past dinner-time, and sometimes part of a weekend. And he was married, with a five-year-old daughter, Karlyn, and a son, Jordan, who was making good progress now after a perilous start a year and a half earlier as a one-pound preemie.

Russ grabbed a six-pack of empty Miller Lite bottles and headed to the Shelburne Falls liquor store, owned by his friend Scott.

At the store Russ swapped the empties for a new six-pack, and almost as an afterthought, he picked up a packet of free state lottery tickets. The Massachusetts lottery was running a promotion. Six free tickets for the six different games the state used to fish for people's money. Russ never took the bait himself. But these were free, so what the hell?

That was Saturday, October 13. When he got home, he took a thumbtack, stuck the tickets to a cork board in the kitchen, and forgot about them.

On Monday evening, Russ thumbed through the local paper—the *Greenfield Recorder*. In the back was a small story about an unclaimed lottery ticket. The winning ticket in the state's Megabucks game had been traced to Scott's store. The paper quoted Scott saying that in all likelihood, the ticket had been picked up by a leaf-peeper—an out-of-state tourist come to admire the fall foliage. Russ put down the paper.

"Well, let's check and see," he thought.

In the middle of the pack he found the Megabucks ticket. All six numbers lined up with the number that was in the newspaper. He called to his wife, who was in the back bedroom.

"Hey Lynn, come here," he said. "Take a look at this. What's wrong with this?"

Lynn walked out, took one look at Gordon and said, "You're white."

Russ called the liquor store. The clerk asked him for the code on the back of the ticket. "Uh, yeah . . . that's the one," the woman said. The jackpot was worth $2.2 million dollars.

"I couldn't eat. I walked between there and there," he says, recalling the incident and pointing to the walls of the high-ceilinged family room just off the kitchen. "I paced, very much like a caged animal, thinking, 'Oh, no, oh, yes' . . . and it scared me . . . scared me to death. Thinking tomorrow I'm going to go down there and I'm gonna get the first installment of two million dollars . . . and what do I do?"

The next morning, Gordon's boss from the plant drove by early to meet him. "Congratulations," he said. "But don't leave now." Gordon assured him he wouldn't.

Much later that day, after driving three hours to Boston to accept a check for $102,000—the first of twenty yearly installments—and driving three hours back with his friend Scott, back to the wooded hills of the Berkshires and back to his simple wood house with the barn out back and the surrounding orchard of eighty-eight Macintosh apple trees, he told the flock of reporters milling at the foot of his driveway that he thought he'd buy some clothes with the money . . . maybe take a trip to the Caribbean. But that's about it. He didn't want the money to change things.

Gordon Russ pauses a moment. It's early spring. We're sitting at his kitchen table talking about his win, and he's looking out the window at the budding apple trees. Was he different than he was eight years ago, before he became a millionaire? Well, yes and no. Had he changed? Yes. But as he sat looking out at the tall pine trees just beyond the orchard, he remembered something that had changed him more than the bigger numbers in his bank account.

Happiness has been variously defined, but perhaps the simplest way of looking at it is the one adopted by David Meyers, a professor of psychology at Hope College in Michigan who has made the study of happiness his life's work. Meyers says happiness is "an enduring sense of positive well-being." The difference between happiness and pleasure, which can certainly *feel* like happiness, is one of duration—happiness being rather like a long-term version of pleasure.

As William James pointed out, everyone pursues happiness—whether consciously or unconsciously—and many people seek happiness through the attainment of various goals: a college education, good health, a loving partner, a rewarding job, social status, or desired material possessions.

By far the most avidly sought means to happiness is money. Despite "poor little rich girl" clichés and innumerable morality tales about the impotence of money as a way to happiness, most people intuitively feel that if they only had enough money, most of their problems would be solved. Asked by researchers what would improve the quality of their lives, the answer most frequently given in survey after survey is "more money." Not more friends. Not more love. Not more status. More money. In one study, people were asked how satisfied they were with thirteen different aspects of their life, including things such as their friends, their schooling, and their homes.[1] The thing participants were *least* satisfied with of all thirteen aspects was the amount of money they had to live on.

As Gordon Russ's story will illustrate—and as careful research corroborates—money can, indeed, contribute to well-being, and certainly the complete absence of money constrains opportunities, exacerbates poor health, increases stress, and has other effects that demonstrably erode happiness. But decades of accumulated research into the nature of happiness proves that, contrary to people's gut instincts, happiness has little to do with money and other external factors. Instead, how happy people are seems to depend on something a good deal more mysterious: an inner quality that allows people to experience happiness regardless of their external circumstances, as long as those circumstances are not completely corrosive or impoverished.

Scientists have found that the link between happiness and the things most people *think* bring happiness is stunningly weak, while the link between internal factors such as outlook, temperament, and personality are robust. This is a crucial insight. If happiness is a function of money and love and stress reduction and education, then the whole notion of using drugs to induce or enhance happiness would be a waste of time at best, and counterproductive at worst. But a huge amount of data demonstrate that external factors have a very limited impact on happiness.

Money is a fine example. If money could buy happiness, then people living in wealthy countries should be happier, on average, than people living in poor countries. The biggest and best study of this question was conducted over several years in the late 1980s.[2] More than 170,000 people in sixteen nations were repeatedly surveyed using standardized questionnaires and interview protocols. It turned out that average happiness levels among countries had little to do with how much money the people in those countries made. West Germans, for instance, made almost twice as much on average as the Irish, but the Irish were significantly happier. Belgians tended to be happier than their wealthier French neighbors, and the Japanese, while among the wealthiest people, were also among the least satisfied.[3]

What about the related question of whether, in any particular country, the rich are happier than the poor?

Psychologist Ed Diener and his colleagues at the University of Illinois at Urbana tested that belief by giving standard psychological tests of well-being to forty-nine of the wealthiest Americans and forty-nine people making only average incomes.[4] The result? On average, the rich were only marginally happier—and many were much less happy than those making far less money. Many more extensive surveys have replicated this finding. Once people's basic needs for shelter, food, clothing, and health have been met, additional wealth has very little power to increase happiness.

Further corroboration of this fact comes from the National Opinion Research Center, which for more than thirty years has been tracking key aspects of American life. Two of the things they measure every year are personal income and self-reported happiness. In 1957 the average annual income was about $7,500. In 1990 that figure had doubled to about $15,000, after adjusting for inflation. Although $15,000 doesn't sound like much, it is significant because it represents a *real* doubling of income. With twice as much money in our pockets, you might think people would be at least *somewhat* happier. But in fact, while the income trend in the past thirty years has shot up, the happiness trend has been virtually flat: people's overall happiness over the years hasn't budged.

The last line of evidence proving that money can't buy happiness—or not much, anyway—comes from lottery winners such as Gordon Russ.

In the late 1970s researchers subjected twenty-two major lottery winners and twenty-two "normal" (i.e., non-lottery-winning) people to extensive batteries of psychological tests and interviews.[5] They compared the overall happiness levels of the winners and the "normals" and also gauged how much pleasure each group, on average, derived from everyday events.

The lottery winners and the controls "were not significantly different in their ratings of how happy they were now, how happy they were before winning (or for controls, how happy they were six months ago), and how happy they expected to be in a couple of years," the study said.

In addition, the lottery winners rated seven ordinary activities such as talking with a friend, watching television, hearing a joke, and buying clothes, as *less* pleasurable than the controls did. Not only were they no happier than "normal" people, in other words, but also the lottery winners experienced less pleasure from daily events.

The explanation for this last observation is that happiness is, to a certain extent, relative. People constantly compare their life circumstances to those of people around them, to their own recent experiences, and also to their beliefs and expectations about what they *think* their lives should be like. This largely unconscious and continuous comparison can cut both ways: compare yourself with others less fortunate, or with other, more difficult times in your life, and you'll feel happier. Compare yourself to people who have more of what you want or with the "glory days" of your own life, and your current situation will dim and feel inadequate. Because life circumstances are constantly changing, the reference against which you measure your happiness changes as well, which is one reason why happiness is a moving target.

Another explanation for the quicksilver nature of happiness is that humans are geniuses at adaptation. We rapidly adjust to new situations. Our desires and our satisfaction levels seem to automatically change to match our changed circumstances. Adaptation is particularly relevant to the quest for wealth: unless you are among the handful of multibillionaires, there are almost always things priced beyond your reach. A once-coveted $500,000 house can become standard once obtained, and $1 million houses begin to look even better.

The twin phenomena of adaptation and the relativity of happiness explain why lottery winners derive less pleasure from ordinary life events—at least in the months following a win. They adapt rapidly to their new situation, and daily events pale relative to the burst of euphoria and high emotion of winning.

Lottery winners usually continue pretty much as they always did—except they may have new houses or cars or jobs.

"Most people wouldn't believe how ordinary my life is," says a twenty-six-year-old woman who won $87.5 million in the Idaho state lottery. "I'm out of the National Guard and in school full-time, so my typical day consists of going to classes, doing chores, and playing with Nicholas. A sitter watches him when I'm at school. My idea of a great time on a Friday night isn't club-hopping but hanging out at home with my best friend, Sheila, eating take-out Chinese, and watching *The X-Files*."

And although some winners quit their jobs, most don't. One study found that only 23 percent of lottery winners leave the job they were in when they won. And even if they do quit, most winners keep working, either by returning to school or by pursuing other work more in line with their interests.

Psychologists such as Diener and Meyers have found that being rich isn't the only thing people tend to wrongly assume equates with happiness: the young are not happier than the old, men are not happier than women, Caucasians are not happier than African Americans, and the college-educated are not happier than high-school dropouts.

What *does* correlate with happiness are strong social connections, long-term loving relationships, a sense of optimism and openness to new experiences, the opportunity to pursue meaningful work, and spiritual belief or identification with an issue or idea larger than oneself. Such variables account for some, but by no means all, of the differences in well-being reported by people. It's important to understand, however, that these are simply correlations.

It's not at all clear whether an optimistic outlook, satisfying work, and friends make for happy people, or whether happy people are simply more likely to be optimistic, enjoy their work, and form strong friendships. Which is cause, and which effect? Does some innate level of happiness drive life events, or do life events drive perceived levels of happiness?

A specific example of this conundrum is determining whether marriage fosters happiness or whether happy people are more likely to marry. A National Opinion Research Center survey of more than thirty-two thousand Americans reveals that 40 percent of married adults but only 24 percent of never-married adults say they are "very happy."[6]

But does marriage enhance happiness, or are happy people simply more likely to marry and stay married?

"The evidence suggests that the causal traffic is two-way," Meyers told me in an interview. "On the one hand, happy people tend to attract and retain marital partners. Misery may love company, but research on the social consequences of depression reveals that company does not love misery. A depressed (and therefore self-focused, irritable, and withdrawn) spouse or roommate is no fun to be around."

On the other hand, Meyers points out, if happier people are more apt to marry, then the happiest people would tend to marry first, leaving older, less happy people to marry later. But, in fact, surveys find no difference in the happiness levels of people who marry early or late.

"This suggests that marital intimacy, commitment, and support really do—for most people—pay emotional dividends," Meyers says.

This is a specific case of a general pattern: happiness arises from a continuous interaction between one's environment (relationships, work, physical health, upbringing) and one's temperament, the inborn tendency toward optimism or pessimism, cheerfulness or dourness, introversion or extroversion. Internal factors such as energy level, openness to new experiences, and emotional resilience can powerfully shape life events, including the quality and character of the relationships a person forms. It is not hyperbole to say that to a certain extent, people create their own environmental reality—and it is created in their own image.

In recent years, these mysterious internal factors have been getting a good deal of attention. Data have been piling up for years suggesting that temperament is genetically based, is extremely stable over the long term, and powerfully affects happiness. Life events may push people temporarily toward elation or depression, but relatively quickly, normal mood returns. And this "normal mood" appears to come from inside, not outside.

A major source of these data is the National Health and Nutrition Examination Survey.[7] In this study, almost seven thousand men and women were interviewed extensively between 1971 and 1975. Ten years later, almost five thousand of these people were tracked down and interviewed again.

"We found that the people who are relatively happiest now will be the happiest ten years from now, despite the day-to-day fluctuations," says Robert McCrae, a research psychologist at the National Institute on Aging who analyzed the data with colleagues Paul Costa and Alan Zonderman. "The forty-year-old who is cheerful, enthusiastic, and fun-loving is likely to become a cheerful, enthusiastic, and fun-loving eighty-year-old."

The study looked carefully at people who experienced significant life changes such as divorce, bereavement, change of jobs, retirement, or moving out of state. None of these changes affected people's well-being over the long term.

To push their theory to the limit, the researchers zeroed in on forty-nine subjects who experienced *all three* major life changes during the study period: they moved to a different state, changed marital status, and changed employment status. But even with these people, overall well-being was strikingly similar to what it had been ten years earlier.

This research demonstrates that most people have long-lasting and stable levels of happiness and well-being, and that this average mood level is surprisingly unaffected by things traditionally thought of as being precursors of happiness.

The stable point around which an individual's mood oscillates has been called the "happiness set point." The nature of this set point—where it comes from and whether it can be changed—is now the subject of intense study, because if the set point is at least partially a biological phenomenon, biological interventions such as drugs can change it.

It was early November 1990. Three weeks earlier, Gordon Russ had won $2.2 million with a lottery ticket he didn't even buy. Now it was his thirty-ninth birthday, and he was going to celebrate in a big way.

Even though it was Saturday, he drove to work that morning to finish up the fourth-quarter inventory. As he had promised his boss, he had continued to work. The company needed him—and he wanted to work while he figured out what to do with his windfall. He knocked off around noon and drove home, along the valleys and then up into the hills and along the dirt road that leads to his house.

It was a beautiful day—clear and unseasonably warm. Almost seventy. He pulled in, parked the car behind the house, and began helping with party preparations. He got out the croquet set and the grill, and set out a tub of ice for the beer.

Many of his friends were already there, hanging out near the house beside the orchard. It was going to be a special party.

Gordon had always wanted to fly, and recently he'd been taking lessons from a buddy named Rick. The two of them would drive in the afternoon to Northampton, hop in Rick's plane, fly the length of the Hudson River at two hundred feet, circle the Statue of Liberty, and be home for dinner. Along the way, Rick would teach Gordon how to do snap rolls, inside loops, outside loops. Gordon was getting the hang of it.

Rick was good enough that he often entered stunt flying competitions and air shows. That weekend he was doing the New England Air Show circuit competition, so he offered to give Gordon and his guests a private show, right over the property.

By two o'clock, all the guests had arrived, including Rick's wife and one-year-old son. On schedule, Rick came by, flying low over the trees in his new Super Decathlon stunt plane. He did a full show—a spectacular display of fast rolls, loops, and turns. Gordon and his guests were thrilled.

On his final pass, Rick came in low—lower than ever—roaring in at treetop level, roaring so close you could see his face clearly through the cockpit glass, roaring in a beautiful snap roll right over the picnic table where his wife sat, roaring off, over the orchard and out over the tall pines behind them.

But not quite over. In the blink of an eye, the right strut of Rick's landing gear caught the top four feet of one of the pines. As everyone watched, the plane flipped and crashed in a fireball fueled by forty gallons of one-hundred-octane low-lead fuel.

"I ran in here and got the fire extinguisher," Gordon says. "We ran out there, but . . . nothing . . . we couldn't get within a hundred feet of it. I mean the forest was on fire. It was a fabric airplane. Gasoline everywhere . . . it was just an explosion. They didn't take Rick's body out of there . . . there was nothing, you know . . . nothing left."

Gordon was in shock for days.

"I wasn't focused. . . . I wasn't able to do my job. . . . I'd find myself just, bang. . . . All of a sudden I was junk. . . . I'd just be crying."

The accident spurred him to renege on his decision about work.

"The next day I told the owners of the company that life's pretty short and it's time to do something else. So let's put together a transition package and I won't strand you without a production and inventory manager, but I'm gonna go spend some time with my kids because I just saw how quick it ends."

Within a few months, the trauma of the accident was gone—though its painful memory was etched permanently in his brain. And for the next four years Gordon Russ, millionaire, spent his days doing the laundry, taking his kids to school, vacuuming the house, feeding the dogs, and living a relatively ordinary, relatively happy life.

But eventually he grew restless.

One day he read that a member of the Buckland board of selectmen was stepping down. Russ ran unopposed for the post, and as soon as the ballots were counted he began working on a pet project: the dump. He became a "landfill czar." Working six and seven days a week, he eventually found the $900,000 needed to safely seal the old dump and create a solid-waste master plan that included an aggressive recycling plan. In 1998 his tiny town of Buckland had the best recycling record of any town in the state, with fully 73 percent of municipal waste diverted to recycling and away from incinerators and landfills.

But after two years of nearly nonstop work, he took a break from his brief political career. By this time Russ's bank account had fattened considerably. Between his wife's salary and his meager wage as a selectman, he was saving most of his winnings. He didn't need to work . . . but when his former boss asked him to oversee the out-of-state move of the plant, he jumped at the chance. Nineteen months later, Gordon watched as the last batch of cotton was run through the 167-year-old factory.

Now, only ten days after that official closing, Gordon is already getting itchy.

"I'm a little bit of a lost soul right now," he says, stretching his legs under the kitchen table. The south-facing room, which he designed himself to take advantage of solar energy, has grown hot with the spring sun as we've talked. I ask him if he's changed in the past eight years.

"Everybody's got their day-to-day issues," he says after a moment. "Money will take some of the pressure off some of those, and it's done that, I acknowledge that. But day-to-day, my concerns are the same as most parents in Franklin County. I don't think there's been any quantum shift pre- to post-lottery win in my day-to-day approach to people and my life and responsibilities. I think I'm very much the same."

The happiness set point is a kind of neutral mood point that is roughly the average of all the moods someone experiences in a given period of time. The idea can be conveyed by creating a simplistic mood scale ranging from abject depression and sadness at the bottom to the heights of euphoria and happiness at the top, and plotting mood over time.

In reality, moods and emotions are generated by independent brain circuits, the outputs of which can mix and overlap in complex patterns that can't be captured on a simple 2-D scale. For instance, you can be sexually aroused, nervous, and happy at the same time. An additional complicating factor is that to a certain extent, happiness and sadness appear to be somewhat independent mood states that are generated by two separate but linked brain areas. Usually, activity in one of these modules inhibits activity in the other, which means that usually when we are happy we are not sad. But under certain circumstances, *both* brain modules may be active, giving rise to a blended emotion that also can't be adequately portrayed on this type of graph.

Despite these qualifications, a cartoon happiness/ depression scale can roughly approximate mood swings over time. The pattern of the fluctuations shows both randomness, due to vagaries of life such as traffic jams and interpersonal conflicts, and rhythms caused by regular patterns of rising and falling energy, wakefulness, and tension. As a result, a typical mood chart looks pretty erratic:

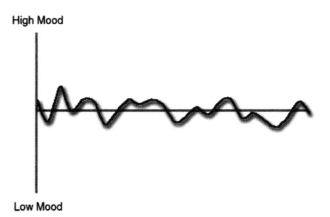

Of course, people vary in the pattern of their moods. Some people, for example, experience only mild and infrequent mood swings:

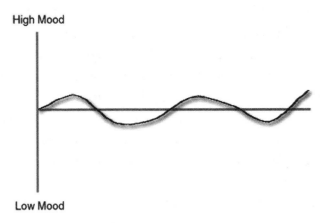

High Mood

Low Mood

Others display great variation in moods, and their moods cycle rapidly from day to day:

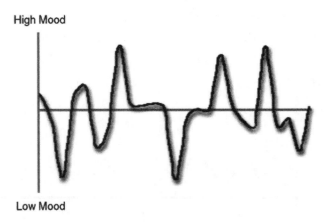

High Mood

Low Mood

Extreme patterns of mood and emotional response are usually dysfunctional. For example, some people suffering from autism have virtually no emotional reactivity. Their mood states are extremely flat, and they have great difficulty perceiving and responding to the emotional cues from people around them. At the other extreme are those suffering from manic-depression, for whom mood swings uncontrollably from a deep and suicidal depression to a giddy and equally self-destructive exuberance. Most people, of course, fall somewhere between the extremes. In all cases, however, there is a midpoint around which the moods cycle—the set point.

Scientists find that people return to their set point relatively quickly following major mood-altering events such as the crash witnessed by Gordon Russ.

"We find that for events like being promoted or losing a lover, most of the effect on people's moods is gone within three months, and there's not a trace by six months," says psychologist Diener.[8] In general, he says, the more extreme the mood-provoking event, the longer it takes to restore a set point baseline mood. Losing a spouse, for example, may take a year or longer to recover from. And very rarely, extreme events such as torture, sexual abuse, long isolation, or war can be so mentally devastating that a person never fully recovers their set point—though it's also true that many people *do* recover emotional health even from the most horrific ordeals.

The capacity to recover normal mood rhythms following either bad or good events appears to be an inborn, hard-wired trait that has been shaped by natural selection.

"Nature uses a sort of carrot and stick method to get us to do what she wants us to do," says David Lykken, a behavioral geneticist at the University of Minnesota who has done extensive research on the happiness set point with coworker Auke Tellegen. "But it would not serve her purpose if either the effects of punishments or reward were to last too long. So if you win the goal you feel great for a while, but after some time, a few months, winning the lottery doesn't mean anything to you. And similarly people who have terrible things happen, loss of loved ones or crippling accidents such as the one suffered by Christopher Reeve, six months to a year later people are back to where they were before."

As with other traits, people vary dramatically in their emotional sensitivity to life events. Psychologists call this "affect tolerance"—the ability to tolerate swings of emotion without denying, repressing, or avoiding them. Some people are capable of experiencing and processing both joyful events and depressing events relatively quickly and easily. Others require much longer times than normal, and the transitions are more difficult.

Diener, Lykken, and others have found that no *universal* set point exists. Everyone oscillates around their own, private set point, which is simply the average of their long-term moods. Some people move around a lower-than-normal average mood, experiencing manic-like highs very seldom, if ever. Others swing around a set point considerably higher than normal, seldom experiencing melancholy and endowed with unusual energy and levity much of the time.

Intriguingly, the *average* human set point appears *not* to be at a neutral spot midway between euphoria and depression, as one might expect. Most people's set points, in fact, are slightly *above* neutral. On average, in other words, most people are moderately happy.

In every single national survey of well-being ever conducted in the United States (and there have been dozens), people on average have reported a positive level of subjective well-being, which is the clinical term for "happiness." For example, a 1976 study found that about 84 percent of respondents scored above neutral. A 1988 study found that *all* socioeconomic groups, and both whites and African Americans, scored well above the neutral point on life satisfaction.[9]

The phenomenon appears to hold worldwide. Studies in France and Japan show that in every year data were collected, the average scores for happiness were above the midpoint of the scale. In an exhaustive compilation of data from different countries conducted in 1993, the average happiness levels in thirty-seven of the forty-three nations studied were above neutral. On a scale from 1 to 10, with 1 being most unhappy and 10 most happy, the overall average from all nations was 6.33.

"Most people are not elated most of the time—they are just mildly happy," Diener reports.

It's true, of course, that happiness is difficult to measure objectively. It could be, for instance, that people say they are happier than they really are. But scientists have found that self-reports of people's own happiness accord well with independent measures of their well-being, such as the opinions of family members and friends, or assessments by trained psychologists. Another reason to trust the finding of a slightly higher-than-expected human happiness set point is that it makes good evolutionary sense.

First of all, a slightly happy baseline makes negative mood states such as fear and anxiety stand out more clearly in consciousness, the same way that a dark object is easier to see against a light background.

"A positive set point gives negative events maximum information value because they stand out as figure against a positive background," says Diener. "A system that is preset to be slightly positive allows threatening events to be noticed quickly."

Second, a generally positive mood enhances survival. Being in a good mood, in other words, makes it more likely that an animal will look for food, mates, and other things, behaviors that scientists call "approach tendencies."

"Approach tendencies must prevail in behavior for people to obtain food, shelter, social support, sex, and so forth," Diener says. "Because positive moods energize approach tendencies, it is desirable that people on average be in a positive mood."

Diener thinks that our built-in slightly positive average mood has played a key role in our success as a species.

"Human approach tendencies are manifest in the rapid exploration and settlement of new frontiers and in the unremitting invention of new ideas and institutions throughout human history," he says. "Thus, not only might humans' large brains and opposable thumbs be responsible for the rapid spread of humanity across the globe, but positive emotions might also be an important factor."

As previously mentioned, it is important not only to have a slightly positive baseline but also to have moods that return fairly quickly to the baseline following either elation or despair.

"It is necessary," Diener says, "to be able to feel negative emotions when a bad event arises. These events grab people's attention, and they act. Then they return to a slightly positive to moderately positive state. Note that very few people are extraordinarily happy. Few people stay ecstatic and euphoric. This is also not a functional state. One is too happy, and therefore one cannot become happier when something good happens. Nothing can serve as a reinforcer; nothing can produce greater pleasure. So the most functional set point is somewhat positive. But extreme and long-lasting elation or depression is dysfunctional."

The slightly positive average human happiness set point amounts to a built-in pair of rose-tinted glasses through which most people gaze without realizing it. An interesting consequence of this arrangement is that "normal" people are actually *less* accurate in many of their perceptions about themselves and their prospects in the world than people who are depressed.

In a paper titled "Painful Truths about Depressives' Cognitions," the social scientist C. Layne writes:

"Empirical research indicates that depressives are cognitively realistic, while nondepressives are cognitively distorted. . . . Normals appear to be less in touch with reality than are depressives. Normals are even less in touch than are depressed outpatients and even hospitalized inpatients! The major implication of the empirical literature is that depressives' thoughts are painfully truthful, whereas nondepressives' thoughts are unrealistically positive."[10]

Research shows that depressed people have a realistic—but maladaptive—awareness of their limitations. They better predict their performance relative to others on a task, they better understand the limits of their control over the outcome of games of chance, they are more accurate at monitoring and assessing their own skilled and unskilled social behavior, and they judge themselves responsible for both past successes and failures rather than seeing themselves as more responsible for their successes than for their failures.

The prevailing evidence, then, shows that humans have an internally generated happiness set point that is calibrated for most people at a slightly positive level, and that this set point mood and mood-regulating mechanisms account for both the long-term stability and evanescent nature of happiness.

In recent years the genetics of the happiness set point have been explored using the experiences of identical twins. Such twins offer one of the best opportunities for teasing apart the influences of genes and environment on mood and temperament. Since identical twins share identical genes, measuring their happiness levels over time and comparing them with happiness scores from nontwins provide a window into the genetic contribution to the happiness set point.

That experiment was recently completed by Lykken and Tellegen of the University of Minnesota. The result was a resounding testament to the power of genes.[11]

"Our estimation of the heritability of the set point is about 80 percent," Lykken says. "So that's a very strong value and I think that's not an unreasonable estimate."

Lykken and Tellegen looked at the scores for twins who had been raised together and compared them with twins who had been separated at birth and raised in different families. The results were practically identical, reinforcing the view that genes, not parenting, or schooling, or learning, are the primary shapers of the happiness set point.

Lykken's 80 percent estimate is the highest ever reported. Other studies suggest lower heritabilities, usually between 50 percent and 60 percent. But no studies have found that genes account for *less* than half of the variation in emotional traits, well-being, or the happiness set point.

Finding strong evidence that happiness levels are controlled by genes is not, of course, the same as understanding what those genes are or how they work. Despite the astonishing progress of the Human Genome Project—the effort to map all of the approximately one hundred forty thousand genes that encode human beings—it will take years to figure out what all those genes do and how they interact to give rise to complicated phenomena such as happiness, intelligence, and personality.

But one thing is already clear: happiness is not controlled by a single gene, the way Huntington's disease or sickle-cell anemia is. Dozens, perhaps hundreds or thousands of genes contribute to this broadest of all traits, and those genes undoubtedly interact in complicated ways.

"Unlike the heritability of stature, where all of the genes involved seem to contribute in a small additive way, and how tall you are is a function of how many tall genes you have, these traits like happiness seem to be based on a kind of configuration of genetic factors rather than a sum," Lykken says.

If 50 percent to 80 percent of our happiness set point is locked in our genes, what does that say about our efforts to maximize happiness? At the end of one of his scientific papers on this topic, Lykken suggested that trying to be happier may be as futile as trying to be taller.

"I regretted that as soon as I saw it in print," he says now. "It was sort of a smart-aleck statement and I really don't believe it."

Lykken, Diener, Meyers, and others believe that, in fact, genes leave plenty of room for the exercise of free will and the pursuit of happiness via such traditional and well-founded routes as establishing long-term relationships, finding satisfying work, and maintaining good physical health.

Happiness is not *purely* a matter of genes and neurotransmitters. Environment matters, especially when one's environment is damaging, limiting, or otherwise negative. In the face of injustice, abuse, malnutrition, prejudice, and poverty, nobody's innate happiness set point will predominate. Genes exert their most powerful influence on happiness, in other words, only when one's environment is otherwise benign—when one's basic needs have been met. This means that efforts to reduce stress, improve relationships, achieve peace and justice in society, and enhance health are vitally important and cannot be trivialized. Like Abraham Maslow's famous hierarchy of needs, such things as health, education, and love are necessary foundations for happiness, even if they are not in themselves sufficient for its attainment.

But scientists studying happiness acknowledge that their research suggests that these efforts are not all-powerful. They are constrained by the biological foundation of the happiness set point. Temperament, outlook, emotional resilience, affect tolerance, energy, and a capacity to engage in life's challenges are all rooted in neurochemistry, in the flux of neurotransmitters, and in the health and complexity of one's neural machinery.

Drugs are a direct, focused way to manipulate that machinery. For millennia, humans have used drugs such as alcohol, cocaine, and amphetamines to tinker with the machinery in order to increase pleasure or to dull pain. But such drugs are primitive, and their actions are so misunderstood that by and large they have been stupendously ineffective in helping people achieve lasting well-being. Transient pleasure, yes. Happiness, no. Often, of course, such drugs *erode* well-being through addiction, brain damage, stress, and a myriad of other negative consequences.

But drugs such as Prozac, Zoloft, and Remeron are different, and the ones on the horizon are even more so. These drugs can alter the happiness set point—at least for a minority of users—in helpful ways, and often make that adjustment with a minimum of side effects. In short, when they work well, they are true happiness enhancers.

Where is this trend headed? What are the limits, if any, to direct mood manipulation? Will it really be possible to adjust one's happiness set point with the precision of a thermostat? That depends critically on the nature of the neural machinery at the heart of this matter. Thousands of scientists in drug company labs around the world are probing this machinery, trying to figure out how it works so they can design better, more effective tools to change it. Already that work has produced some surprising results.

CHAPTER 3

The Machinery
of Mood

W HAT HAPPENS IN PEOPLE'S BRAINS WHEN THEY
take Prozac? How can a drug change their outlook on
life? Why are scientists even considering the possibility of
a drug that will enhance or facilitate happiness—both for
those with clinical depression and those now considered
"normal" who, although perfectly "functional," seldom
feel the zest, the poise, the sense of deep meaning that
others seem to have?

Answers to these questions come from the field of
neuroscience—the study of the brain. The explosion of
neuroscientific research has laid the empirical foundation
for the related explosion in the development of more perfect mood-altering drugs. Out of that research has come

a clearer understanding of how the mind works, where moods come from, and how drugs such as Prozac may work.

The most basic message of modern neuroscience is one that many people still have some difficulty accepting: that the brain is a biological machine and that who we are, or who we think we are, is the product of that machine. It's easy to think otherwise: the sense that "we" are separate from our bodies is very powerful. When "we" remain unchanged despite accidents to our bodies—even despite the use of drugs such as alcohol and caffeine, which can temporarily skew our personalities, we acquire the sense that our "true" selves—our "soul"—is a kind of immaterial ghost that inhabits our physical body the way water fills a sponge.

Most people, of course, recognize that this ghost "lives" in the brain. Clearly people's personality, memories, and attitudes don't change when they injure a leg, have a heart transplant, or lose an arm. But damage the brain, and it's another story. People watching as a loved one's brain erodes from Alzheimer's disease will talk of "losing" the person long before that person's body actually dies. Likewise, if the custard-soft brain gets slammed hard enough against the rock-hard skull in an accident, personality can be permanently changed.

Despite these facts, it remains difficult to look at a wet, wrinkled, dull-looking brain and see a machine of such enormous complexity and subtlety that it is capable of producing something as holy and splendid as a human soul.

This is what tripped up the great French thinker René Descartes. Like most people, he couldn't shake the strong sense of himself as an immaterial being inhabiting his body, and yet he, too, was faced with obvious evidence that the brain was necessary to support this being. After much thought, some laborious intellectual gymnastics, and a dash of pure whimsy, he decided that the soul—the true "us"—connects to the brain via the pea-sized pineal gland buried deep within it. This was patently absurd, but such was the fame and respect accorded to Descartes that the explanation survived for many years.

Today the "mind/body" problem that so tortured Descartes is old hat—a minor exercise in introductory philosophy courses.

Descartes's problem was that in the seventeenth century nobody guessed what a remarkable lump of tissue the brain is. Now we know better. The brain is, indeed, a machine—but a machine built on a vastly different scale than those with which we are familiar. Even today, when a hundred million transistors can be crammed onto a computer chip the size of a thumbnail, the brain's machinery is impressive. First of all, an average three-pound brain contains roughly 100 billion working brain cells, or neurons. This is such a staggeringly large number that the brain itself has difficulty grasping it. Nonetheless, the sheer number of parts of our cerebral machinery doesn't begin to convey its true size and sophistication.

Neurons communicate with one another with delicate, treelike extensions called dendrites and axons. Generally speaking, a neuron "listens" to incoming signals with its dendrites and "talks" to other neurons by sending signals out along its axon. A single neuron can "listen" simultaneously to as many as 50,000 other neurons this way. And each of those connections—actually, tiny gaps called synapses—is a vitally important link in the brain's information-processing abilities. In fact synapses—not whole neurons—are the fundamental unit of information storage and manipulation in the brain—the brain's equivalent to a transistor.

A better estimate, therefore, of the brain's true size can be found by multiplying 100 billion neurons by 1,000— a rather conservative average of the number of dendritic connections each neuron makes with another. The result? A hundred trillion synapses. A hundred trillion functional units. As one neuroscientist quipped, "A hundred trillion synapses—hell, you can do anything with that. That's more than enough to contain a soul."[1]

But even this number doesn't fully capture the brain's phenomenal power. That's because, unlike a computer chip, the brain's circuitry is malleable. The brain's "wiring" is sculpted by experience. New synapses form, old ones disappear. Information streaming in through our eyes, ears, and other sense organs is captured when the connections between neurons change in a split second, forming new and unique circuits. This is how memories form and how thoughts can be manipulated. Consciousness itself is a rippling, ever-changing flux of electrochemical activity skittering across hundreds of thousands of discrete neural nets that themselves consist of thousands or millions of simultaneously firing neurons.

Thus the true measure of the brain's complexity isn't just the raw number of neurons or synapses in the brain at any given point in time, but the total *possible* number of connections—the number of ways in which these billions of neurons can be linked into discrete patterns. This number can't be reliably estimated, though it is widely viewed as so staggeringly large that for all practical purposes it might as well be infinite.

This is why Descartes couldn't fathom how his brain could generate himself pondering his own brain. He didn't understand just how mind-bogglingly intricate the brain is. It didn't help that he was also confusing two different kinds of properties.

Neuroscientists today view the mind as an emergent, nonmaterial entity arising from the working of a living brain. The mind is what the brain does, in other words. Emergent qualities are not uncommon. The plot of a story is an emergent quality of the individual words in a book. The words are physical, the plot is nonphysical. (Wednesdays, truth, beauty, and pi are other examples of nonphysical but still perfectly real entities.)

The mind—and by extension that core of self-awareness and memory that we call "ourselves"—emerges from the coordinated firing of billions of individual neurons. In some ways, then, we *are* like ghosts—but we are created by and are utterly dependent on a ghost-producing machine: the brain. One obvious implication of this situation is that changing the machinery can change *us*.

This brings us to drugs such as Prozac and the newer, more perfect descendants on the horizon.

Prozac and other antidepressants, unlike short-acting drugs such as alcohol and caffeine, seem capable of shifting personality—at least for a minority of users. The term "cosmetic pharmacology" was coined precisely because these drugs can sculpt personality the way some people reshape their faces, thighs, and buttocks. This power to zero in on and tinker with the neural machinery at the very core of who we think we really are is what some people find troubling about antidepressants. (Many others, of course, embrace the changes wrought by antidepressants and feel that, far from being "cosmetic," the drugs have literally saved them from a hopeless, suicidal depression and have helped restore them to their "normal" selves.)

When they work, antidepressants somehow punch the right buttons, move the right levers, adjust the right neural dials to lift hopelessness and despair, to rekindle zest, to restore a capacity for pleasure, and to bring the senses back to life. As a result, many people using these drugs are simply *happier* than they were before.

Today's antidepressants thus appear to be acting on at least a part of the neural machinery of happiness itself— the machinery that regulates the happiness set point, perhaps. It's the machinery dozens of pharmaceutical companies would dearly love to understand so that they can create drugs that stimulate happiness faster and more effectively with fewer side effects.

For some people, today's drugs are as good as they need. For these "good responders" antidepressants effectively boost mood with no or few side effects. But such people are a distinct minority. Only about a third of those who try any given antidepressant will respond well—and many of these respond well but suffer pronounced side effects at the same time. Another third experience a limited or partial response, and the final third do not improve at all.

Thus the potential profits from a truly safe, effective, and side-effect-free antidepressant are vast, and research into the nature and functioning of the brain's mood machinery is frenzied.

Neuroscientists have advanced farther toward the goal of understanding the biological components of mood than most people think. Not as far as anyone would like, but far enough to offer some tantalizing clues about where in the brain happiness lies and how happiness-enhancing drugs work. The outline of the machine, in other words, is emerging. In fact, the field of psychopharmacology is now buzzing with so many new discoveries that it is suffering a kind of intellectual anxiety attack. Research coming from diverse quarters has effectively trashed the previous best theory about how moods are regulated: the "biogenic amine" theory.

The idea was that mental illness—and depression in particular—is caused by insufficient levels of the so-called amine neurotransmitters: serotonin, norepinephrine, and dopamine. Neurotransmitters are chemicals that relay messages from one nerve cell to another. The chemicals are released in little packets from a "sending" axon into a tiny gap between cells: the synaptic cleft. In milliseconds, the neurotransmitter molecules cross the synapse and dock at special receiving stations on the outside of the "receiving" neuron. These receiving stations, or receptors, act like triggers for a new sequence of events that relay the message and make the receiving neuron either more or less likely to fire off a signal of its own. Some neurotransmitters send messages to fire signals; others make it *harder* for a neuron to fire. Just as a car needs both an accelerator and a brake pedal to function effectively, so the brain needs both kinds of neurotransmitters to keep the overall electrical activity balanced.

The biogenic amine theory proposed that when levels of stimulating neurotransmitters dropped, electrical activity declined as well, resulting in depression. This was a cartoonish idea at best, but its many problems were overlooked largely because there was nothing better to take its place.

"Back in the 1960s people recognized that antidepressants alter the levels of synaptic serotonin or norepinephrine or dopamine," says Steven Hyman, director of the National Institute of Mental Health. "And even though everybody should have known better, it was very attractive to think that depression must be *caused* by inadequate serotonin or norepinephrine, and that somehow the drugs were addressing that imbalance."

It's now clear that this notion is dead wrong. Not only is depression *not* caused by a lack of serotonin, norepinephrine, or dopamine (the proof of which we'll get to in a moment), but also these are not the only—or even perhaps the most important—neurotransmitters related to mood. This was dramatically illustrated by the recent discovery, mentioned earlier, of an antidepressant molecule that works by blocking a compound in the brain called substance P. The Merck scientists found that their substance-P-blocking molecule lifts depression as well as Paxil, a popular drug in the same class as Prozac. And yet it doesn't do a thing to levels of serotonin, norepinephrine, or dopamine.

Many clinicians and researchers now suspect that the

altered levels of serotonin, norepinephrine, and dopamine found in depressed patients are the *result* of depression, not its *cause*. In other words, whatever problem is causing the depression may be directly or indirectly altering levels of neurotransmitters as well. The odd thing is that drugs that directly *raise* the levels of these neurotransmitters do, indeed, seem to alleviate symptoms of depression, at least in some patients.

Some progress has recently been made toward explaining this enigma.

An aspect of antidepressant therapy that has been recognized—and puzzled over—for more than thirty years is the "lag time" problem: Why does it take from a week to six weeks for all known antidepressants to "kick in"?

When a person swallows Prozac or any other antidepressant, the drug quickly enters the bloodstream and, within minutes, the levels of serotonin, norepinephrine, dopamine, or some combination of the three begin to rise. The drugs do this by physically jamming little molecular pumps that suck neurotransmitter molecules back up into a neuron after they've done their job carrying a message across the synapse. These pumps recycle the valuable neurotransmitter molecules for use again and again. Technically, they're called "reuptake" pumps. Prozac molecules are shaped just right for jamming the pumps that suck up serotonin—hence it and other drugs in the same class (such as Paxil and Zoloft) are called "selective serotonin reuptake inhibitors." Other drugs, such as Effexor, block the pumps that suck up norepinephrine *and* serotonin. And many of the original antidepressants interfere with the pumps for all three amine neurotransmitters—

plus a few others, which leads to their annoying or potentially dangerous side effects.

The fact that it takes weeks for mood to improve even though neurotransmitter levels begin to rise immediately after the drug is taken proves that low levels of these neurotransmitters do not *cause* depression.[2] Contrary to many of the messages in the popular media, in other words, depression is not a "serotonin-deficit disorder" or a "norepinephrine-deficit disorder." If it were, antidepressants would work immediately. People who are depressed may, indeed, have lower-than-normal neurotransmitter levels—but again, it now appears that this is a secondary effect of some more basic process.

A second long-standing mystery is why drugs that target very different neurotransmitter systems are roughly equivalent at relieving depression. For example, Prozac, which targets serotonin, is no better at raising mood than one of the very first antidepressant drugs ever discovered, Imipramine, which blocks reuptake of serotonin, norepinephrine, and acetylcholine.

For decades, researchers looked for clues to these two mysteries—the therapeutic lag time and the uniform response rates across drug classes—in and around the synapse. Perhaps, it was thought, neurons somehow adjusted their synapses in response to artificially raised neurotransmitter levels. Or maybe the number or sensitivity of the receptors on either side of the synapse changed. Or perhaps the key lay in the specific *types* of synaptic receptors being stimulated. Maybe just one or two of the fourteen different serotonin receptors, for example, were important in mood.

All of these ideas are at least partially correct. Neurons *do* adjust to higher neurotransmitter levels, but the adjustments are either temporary or unrelated to the lifting of depression. And some receptors *have* been more strongly linked to depression than others, but the differences have not been significant. Faced with these dead ends, neuroscientists are now looking beyond the synapse, down into the complicated innards of neurons themselves. They're trying to find out what happens *after* serotonin or norepinephrine or substance P bind to their respective receptors on the "receiving" side of the synapse. And here, at long last, they may have struck pay dirt.

The latest neuroscientific research suggests that one reason it may take weeks for an antidepressant to kick in is because the drugs are spurring the brain to start *growing*.

As many people know, the brain is the one organ in the body that doesn't constantly renew its cells. That's because brain cells—neurons—are the fundamental units of information storage. A constant turnover of neurons would result in an animal with constant amnesia—hardly an adaptive situation.[3]

Instead of adding new neurons, the brain grows in another way—by building new dendritic branches on existing neuronal trees. Again, the synapses formed by connections are the true units of information storage and transfer in the brain. Thus the more connections, the more information can flow, the more resiliency and versatility the brain will have, and the more resistant to disease, aging, and stress the brain will be.

The excitement now animating the field of neuro-pharmacology comes from research showing that antidepressants boost the levels of special chemicals called growth factors that stimulate neurons to grow new dendritic branches. The link between antidepressants and nerve growth factors was totally unexpected. Scientists were used to focusing on the immediate actions of antidepressants—the blockade of reuptake, for instance, an action that very quickly changes the electrical activity of neurons. The process of neuronal sprouting, however, takes time and is controlled by genes in the nucleus, far from the immediate synaptic site of antidepressant activity. But it's precisely *because* dendritic sprouting takes weeks to occur that this mechanism is now being keenly eyed as the reason it takes so long for antidepressants to kick in. Almost as a bonus, this new insight suggests a solution to the question of why drugs in very different classes acting on very different neurotransmitter systems function with roughly equivalent efficacy as antidepressants.

The new research began with the attempt to understand exactly what happens after neurotransmitters such as serotonin and norepinephrine cross the synapse and dock at their respective receptors, like so many baseballs slapping into so many mitts. It turned out that this physical docking triggers both the rapid responses scientists were familiar with *and* a much slower response as well. This slow response is the result of a long, dominolike chain of chemical reactions that starts at a synaptic receptor and ends up deep in the neuron's heart, in the genes that regulate the cell's functioning.

If you picture DNA as a string of pearls, a gene is one

pearl: a specific stretch of DNA that serves as a blueprint for the construction of a single, particular molecule. Genes are constantly being switched on and off inside all of the body's cells so that the proper levels of enzymes, hormones, neurotransmitters, and other compounds can be maintained. A handful of the genes in neurons are blueprints for manufacturing nerve growth factors—factors vital for embryos and babies because they guide the "wiring up" of the human brain. But nerve growth factors play an important role throughout life by encouraging the sprouting of new dendritic branches on neurons. Again, the number and strength of dendrites have everything to do with the health of the brain as a whole. When dendrites die—from lack of use, stress, injury, or disease—the electrical signals they carry weaken or disappear. Memories fade. Muscle coordination fails. Hormone production drops. Mood and personality change.

Increase the number of dendrites, on the other hand, and the reverse effects are seen: cognitive abilities such as memory and the capacity for abstraction improve, coordination improves, and mental health returns. By stimulating dendritic sprouting, nerve growth factors play a critical role in brain health.

The new hypothesis is that by switching on the genes that control nerve growth factor, antidepressants stimulate the growth of new dendrites and new synapses between neurons. The result is more "wires" and better electrical conduction in existing neuronal circuits. The overall effect is an increase in the electrical activity of the neural networks underlying mood, emotional response, and perhaps happiness itself.

When these processes are modeled in the lab they take roughly two to four weeks to complete—the same general time it takes for antidepressants to kick in. The process is slow because the machinery required to build all of the different molecules needed to construct new dendrites is extremely elaborate.

The genes regulating nerve growth factors are found in neurons that are, in turn, affected by serotonin, norepinephrine, *and* dopamine. Nerve growth factor, in other words, could be a "common pathway" by which antidepressants of widely varying classes achieve similar effects on mood. The possibility that antidepressants work by turning on a complicated dendrite-building machinery in the brain has opened up entirely new vistas for pharmacological interventions. The more steps there are in a process, the more potential targets there are for drugs that either block or enhance a particular step. For instance, if drugs could be found that aim directly at the genes for nerve growth factors or that mimic nerve growth factors, the therapeutic lag time might be reduced. Another advantage of aiming drugs at the real machinery of mood regulation rather than some of the peripheral biochemical effects is that the severity of side effects may be reduced even farther.

The emerging picture of the neuronal machinery regulating mood and emotion is of a vast, complicated apparatus constructed using genetic blueprints that vary from person to person with the subtlety and uniqueness of faces. The complexity of the machinery means that it can fail or become damaged in many ways. For instance, the processes by which neurotransmitter molecules are manufactured and transported inside a neuron might malfunction. Or the machinery that makes neurotransmitter receptors might be at fault. Or the problem might lie in a completely different area, in a defect in the support elements—the "girders"—that maintain a neuron's physical shape. In short, disorders of mood come in an infinity of variations not only because everyone grows up in a unique environment but also because everyone's neural machinery is subtly different to begin with and can fail in so many different ways.

As cell biologists have been clarifying the ways in which antidepressants work at the cellular level, other scientists have been approaching the question looking for where in the brain as a whole mood and emotions seem to be generated. This has been a long-standing endeavor, and one of the very first mood states ever localized to a specific part of the brain was a close cousin of happiness: pleasure.

It was 1954, and two Canadian neuroscientists, James Olds and Peter Milner, were interested in a small spot on the brainstem called the reticular formation. They wanted to see whether this area controlled the brain's overall state of arousal—its degree of wakefulness. They did their exploration using rats, which have brains remarkably similar to human brains, except for the obvious size differences. Olds and Milner decided to try a new technique: drilling tiny holes in the skull and sliding very fine electrodes deep into the brain. Once installed, the electrodes were held in place on top of a living rat's head with dental cement. Thus wired, a rat could roam relatively freely in the cage, and the scientists could stimulate the rat's brain at will and observe the response.

After placing a few practice electrodes, Olds tried one for real. Unfortunately, he didn't let the dental cement set fully after the procedure, and he accidentally hit the electrode. He didn't know it at the time, but he had pushed the tip of the electrode into the mesolimbic area of the rat's brain instead of the planned reticular formation.

To his surprise, Olds found that stimulating the electrode allowed him to very easily get the rat to do whatever he wanted. For instance, the rat learned to negotiate complex mazes just to get a few zaps. The rat *wanted* the stimulation . . . and wanted it very badly.

When the rat was finally sacrificed and its brain removed, the error was discovered. The mesolimbic area quickly became the focus of intense experimentation. Scientists implanted electrodes into other rats and rigged up a lever that let the rats stimulate themselves at will. The rats quickly discovered the lever's effect and would sometimes give themselves more than a hundred "hits" a minute for hours on end. In fact, some animals—the lever addicts—starved themselves rather than give up their electrical paradise.

Olds and Milner had stumbled onto the brain's pleasure circuitry. The portion of the mesolimbic system they found has come to be known as the "reward center" because it seems to have evolved to reward behavior that improves the chances that an animal will pass its genes to the next generation. Behaviors such as sex, eating food, and achieving social rank trigger the pleasure centers, reinforcing those behaviors. The salient point is that in humans as well as rats, pleasure emerges from the healthy functioning of a discrete brain region comprised of millions of individual neurons.

Is there a discrete brain area controlling the happiness set point? Perhaps. For more than twenty years, neuroscientist Richard Davidson at the University of Wisconsin in Madison has focused his attention on a tantalizing section of the brain called the prefrontal cortex. This area, which lies behind the forehead in the front of the brain, has long been viewed as the seat of human consciousness and "higher" cognitive abilities such as the capacity for abstract reasoning, complex analysis, and foresight. It is here that the "executive" functions are thought to exist— our capacities to organize the disparate signals arising from our senses and other brain modules and synthesize these inputs into a consistent, stable, integrated whole that we can use as a platform for understanding ourselves and the world around us. In addition to these roles, the prefrontal cortex also plays a major role in the regulation of emotions. It is directly linked to brain structures such as the amygdala that generate strong emotional reactions. The connections between the prefrontal cortex and these emotion-producing hardware modules are unbalanced. More nerve fibers run from the emotion centers to the prefrontal cortex than from the prefrontal cortex back down to the emotion centers.

This mismatch in the wiring between our emotions and our linear, rational, consciousness-generating prefrontal cortex means that the limbic system can physically outgun the prefrontal cortex with electrical signals. This is one reason why it's notoriously difficult for humans to control their emotions. When the emotion centers are aroused, strong excitatory signals are sent out in all directions, including the prefrontal cortex. The prefrontal cortex can dampen activity in the emotion centers by firing off inhibitory signals, but when things get emotionally intense—in either a positive or a negative direction—the prefrontal cortex is electrically overwhelmed and emotions prevail.

The prefrontal cortex is thus an interesting piece of neurological real estate. It sits at a crossroad between emotions and abstract thinking, and is the most likely candidate for the location of the neural networks that encode our representation of ourselves—our self-awareness. Not surprisingly, people with damaged prefrontal regions are prone to emotional outbursts, have difficulty forming and manipulating abstract thoughts, and have a diminished capacity for self-awareness.

Given the critical importance of the prefrontal cortex, it's not surprising that changing the electrical activity in this area has profound effects on mood. It's also not surprising that if happiness emerges anywhere in the brain, it's here.

Like the brain as a whole, the prefrontal cortex is split in half. Davidson has found that the right and the left prefrontal regions perform separate but equally important mood-related functions. The left side prompts us to take actions that increase our chances for survival; the right controls our responses to external threats. The left prefrontal cortex is the biological substrate of the behavioral approach system—a coordinated circuitry that guides our response to incentives. The behavioral approach system prompts us to engage in energy-demanding, outwardly directed social behaviors, exploratory activity, and all manner of tasks required to attain goals that will increase our chances of survival and procreation. The left prefrontal cortex must, therefore, draw on many different aspects of cognition and emotional functioning to obtain these goals. When such a goal is attained, we are rewarded by bursts of pleasure arising from the firing of networks in the mesolimbic area.

Playing yin to the left prefrontal cortex's yang, the right prefrontal cortex is the seat of the behavioral inhibition system, responsible for guiding our responses to threats and risky situations. Such responses range from simple flight or fight to much more complex behaviors such as changing jobs, partners, or life situations when these are unsatisfying, painful, or dysfunctional.

Healthy animals—humans included—need both systems to respond effectively to opportunities and threats in their environment. Approach behaviors are needed to acquire food, mates, desired material objects or locations, and social dominance. Inhibitory behaviors are required when dealing with threats from predators, other people, scarcity of resources, social domination, or unsuccessful attempts to obtain a given goal.

Davidson has discovered that people vary considerably in the strength and balance of the electrical activity in these all-important brain regions—and the differences he's found correlate strongly with mood. People with higher than normal activity in their outward-oriented left prefrontal cortex tend to experience more positive moods than people with lower than normal left-side activity (or, conversely, above-average activity in the right prefrontal cortex). Other things being equal, Davidson says that people with active left prefrontal cortices tend to be the kind of people who get out of bed in the morning and want to take on the world.

"They're very actively engaged, real problem-solvers," he says. "They're people who will not get discouraged in response to failure."

On the other hand, people with relatively more activity in their right prefrontal cortex tend to be inwardly directed, withdrawn, shy, anxious, and depressed.

Supporting these ideas is the observation that patients with damage only to their left prefrontal cortex (thereby giving their right prefrontal cortex much greater prominence) are likely to be depressed or exhibit depressive symptoms.

Correlations between activity in the left and right prefrontal regions and overall mood and personality have been found in children as well as adults. In one experiment, children were brought into the lab and asked to play with an experimenter who was blowing bubbles. Some children jumped up enthusiastically to catch the bubbles, squealing with delight and exhibiting obvious pleasure in the activity. Other children jumped less or not at all and tended not to be as involved with the activity. When the children were later wired to an electroencephalograph—a machine that measures electrical activity in the brain—the exuberant children were the ones with greater left prefrontal brain activity, and the inhibited children were found to have more right prefrontal activity.

That the left prefrontal cortex plays a major role in positive mood is also supported by the experiences of some rare individuals who have had their prefrontal regions artificially stimulated. These patients were undergoing brain operations for epilepsy. Under local anesthesia, their skulls were opened to provide access to the brain regions thought to be causing their seizures. When their left prefrontal cortex was stimulated, some patients reported an immediate rise in mood. Other patients reported a range of mood states.

"Their responses began with relaxation and feelings of well-being, smiling, and euphoria," says neuroscientist James Austin of the University of Colorado. "Next, they developed a further extension of the euphoria with outbursts of emotion either in positive or negative direction. Finally, there occurred an abrupt, sudden positive emotional response. This was followed by a satisfaction so sudden and complete that it precluded further attempts at stimulation."[4]

All of this raises the possibility of increasing left prefrontal cortex activity with drugs, thus raising the happiness set point and facilitating an adaptive level of well-being. A drug that stimulated electrical activity in the left prefrontal cortex—or conversely, that inhibited activity in the right prefrontal cortex—might induce a more buoyant, outgoing, optimistic attitude. In short, it might be an antidepressant. Some of Davidson's most recent work supports this idea.

He measured the electrical activity in the prefrontal regions of people before they started taking an antidepressant and then six weeks after they began. He found, as predicted, higher levels of activity in the left prefrontal cortex in those who responded to the medication. Somehow, antidepressant molecules induce greater electrical activity in the left prefrontal cortex. The research mentioned earlier suggests that one way the drugs might achieve this effect is by turning on selected genes in the relevant neurons, causing them to sprout more dendrites and make more connections between neurons in the left prefrontal cortex. The effect of this microscopic activity would show up in the macroscopic views of the entire brain region studied by Davidson.

These preliminary findings have kick-started the field of mood research.

"I think the field is still very much in its infancy," Davidson says. "But it's an exciting time because we now have methods that we never had before, and that is really revolutionizing how we study the brain and emotion."

The picture that is forming of the machinery underneath the happiness set point thus looks like this: The set point—and happiness itself—is an emergent property of a brain in which activity in the left prefrontal cortex predominates and in which neurotransmissions between the prefrontal cortex and other discrete mood-related areas, such as the pleasure center, the amygdala, and the right prefrontal cortex are balanced, robust, and unimpeded. The machinery of these networks depends critically on the number and strength of the dendrites along which neural information flows. These dendrites, and the functioning of each individual neuron, depend, in turn, on the proper functioning of millions of even smaller machines—the neurotransmitter receptors, reuptake pumps, storage and release mechanisms, and the long chains of chemical reactions required to relay messages to genes.

The machinery of happiness, in other words, is complicated indeed. The details fill thousands of pages of scientific journals every year. But the direction of the research is clear: Eventually the machinery of mood, of depression, and of happiness will be *completely* laid bare. All the circuitry will be revealed. All the neurotransmitter actions will be cataloged and their actions traced to specific brain areas. All the receptors will be understood in vivid, three-dimensional splendor, every atom of every molecule accounted for. All of the secondary pathways of neurotransmission, all of the genes that are turned on or off, all of the cascades of reactions those genes set off—*all* of it will be understood.

This is the knowledge that will allow drug companies to make the perfect drug—the drug that will allow people to shift the electrical activity in their mood-generating circuitry to produce more positive feelings—more pleasure and happiness—and fewer negative feelings—sadness, anxiety, and depression. Not a "happy pill," which, like heroin, induces pleasure—even bliss—regardless of one's life situation, but drugs that notch up the happiness set point so that, on average, a person can feel good more often than not.

The question will then become how to use this new technology effectively. How happy is *too* happy? To what degree can negative feelings such as sadness, guilt, fear, anxiety, and depression be safely wiped out? Is there an ideal mood state? An ideal range of emotions?

These are vitally important questions, not just for individuals interested in using the new drugs, but for society as a whole. Because, paradoxically, bad moods may actually be good for people—and good for society.

CHAPTER 4

Listening to
Depression

S HE'S KNOWN ONLY AS "MISS C."

It was her choice. Although willing—even eager—to participate in the research that was later published about her, she felt uncomfortable revealing her true identity. She was in her third year of college, and she didn't even tell her friends—much less complete strangers—about her condition. No, she decided, she didn't want her real name published.

And so, in the article appearing in volume 64 of the 1950 *Annals of Psychiatry and Neurology,* she is simply called "Miss C"—for "Canada," because that's where she lived—Montréal, to be exact. And that's where the research on her condition was conducted—in the laboratory of

Dr. F. L. McNaughton of the Montréal Neurological Institute.

The article appearing as a result of that research was titled "Experimental Study of a Case of Insensitivity to Pain." It didn't get much attention at the time and quickly disappeared, a curious case study of interest to only a handful of researchers probing the nature of pain. But the article remains one of the best chronicles of a remarkable and exceedingly rare condition: the complete inability to feel pain.

Miss C, who was twenty-two at the time of the research, had never felt the slightest hint of a headache. She never had a toothache, a stomachache, an earache, or any discomfort from menstrual periods. She also never felt an itch—even when exposed to chicken pox, sunburn, or the drying of the long Canadian winters—conditions that made those around her miserable with the overpowering urge to scratch. But not Miss C. She was simply—and permanently—pain-free.

At first glance, Miss C's condition sounds appealing. Certainly anybody who has experienced the constant throbbing ache of chronic back pain, or the blindingly acute pain caused by a broken bone, a severe burn, or an illness such as appendicitis, might view Miss C's condition with some envy. And, indeed, Miss C's condition was not, at first, seen as anything more than a quirk of nature—a benign oddity.

Miss C was born to healthy, well-educated parents. Her father was a physician, and she attended a French nursery school. From her own reports, taken from interviews conducted during the research on her, she was a "highly excitable" child who hit herself or bit her tongue and hands when frustrated. These behaviors undoubtedly troubled her parents, but Miss C herself did not suffer directly from her self-inflicted mutilations.

The first "official" recognition of her condition came when she was a toddler—at twenty-one months old. She had a large, soft swelling on the back of her head, an abscess that resembled a large blister. At a hospital, a small incision was made to drain the abscess. The hospital records note that Miss C never showed any signs of pain during or after the procedure.

When she was three, she was hospitalized three times for osteomyelitis in her right heelbone. Osteomyelitis is an inflammation of the bone marrow due to a bacterial infection. It is a hazard of bone fractures or of any other damage that exposes or irritates the marrow. To the eye, osteomyelitis reveals itself as a tender, swollen, reddened area. To the sufferer, the primary indication is extreme pain in the affected area. Since it is a bacterial infection, osteomyelitis can usually be treated quickly and effectively with high doses of antibiotics. And because the condition is so painful, most cases do not progress far before treatment is sought.

But, of course, Miss C felt nothing during her attacks. It was only because her mother noticed the redness and swelling that Miss C was brought to the hospital.

It was now becoming clear to everyone—including Miss C—that her condition was more serious than a mere oddity. In fact, it was a devastating loss of function. If her bouts with osteomyelitis weren't enough to prove the point, another incident in the same year made it plain.

Alone in her room one winter's day, Miss C heard some children playing in the snowy street outside. She went to her window and, to see more clearly, knelt on the radiator, which was scalding hot. Minutes passed until she grew tired of watching the street scene. Then she got off the radiator and walked away.

She had sustained extremely serious burns, discovered immediately by her parents, who rushed her to the hospital. There she underwent extensive skin grafts to repair the damage.

When she was nine she was hospitalized four times, once for a bacterial infection of her kidney—pyelitis—which is typically caused by unusual retention of urine. This may have been due, in turn, to Miss C's inability to detect the pain of an overdistended bladder. The three other times were all for osteomyelitis, this time at the lower end of her left femur—the thighbone.

In addition to these major episodes, there were frequent small injuries. Miss C learned to check herself carefully for injuries. She recalls returning from a day at the beach when a friend noticed she was bleeding. She had cut her foot deeply on a sharp shell. From then on she inspected her feet and legs regularly for signs of injury. By the time she was formally evaluated in 1948, her hands, legs, and feet were scarred from cuts, bites, burns, scratches, and frostbite. In addition, her tongue was deformed from severe biting—some intentional during childhood, some unintentional in later years as a result of normal accidents during eating that went unnoticed.

Despite all these injuries and hospitalizations, Miss C had a relatively normal upbringing, with the exception of the sudden death of her father when she was eleven. She outgrew her childhood frustrations and, by the time she was extensively examined, possessed an above-average intelligence (as measured by standard IQ tests) and normal emotional maturity (as measured by a variety of psychological indices such as the McFarland and Seitz Psychosomatic Inventory). She was described by the investigators as "very capable and cooperative and displaying remarkable initiative" in her work as an assistant in the psychology division of the Allan Memorial Institute.

The examinations conducted by Dr. McNaughton in his attempts to quantify and characterize Miss C's condition were rather obsessively thorough. For instance, he had her immerse her hand in a bucket of ice water—a situation normal people find unbearable within fifteen to twenty seconds. The pain of the ice water is easily detected in people with normal sensation as a sharp rise in blood pressure at the moment of immersion. Miss C could calmly keep her hand in the ice water for minutes, and her blood pressure never varied. McNaughton then tried to elicit pain in other ways: hypodermic needle (Miss C simply reported a vague "pulling" feeling); electric shocks (control subjects found the shocks "very unpleasant" and couldn't control a reaction to withdraw their hands—Miss C reported no sensation and never withdrew her hand); gentle insertion of a small stick into the nostrils (no reaction or sneeze reflex); and heating of various parts of her body (no reported pain even when the heat was increased to the point of blistering the skin). Microscopic examination of tiny specimens of Miss C's peripheral nerves revealed nothing abnormal.

In the end, McNaughton succeeded only in convincing himself that Miss C was neither a charlatan nor a "hysterical neurotic." He documented what he called "this peculiar disorder" with unusual detail, but he could shed no light on its cause. Only two facts appeared to him worthy of mentioning: that Miss C could easily feel light touches on her skin even though she lacked pain perception; and she lacked the sensation of itch.

McNaughton thus missed the most important point: Miss C's "peculiar condition" could kill her.

Miss C finished college. But her health problems began to multiply. The major problem was the first one that attacked her: osteomyelitis. When normal people twist an ankle, sprain a muscle, or overextend a joint, the pain caused by the tissue damage forces protective measures. Crutches are used, a muscle is favored, a joint is immobilized. Miss C, with her pain alarm system disabled, was deaf to her body's screams. She would continue to walk on a sprained ankle, use a torn muscle, or flex a damaged joint. Tissue in the affected areas would die— and dead tissue is a perfect growth medium for bacteria.

Within several years, Miss C's bones and joints were disintegrating from the years of unrestrained pummeling. Infections became harder to control. The swelling was worse. She became crippled as her bones deformed from the damage.

In 1957 Miss C was hospitalized again for severe osteomyelitis. But this time the doctors were helpless against the infections that raged through her body. Despite massive infusions of the most powerful antibiotics, Miss C's condition worsened. The traumas occurring in Miss C's tissues finally reached such monumental proportions that she began to feel pain for the first time in her life. Traditional analgesia eased that pain. But nothing else could be done.

A month after she was admitted to the hospital, at age twenty-nine, Miss C was dead.

Miss C's story is a compelling reminder that pain, as horrific as it may be, is not a defect or malfunction of nature. In fact, it's a precious and exquisitely engineered neural capacity honed by millions of years of natural selection to provide us with the instantaneous information required to ensure our physical survival. Far from being an ideal state, the inability to feel pain is dangerous and almost always lethal.

It takes an extreme case like that of Miss C to point this out because we are so accustomed to viewing pain as an enemy—something to be "killed" as quickly and as completely as possible. But the simplistic idea that pain is always bad and should never be tolerated—an idea reinforced by an unending barrage of advertising from the pain-relief industry—can create problems.

For instance, many headaches result from muscle tension, which, in turn, is caused by stress from demanding jobs, parental responsibilities, and fast-paced lifestyles. If we view headache pain as simply a defect to be fixed or a malfunction to be corrected, then using a painkiller makes perfect sense. But if we view the pain, instead, as a warning signal arising from the proper functioning of a healthy—though unpleasant—human capacity, we would see the headache as a sign that we are doing something wrong, something that is harming our bodies. Rather than kill the messenger with a strong dose of ibuprofen or aspirin, we would heed the message that we should change the circumstances that are producing the stress at the root of the pain. Using a painkiller, in fact, could easily make the problem much worse. Like a drugged-up professional athlete who continues playing on an injured knee, only to sustain far greater knee damage as a result, the headache sufferer might continue struggling under stressful conditions to the extent that both the physical and the mental tension are amplified to the point of a more serious muscle or mood breakdown.

Of course, just because pain is "natural" doesn't mean it is always necessary. Our capacity for pain, for instance, did not evolve in the context of modern surgical methods. I recently underwent a minor surgical procedure, and I'm supremely grateful for the anesthesia that allowed me to chat amiably with the surgeon while he cut into my body to perform the work. I'm equally thankful for the ibuprofen that at this moment is taking the edge off the lingering pain from the incisions.

Nobody would argue against the use of anesthesia during surgery, or against the use of powerful analgesics—even opioids—for treating postsurgical, cancer, or chronic pain. Such uses are "unnatural" but wholly justified and humane. And, on the other hand, few would sanction the use of powerful painkillers in situations where it would be more reasonable to simply remove the source of the pain. And nobody would suggest that normal people use drugs that dampen or eliminate their capacity for pain.

All of these considerations apply to the field of psychopharmacology, though many factors make it more difficult to determine when mood-altering drugs are appropriate and when such use is unwise. Pain provides a helpful and closely related analogy for thinking about these dynamics.

Like pain, emotions and moods are coordinated systems of responses that have been shaped by natural selection to protect us and guide our behavior. Fitting emotions and moods into the larger picture of human evolution is a fairly recent endeavor and has been christened Darwinian psychiatry.[1] It is an approach to mental life—both normal and dysfunctional—that embraces a wide range of existing theories of behavior while adding a fresh and overarching appreciation for the ultimate evolutionary explanations for our many mental traits and functions. One of the founders of the field is Randolph Nesse, a practicing psychiatrist and professor at the University of Michigan. He defines emotions as "specialized modes of operation shaped by natural selection to adjust the physiological, psychological, and behavioral parameters of an organism in ways that increase its capacity and tendency to respond adaptively to the threats and opportunities characteristic of specific kinds of situations."[2]

That's a bit of a mouthful, but it captures the essential idea. Our emotions—both pleasant and unpleasant—exist because they have served useful functions in the past. Fear and panic, for instance, shape our response when our physical, mental, or social lives are immediately threatened. Fear is evoked by situations that could hurt us or endanger our social standing, our chances for success-ful mating, or our ability to acquire valuable resources.

Anxiety tracks *potential* threats or danger. It is a future-oriented version of fear that helps us predict, and thus avoid, immediate danger. Love is a response to opportunities for intimacy, companionship, and repro-duction and generates powerful bonding feelings between parents and children, lovers, and kin. Anger is triggered by perceptions of unfairness, cheating (in the largest sense), and spiteful threats to harm another person.

Emotions thus coordinate our responses and provide a kind of "radar" that constantly tracks important aspects of our surroundings. Emotions also give rise to *affects*—actions, physical responses, or behaviors that attract the attention of others. The inward experience of anger, for example, immediately produces an outward affect signal-ing to others that a potential unfairness has been detected and will not be tolerated. Love signals an openness and an availability for intimacy. Pain and fear signal a need for assistance from others.

Both the signal-detection and communication func-tions of emotions have been honed by natural selection, and have served to increase our chances for survival and reproduction in eons past.

It is fairly easy to see how happiness fits into this pic-ture. Happiness is obviously adaptive: happy people are energetic, gregarious, socially outgoing, willing to make investments of time and energy for future rewards, and sexually alive. Nesse says that happiness is aroused by information that is often correlated with increasing repro-ductive success—being admired, being loved, having sex, watching children succeed, and having grandchildren. In humans, of course, happiness also can arise from situations less immediately linked to reproduction—for instance, the satisfaction of solving an intellectual problem, the happiness of creating an evocative work of art or literature, or the attainment of any of a million other possible goals or objectives.

But what about sadness and depression? Unlike the capacity for physical pain, or the capacity for happiness, the purpose of these negative emotions is less immediately obvious. After all, unhappy people often withdraw from social activity. They typically lose their appetite, have disturbed sleep, are lethargic, and lose interest in sex. What could be *less* adaptive, from a Darwinian standpoint, than such behaviors? Why hasn't the capacity for depression been weeded out of the human genome millions of years ago? What possible utility could unhappiness and depression serve?

Such questions come naturally in this age, when depression—and even just ordinary sadness—are often viewed as emotional defects or as malfunctions of nature. The prevailing notion that depression is a dysfunction caused by unbalanced neurotransmitters has become so deeply entrenched that it's hard to grasp the notion that a capacity for unhappiness—even depression—might be *good* for us, just as a capacity for pain is good for us, even though it is unpleasant.

But in fact, as heretical as it sounds, the pain of depression can indeed be every bit as vital as the pain of injury.

The potential utility of depression has been most clearly articulated by the Swedish psychotherapist Emmy

Gut. In her book *Productive and Unproductive Depression* Gut draws a distinction between depression serving a valuable and ultimately healthy purpose, and depression that does not. Generally speaking, she says, the less severe forms of depression tend to be potentially productive, but in her view even a profound depression can be healthy and should be carefully examined as a potentially valuable sign before it is actively treated with medications.

According to Gut, Nesse, and other proponents of Darwinian psychiatry, depressive moods are to our mental life what pain is to our physical life: potentially valuable signals that something is reducing our chances for survival, reproduction, and well-being. Most often, depressive moods are telling us that something is wrong with our intimate relationships, our life situation, or our efforts to achieve a goal.

"We are not familiar with the idea that becoming depressed under certain circumstances could be as vital, universal, and adaptive an emotional response as the emotions of anxiety, grief, or anger are in their own appropriate context," Gut wrote in 1989, presaging the current interest in Darwinian psychiatry. "We are not reminded by the word 'depression' of a specific type of problem with which the basic depressed response is uniquely suited to help us, as anger or grief do with other problems. Instead, we are likely to think of depression as something 'sick,' or as some undesirable weakness."

In Gut's view, depressed moods are most often telling us that we are experiencing an unconscious crisis, frustration, breakdown, or problem that needs our attention. She emphasizes the unconscious nature of the problems because being aware of a loss or a crisis changes how they feel. Grief, for instance, is a negative, depressionlike emotion associated with the conscious loss of companionship, whether from a spouse, friend, relative, or pet. Sadness can result from other types of conscious loss, such as loss of money, prestige, social power, or health.

Depression, however, has a distinctive feel to it—a feel that is tinged with the frustration, perplexity, and fear that come from experiencing a powerful emotion without knowing fully *why* one is experiencing it.

If, as Gut suggests, depression has evolved as a signal of an unconscious loss of Darwinian fitness, it makes a good deal of sense that depressed feelings should be relatively common. That's because unconscious mental conflict is a hallmark of the human experience and an unavoidable result of the brain's architecture. The past two decades of neuroscientific research have firmly established the modular nature of human consciousness. The brain, in other words, functions not as a single entity, but as a collection of interdependent (and often independent) functional modules that have been evolving for millions of years. Some modules control automatic processes such as heartbeat and breathing. Some modules process incoming sensory information. Some generate emotional signals. Some store and process long-term memories. Some generate positive affect, some generate negative affect.

The point is that often the activities of two or more modules collide. Giving a public lecture, for instance, can generate conflicting emotions because the situation is at once an opportunity to acquire social status and a potential threat to that status. Likewise, our capacity to feel love for multiple individuals and our urge to reproduce widely so as to maximize the distribution of our genes can easily collide with our simultaneous desire to remain faithful to a single partner—a desire with roots in cultural norms and in fundamental Darwinian genetic self-interest.

Conflicts between different brain modules—the different parts of ourselves—are not necessarily obvious. In fact, we strive to avoid, suppress, or ignore cognitive dissonance—the unpleasant awareness of an internal mental conflict. Depression can thus act like a warning light on a car dashboard signaling engine trouble; it can be our only indicator of the existence of such mental roadblocks and breakdowns.

The fact that the mental conflicts that can lie at the root of depression are *unconscious* poses an interesting difficulty: because the precipitating factor in depression is often unknown, the symptoms may be wholly inexplicable to the sufferer—it appears that nothing has happened in his or her life to bring about the depressed feelings. The result is that depression can feel unconnected to life events, which leaves the door wide open to interpret the depression not as a sign of psychological distress but as biological dysfunction.

As sensible as it may be to have an emotional warning system for unconscious conflicts and losses of Darwinian fitness, it still isn't immediately clear how depressive symptoms are helpful. A closer look, however, reveals nature's logic.

For example, the decreased energy, withdrawal from social interaction, and inward-turned focus typical of depression would deter an animal from pursuing hopeless goals such as chasing after game that is too fast, attempting to mate with females who are either unfertile or unavailable, or trying to achieve social dominance over a rival who is physically superior. The depressive response would prevent further wasted energy and would allow time for a reconsideration of goals and methods for attaining those goals.

An equally valuable aspect of the depressed response is the forced dropping of the rose-colored glasses worn by "normals." As mentioned previously, a great deal of research has shown that depressed people have a more realistic view of themselves and their surroundings. They are better able to predict their performance relative to others, they better understand the limits of their control, they are more accurate at monitoring and assessing their own social behavior, and they judge themselves equally responsible for previous successes and failures on a task rather than seeing themselves as more responsible for their successes than for their failures. The sometimes harsh reality revealed by depression may allow for a more accurate appraisal of a situation and lead to a more successful outcome.

Summarizing the potential utility of depression, Gut draws a comparison with digestive failure.

"It is not the vomiting, diarrhea, or fever that are illnesses in themselves," she says. "On the contrary, if we were unable to vomit, or get diarrhea or a fever, we might die of the poisons or infection. These unpleasant reactions tell us that our body is making an effort to remedy a disturbance and that this effort requires our consideration. Likewise, if we were not equipped to withdraw into ourselves, lie awake, or dream restlessly, and generally slow down until the cognitive and emotional problem is solved, the continuation of our psychic functioning would be in serious danger whenever part of our information processing—our psychic digestion—temporarily comes to a dead end. This is why depressed reactions require consideration as much as do symptoms of physiological dysfunction. The remedial effort they announce should be given a chance by a restriction or change of our activities."

Our capacity for the unpleasant emotion of depression can be just as normal and just as vital for our health as our capacity for pain. Contrary to the prevailing attitude, in other words, depression is not necessarily an illness that must be "cured" at all costs. Indeed, completely wiping out one's capacity for depression with drugs—as appealing as that might sound—could be as ultimately harmful as wiping out one's capacity to feel pain. A healthy person *needs* to be able to feel depressed—because conflicts, frustrations, communication breakdowns, and all manner of other psychic difficulties that threaten our overall fitness are inevitable parts of the human condition.

But just as appreciating the utility of pain doesn't mean one should never use painkillers, so embracing a Darwinian perspective of depression does not mean that all depressions are valuable. Nor does it mean that depression is *always* the product of unresolved mental conflicts or the experience of a loss of reproductive resources. And it certainly doesn't imply that all pharmacological interventions for depression are misguided. Far from it. A deeper understanding of the way natural selection works strongly suggests that controlling negative emotions—like pain—may, in fact, be entirely reasonable.

As valuable as a capacity for pain may be, it is not a perfectly designed system. Often pain signals are more intense and longer-lasting than they really need to be, particularly in our modern world. The pain of a cut, for instance, continues long after we have become aware of the cut and stopped whatever action brought it on. The pain is also more intense than it needs to be to ensure that we remember to avoid whatever action led to the cut. This "excess" pain can be safely eliminated with drugs without compromising our Darwinian fitness. This is a specific example of a general principle: natural selection has honed many of our physical and mental defense systems to be trigger-happy. This is particularly true with emotions. Natural selection favors emotional responses that go off more frequently and with greater intensity than is required in a purely objective sense. This is because animals with slightly oversensitive danger detectors tend to reproduce more than animals with "normal" danger detectors, even though the extra sensitivity requires a short-term waste of energy.

Consider two rabbits. One has a slightly oversensitive fear response. This rabbit runs and hides from any vaguely predator-shaped object. As long as the running and the hiding do not seriously interfere with other normal behavior, this pattern will keep the rabbit safe even though some energy is wasted in the false alarms. Another rabbit has less sensitive fear circuitry. This rabbit is not spooked by oddly shaped rocks, stumps, deer, and other harmless objects and thus it doesn't waste time and energy running and hiding. But this rabbit has less margin for error than his slightly oversensitive brother. The one time that an ambiguous shape actually *is* a wolf could easily terminate that rabbit's gene pool—and hence the blueprints for a "normal" fear response.

Our emotional responses appear to have been shaped along these lines. Just as it is "normal" to have a slightly rosy view of the world—a view that promotes survival-enhancing behaviors—it is also "normal" to have slightly overreactive emotional responses. This may hold true for the depressive response as much as it holds for anxiety, fear, anger, and other negative emotions. We may respond with a depressive response that is out of proportion to the problem it has detected and is longer-lasting than it needs to be to serve its warning functions.[3]

"I've come to the conclusion that in many cases these emotional responses have been shaped by natural selection to go off too easily, too much, and too long—at least for our circumstances in the modern world," Nesse says.

In other words, in the same way that some pain is unnecessary and can be safely eliminated by the judicious application of an appropriate analgesic technology, some anxiety, fear, and depression may be unnecessary and can be safely eliminated as well. The obvious trick is determining when an emotional reaction or response is a valid and helpful signal of distress or dysfunction and when it is excessive, unhelpful, and dispensable.

Depression is a fundamentally valuable capacity of a healthy organism that we should alter cautiously. But it is equally true that appropriate use of drug or therapeutic interventions can relieve much unnecessary suffering. It is vitally important, in other words, to listen to depression, to consider whether it is telling us something important about our lives. But listening to depression can be confusing and frustrating not just because it can be hard to draw a clear line between "necessary" and "unnecessary" depression but also because depression is a set of symptoms arising from a bewildering number of causes. The following case studies illustrate the diverse ways in which depressive moods can manifest in the human experience.

Ms. E

After having spent three years in a nearly full-time effort to write a book, Ms. E was unable to obtain a publisher. Following her eleventh rejection by publishers, she became depressed, refused to leave her home, and avoided social interaction. Friends and family continued to provide support, and a close friend took it upon herself to contact other publishers, one of which took an interest in Ms. E's book. Book negotiations followed, and eventually a contract for the book was signed. Within a month, the signs and symptoms of Ms. E's depression began to resolve. After three months she was functioning normally and was actively involved in the final editing of her book.[4]

Mrs. N

Mrs. N, sixty-four, was in good physical health and lived with her husband. She was an active member of a close and supportive family, and her three daughters and two sons lived nearby, as did her fourteen grandchildren. She had no prior history of depression. Without any evidence of precipitating incidents, Mrs. N developed signs and symptoms of depression. Weight loss, as well as withdrawal from her family and friends, followed. An array of antidepressant medications minimally altered her condition. Eventually she received electroconvulsive treatment (shock therapy), which resulted in a complete recovery.

Mr. A and Mr. B

Mr. A and Mr. B were identical twins who were separated at birth and who did not know of each other's existence until they met in their late twenties. One had grown up in a warm and supportive family, the other in a stern and often verbally abusive family. Both had graduated from college; both had jobs in which they were successful; and both were married and had children. Each had suffered periods of moderate to severe depression, beginning when they were teenagers. Psychotherapy (Mr. A) and multiple trials of antidepressants (Mr. B) did not alter their clinical conditions significantly.

Margaret

Raised by a distant and emotionally unavailable mother and affected by the suicide of her older brother when she was eighteen, Margaret suffered repeated bouts of depression as an adult. During a particularly intense depression, when she was full of despair, devoid of energy, and prone to nightmares and violent night tremors, she sought psychotherapy. Over the course of a year of weekly sessions,

Margaret confronted many traumas in her past and gained insight into the sources of her present feelings and attitudes. Her therapy was marked by repeated setbacks and emotional ambivalence toward her therapist; nonetheless, Margaret made progress. Her symptoms slowly declined, her mood improved, and she returned to work. As therapy continued, she ended an unsatisfying relationship, decided to move farther from her parents, and took a job as a midwife that she found more personally rewarding. After a year and a half of therapy, she decided to terminate the process, feeling she could reach her goals without further assistance.[5]

Tess

Tess was the eldest of ten children born in the poorest public housing project in her city. She was physically and sexually abused in childhood and, when she was twelve, her father died and her mother entered a clinical depression from which she never recovered. Nonetheless, Tess remained in school, helped raise her nine siblings, and carved out a career as a capable business administrator.

Her first marriage, at seventeen, ended quickly because her husband was alcoholic and abusive. After a series of short-term relationships, Tess became involved with a married man. When that relationship ended after four years, she became depressed and sought treatment. After months of psychotherapy in which she willingly faced the difficult aspects of her life and yet remained depressed, she was prescribed Prozac. Two weeks later, she reported feeling much better. In the coming months she continued to improve. The split with her former lover ceased to obsess her, and she began dating other men with an unaccustomed ease. She was more assertive, clear-headed, and decisive at work. After nine months on Prozac, she went off the medication and did well for another eight months. She then reported to her therapist that she was "slipping." She said she wanted the sense of stability and invulnerability to attack that Prozac gave her. She resumed the medication and responded favorably.[6]

These real-life case studies demonstrate that depression or depressive feelings are always telling us something—but exactly what is seldom clear, at least at the start. A given depression may be saying something important about one's life, one's family, one's neurochemistry, or some combination of such factors. As Gut, Nesse, and many others point out, depression can be the normal response of a healthy psyche to psychological conflicts, unresolved interpersonal problems, and life situations in which our Darwinian fitness is being compromised. And, as a vast amount of evidence also shows, depression can also be a sign that a normally healthy brain is malfunctioning. To complicate matters, dysfunctional brains can lead to dysfunctional lives, and vice versa.

How depression is viewed depends on the prism used for the examination. These prisms are formulated as models of depression that are promulgated by ardent and often highly articulate teachers, and perpetuated by schools that derive their identity from their particular prism.

The biomedical model now held in such high public regard, for instance, views depression as most often the result of defects in brain chemistry or neurology stemming from either genetic mistakes or environmental stressors. From the developmental perspective depression arises when the bonding between an infant and a caregiver is disrupted and the normal maturational process is stunted or warped. From a cognitive-psychological perspective depression stems from faulty, illogical, or dysfunctional thought patterns and information processing. Sociocultural models emphasize the role that poverty, injustice, political oppression, and excessive stress can play in depression. Finally, some depressive symptoms have been correlated to declining light levels in winter, inadequate dietary intake of certain amino acids, and a variety of medical conditions such as hypothyroidism.

There is a growing appreciation that *all* of these models have validity. The emerging paradigm of Darwinian psychiatry provides a unifying framework into which all of the current models can fit. From the Darwinian standpoint, depression is a specific emotional response arising from a complex biological and neurological substrate that has been shaped by natural selection to provide adaptive advantages. That means depression—like pain—can serve valuable functions and should be viewed as a fundamentally healthy capacity. It also means that the neural machinery underlying this capacity is fallible and subject to dysfunction. Even though the machinery may exist for good and potentially valuable reasons, it may malfunction nonetheless. And it may malfunction for a host of reasons, including defects in upbringing, genetic mistakes, or damage, stress, and other causes represented by one or the other of the current models of depression.

Darwinian psychiatry also stresses the inevitably tangled roots of depression. For instance, an essentially healthy depressive response to unconscious conflict or a loss of resources can degenerate into frankly dysfunctional, full-blown depression when exacerbated by stress, poverty, or genetically compromised mood-regulating machinery. "Pure form" cases of depression—cases resulting exclusively from a single cause—are thus extremely rare. The vast majority of depressions result from a messy knot of factors that can be difficult to untangle.

Depression's message is thus as stark and as simple as a red, blinking warning light. In itself, the blinking light simply means "trouble." The task of determining what the trouble is and how best to fix it falls to each individual and the professionals they may enlist to help him or her with the process.

If depression results from frustration in attaining a goal, or a repressed conflict in a primary relationship, a drug that acts only on neurotransmitter levels will not address the problem.

"I can think of five people I've known who were admitted over and over for five-year periods of depression and who appear to have gotten miraculously better when they finally got divorced," chuckles Jonathan Cole, a psychiatrist at Boston's McLean Hospital and a pioneer in antidepressant research.

On the other hand, years of competent psychotherapy will be of no avail if the primary problem in a case of depression is a malfunction in some part of the brain's complicated mood machinery.

"You know you can sit with someone with a major depression week after week and you're not really going anywhere," says Mark Weber, a psychotherapist in private practice in Boston. "They just don't have the energy. It's very, very slow. And if you give somebody like that some medicine, after about a month or so they start to perk up. They're still not happy, but at least they're able to try."

Of course, both of these scenarios are oversimplified. The multicausal nature of mood and depression implies that the most effective treatment plan will use multiple strategies. For instance, even if a bout of depression is primarily due to a life crisis or an unconscious mental conflict, brain function may secondarily be affected. If the depression lingers, a person may become less and less able to muster the physical and mental energy he or she needs to tackle the psychological roots of the problem. Giving such persons a drug that increases their available psychic energy may facilitate their insight and learning, thus speeding the resolution of the fundamental problem.

Similarly, even if the fundamental problem is a genetically grounded dysfunction in some part of one's neural machinery, this dysfunction will result in a host of psychological adaptations and accommodations that may contribute to the problem. Therefore, talking with a trained therapist and confronting potentially painful truths about one's life may greatly enhance the effects of antidepressant medication.

Although it is minimized in today's climate of biological psychiatry and the popular view of depression as a physical illness, the effort to gain psychological insight is a necessary part of overcoming depression, according to many practitioners. That is because learning can't be put in a pill. And it is learning that builds a mind and makes that mind useful to an individual.

Think of a Christmas tree strung with lights. If the tree represents the brain, the lights are the neural networks that encode memories, ideas, and thoughts. We are born with a sparse set of lights—the rudimentary circuitry needed for initial survival. But as we grow, thousands of new lights—new constellations of neural connections—are added to the tree every time we learn something. By adulthood, the diversity of light patterns is immense. In fact, no two trees, no two brains (even those of identical twins) are the same. Some people's neural trees glow brilliantly with elaborate patterns of multicolored lights installed and maintained by a lifetime of active learning and rich experience. Other people's trees burn less brightly or glow with only a limited range of colors.

Drugs can act like a dimmer switch for the entire set of lights or particular circuits on the tree. Stimulants such as amphetamine can make the lights blaze briefly, while depressants such as Valium can dim the entire tree. Other drugs, such as LSD, can scramble the color and patterns of the twinkling lights, producing unusual or bizarre patterns.

But *no* drug can *add* new lights. Some drugs can extinguish lights, of course, but that's a different story. Only learning adds lights, adds color, adds complexity, adds pattern. And there is simply no way to learn about one's self without talking, listening, thinking, and wrestling with the conflicts, the fears, and the emotions that can arise in the process.

"Talk" therapy, in other words, is a vitally important intervention. And although it is not usually viewed as a biological intervention, it shares this trait with drugs.

"Psychotherapy works because it works on the brain," says Steven Hyman, director of the National Institute of Mental Health. "Any time you learn anything you are laying down memories—certain synapses have grown, new ones have grown, some have been strengthened, others have been weakened and some have been pruned so that you have an altered set of circuits that can reassemble memories out of visual stores elsewhere in the brain. Psychotherapy is a specialized form of learning, and it almost certainly does some similar things to drugs—and maybe different things that can be very beneficial."

Unfortunately, the current medical and cultural climate favors the biomedical model of depression, and that makes it difficult to fairly assess any particular instance of depression. It also has led to a profound shift in attitude toward treatment for depression.

"When I came into psychiatry I had to twist people's arms to take medication," says Nesse. "And quite uniformly the public attitude was 'But isn't that tampering with my brain? Isn't it abnormal to use drugs to influence moods? Don't I need my emotions? Aren't they normally useful?' And partly that was the result of the psychoanalytic influence of therapists telling people that if they took drugs they couldn't get therapy properly. So that was part of the ideology behind it. But nowadays it's exactly the opposite. Now patients very often almost demand medications even when it's very clear that their unhappiness is due to their life circumstances. And now I'm very often trying to insist that people get into psychotherapy or consider looking at their lives instead of just taking medication to make themselves feel better. So it's been an incredible sea change just in the past fifteen years."

One of the most potent agents behind this change is the simple fact that for some people, antidepressants work. Despite the fact that a significant fraction of antidepressant response has been repeatedly demonstrated to be a placebo effect, the fact is that millions of people try antidepressants and feel remarkably better. Popular books such as Peter Kramer's thoughtful *Listening to Prozac* and William Styron's powerful autobiographical account of his depression, *Darkness Visible,* offer compelling examples of the effectiveness of antidepressant drug therapy.

Viewing depression as a physical illness akin to diabetes is also far more palatable to both patients and their families than seeing depression as a normal capacity for detecting psychological problems. To this day, mental illness carries a negative stigma completely absent from the attitude surrounding physical illness. Mental illness has always been more frightening than physical illness because for so many centuries it was inexplicable and the changes wrought in personality were often so bizarre or threatening. In addition, psychological problems often involve other people—and the people most connected are spouses and family members. If depression is a sickness— a simple matter of out-of-balance brain chemicals—then those close to the affected person bear no responsibility and don't need to feel burdened with treatment. But if depression is a complex phenomenon that almost always involves suboptimal psychological adjustments, either as a primary or a secondary effect, then those around an affected individual are unavoidably involved. Sometimes, in fact, depression in one person can actually result from a primary dysfunction in *another* individual— such as when a wife is depressed as a result of a difficult or abusive husband.

Another factor pushing the biomedical perspective of mental illness is the simple lack of time experienced by many people today. Parents holding down jobs, paying bills, and raising children can be hard-pressed to find time to exercise occasionally or to go out for a quiet dinner together once a week, much less spend an hour a week for ten or more weeks wrestling with a difficult psychological conundrum. It's much, much easier to believe that a depressive episode is a simple serotonin deficiency curable with one pill a day.

Rounding out the phalanx of forces arrayed against a holistic view of mental illness are the twin forces of managed care and drug company promotional efforts.

Psychotherapeutic drugs are a boon to managed care companies because, at least initially, they are cheap compared to multiple sessions with a human therapist. The fact that they do work for at least some of the people who take them provides abundant justification for policies that restrict access to psychotherapy. Elliot Valenstein, a historian of psychiatry and professor at the University of Michigan, writes in his recent book *Blaming the Brain* that "many health plans pay 80 percent of the average fee of physicians who dispense antidepressants, but only 50 percent of a psychotherapist's normal fee. In some instances, managed-care employees have been instructed to recommend using drug treatment and to discourage hospitalizing mental patients."[7]

Finally, the profits to be made from a successful drug such as Prozac drive an enormous "education" program aimed at physicians, psychologists, and the public at large, the goal of which is to build a context that supports the sale and use of drugs for solving psychological problems. It is estimated that the drug industry spends more than $12.3 billion promoting drugs every year in the United States alone. In addition, more than $5,000 per physician are spent annually on promotional or educational efforts by drug companies.[8]

Drug companies are large, centralized, multinational businesses with vast financial resources at their disposal to create "educational" and advertising materials to promote the biomedical paradigm of mental illness. Psychotherapists, on the other hand, are only loosely organized, operate largely autonomously, and have very limited resources to promote a more holistic perspective of mental illness. This situation leads to a very lopsided theoretical and ideological "playing field." The public is awash in messages touting the biological dimension of depression and depressive feelings—and often these messages subtly minimize or discredit the psychological and environmental dimensions of the problem. Appreciating this huge imbalance is critical as the age of pharmacology unfolds and drug companies offer the public ever more perfect mood-altering drugs.

CHAPTER 5

Selling Happiness

SOONER OR LATER, SOME DRUG COMPANY IS GOING to discover the next antidepressant blockbuster—the sequel to Prozac, the new breakthrough, the more perfect drug. But that discovery alone will not win the prize. The discovery of a truly superior mood-altering molecule will be just the beginning. Getting clearance from the U.S. Food and Drug Administration to sell the drug, and then convincing doctors and the public to actually *buy* the drug are monumental challenges in their own right.

With hundreds of millions of dollars already spent on discovery, these struggles are supercharged with the specter of failure. So much rides on the success of a new molecular entity that the pressures are enormous on corporate executives answering to hungry shareholders, on product team leaders answering to corporate executives, on advertising agencies answering to team leaders, on copywriters answering to ad agency executives, and, supporting the entire structure, on the "detail men"—the hundreds of salespeople who fan out to physician and HMO customers around the world to hawk the new molecules and who answer to everyone in the chain of command above them.

And danger lurks in that pressure.

The drug industry is no more or less scrupulous, altruistic, or ethical than any other industry. It is composed of human beings who vary widely in their integrity, honesty, and intelligence. Many, perhaps most, workers are honorable people whose sense of integrity and scientific honesty counterbalance unbridled interest in the bottom line. But in any industry and in any group of human beings there will also be those who make mistakes—intentional or unintentional, those who respond to pressure by bending the truth, and those who follow the path of least resistance even if, for instance, that path involves creating and disseminating ideas or theories that they know are simplistic, deceptive, or simply untrue.

Falsehoods can creep into every step of the long drug development and marketing pipeline. The clinical trials used to test drug effectiveness can be arranged to favor a candidate drug—for instance, when a drug company can handpick the scientists who conduct the trials. The data from those studies can be manipulated in ways that emphasize effectiveness and deemphasize negative results or unwanted side effects. Pressure can be exerted on individual authors and entire institutions to block publication of studies unfavorable to a drug company's interests. Public "educational" materials can distort the reality of mental illness, promulgate outright falsehoods, and unjustifiably tout the efficacy of drug therapy. Marketing efforts can blatantly attempt to redefine an illness to broaden the pool of potential "patients." And occasionally drugs can be marketed and sold despite evidence that the drugs in question could be harmful or even fatal under certain circumstances.

These are not idle or speculative assertions, nor do they exhaust the ways in which dishonesty can infiltrate drug development and marketing efforts. Case studies illustrating each of these abuses will be presented in this chapter, not in an attempt to demonize the drug industry, but as a reminder that the issues surrounding the development of more perfect mood-altering drugs extend beyond the drugs themselves and include how those drugs are marketed and sold. A more perfect drug of the type I've been describing will be enormously valuable—undoubtedly just as valuable as Prozac, which now generates sales of almost $3 billion each year.

The drug industry can, and frequently does, point to several historical instances of altruistic behavior: Merck's 1942 delivery of free penicillin to the victims of a nightclub fire in Boston, for instance.[1] But a few such isolated instances do not shield the industry from the harsh realities of today's marketplace, nor set the industry on some higher moral plane than, say, the auto industry, the oil industry, or the computer industry.

The following case studies provide the darker tones

required in any realistic portrait of a complex human enterprise. These tones are needed because they are so conspicuously absent from the cheery, sanitized colors used by the industry itself in its tireless self-promotion efforts. These are documented instances of dishonesty, marketing manipulation, and business interests prevailing over safety concerns. The examples involve a range of drug types, but the morals in each case apply to the development and marketing of future mood-enhancing drugs. They should serve as warning lights to an uncritical embrace of drug-industry "facts"; to advertising for both drugs and the general issue of mental illness; and to assurances of "proven" efficacy, "demonstrated" safety, and "clinically tested" benefits.

People are accustomed to buying cars with a good deal of skepticism for auto industry claims and, in particular, the sales tactics of car dealer sales personnel. Most consumers try to obtain reports by unbiased reviewers, and they enter sales negotiations with an understanding that they must be vigilant for dishonesty, manipulation, and distortion.

In contrast, most people are not accustomed to buying drugs with this attitude, particularly because the "salespeople" wear the honored and respected white coat of medicine. But as the following examples suggest, consumers proceed with this naïveté at their peril.

Case Study 1: Redefining "Normal"

Genentech, one of the hottest of a new breed of companies using genetic engineering to create drugs, had a major problem back in 1985. Company scientists had achieved a phenomenal feat: they managed to insert human genes into bacteria so that they would manufacture human growth hormone in mass quantities. This hormone, which the company named Protropin, was a godsend for children who suffer from pituitary dwarfism—stunted growth caused by an underactive pituitary gland.

There was just one small difficulty: only about seven thousand U.S. children are born with this defect every year.

Because of its enormous start-up costs, Genentech, like all new biotech companies, was under intense pressure to begin turning a profit. As spectacular as its drug was, and even pricing the drug so that a typical year's supply for one child ranged from $10,000 to $50,000, Protropin wasn't going to earn the company the kind of profits it needed with a patient pool of only seven thousand children.

And then someone had a brilliant idea.

The company recognized that each year about ninety thousand children are born whose height falls in the bottom 5 percent of the "normal" distribution of height. Such children are not dwarfs—they're simply shorter than normal. Genentech calculated that if it could sell Protropin to the doctors and parents of these children, it could earn $8 billion to $10 billion annually. A concerted campaign was begun aimed at both doctors and parents and that was designed to bring to light this previously unrecognized "problem."

Genentech, along with Eli Lilly, which sold a competing growth hormone, provided funding to two foundations, the Human Growth Foundation and the Magic Foundation, to support a height screening program for children conducted in schools, shopping malls, and at state fairs. When a child was found who fell in the bottom 5 percent of normal, a letter was sent to school officials and parents, identifying the children with the height "problem."

Meanwhile, doctors, particularly pediatricians, received company-produced information about the availability of growth hormone and its effectiveness in dealing with this "medical" problem.

The strategy paid off. By 1997, about thirty thousand children in the United States were being given injections of growth hormone three times weekly.

Genentech had successfully redefined "normal" height. Tens of thousands of children suddenly became "deficient" and in need of "treatment." The company claimed that about 90 percent of the children getting their drug had a true hormone deficiency. A study conducted by the independent National Institutes of Health, however, said the figure was closer to half.

It is true, of course, that using Protropin to boost height for "normal" but short people is not morally different from any other form of cosmetic manipulation. But in this case, the decisions to engage in the manipulation were being made by parents, not by the "patients" themselves. And on a more practical level, the hormone intervention doesn't work. Medical research now shows that giving growth hormone to children who don't actually have a hormone deficit fails to boost their long-term height. One Japanese study found that boys without a true hormone deficiency who nonetheless took the hormones ended up three inches *shorter* than an unmatched control group. The *British Medical Journal,* in an editorial, concluded that "the treatment of short normal patients in the mistaken belief that the treatment could improve final height is a cruel illusion and an expensive mistake."[2]

Despite such editorials and more recent negative results about the use of growth hormone in normal children, Protopin and other growth hormones continue to sell well—though screenings for height have been discontinued.[3]

Case Study 2: Hardball

About eight million people in the United States suffer from an underactive thyroid gland and thus feel constantly tired, stiff, and chilled. Since 1958, however, replacement synthetic thyroid hormone has been available, freeing such people from these troubling symptoms.

For years the best-selling synthetic thyroid hormone has been Synthroid, which back in the late 1980s was generating about $600 million a year for its owner, the Boots Company of Britain. Synthroid's success drew competition from companies making generic versions of thyroid hormone and, about a decade ago, several of these drugs began to threaten the Synthroid cash cow.

"As a businessman, I had to do something about it," said Carter Eckert, then an executive at Boots, to the *Wall Street Journal.*

What he did was commission a $250,000 study with Dr. Betty Dong, a pharmacy professor at the University of

California at San Francisco, who had written articles about the possible risks of switching patients from brand-name thyroid hormones such as Synthroid to generics.

Dong was given the contract and, in 1987, she and her colleagues began to test Synthroid against three generic hormones in twenty-two women. Boots executives and scientists collaborated closely with Dong at every step in the process, reviewing all procedures and protocols of the study to make sure there were no mistakes that might bias the results. Some minor changes were suggested and implemented. The study continued—each woman received a randomly assigned version of the thyroid hormone for a six-week period. As is common with such studies, neither Dr. Dong nor any of the other investigators knew which versions of the hormones the women were taking. They were "blinded" to minimize any bias they might have during the study and subsequent data analysis.

Finally the trial was complete, and the results were carefully analyzed and reanalyzed. Then the codes labeling the different drugs were broken.

Dr. Dong and Boots were shocked: the data clearly showed that Synthroid was no better than the generics. It was "bioequivalent," meaning that the human body couldn't tell the drugs apart.

When he read Dr. Dong's report of the results, Steve Freeman, then vice president of marketing of Boots, was obviously aware of its implications. He scrawled the following notes: "Tackle therapeutic equivalence issue head on," "Must review harshly," and "Begin to get our ducks in order with the sales force."

Dong, meanwhile, proceeded with the original plan of

publishing the study results in a medical journal. At stake were millions of dollars that could be saved by switching patients to the cheaper generics.

But Boots was adamantly opposed to publication, and began a concerted effort to discredit Dong's work.

Ignoring numerous letters from the company threatening to take actions against her if she proceeded, Dong wrote up her study and submitted it to the prestigious *Journal of the American Medical Association (JAMA)*, which had the study reviewed by five independent physicians. All five recommended that the study be published.

But Boots executives had an important ace up their sleeve. Buried in the twenty-one-page contract that Dong had signed was a clause stating that the results were "not to be published or otherwise released without written consent" of the company. That clause, in fact, violated a UCSF rule designed to protect academic freedom and its researchers from exactly this kind of pressure. But Dong had neglected to run the contract by university lawyers before she signed it.

Dong had goofed. The clause gave sharp teeth to the company's threats to sue, and the university knew it. After standing with Dong for months, the university reversed itself, telling Dong that it could not defend her if she continued, and urging her to withdraw the article.

On the night before the article was to go to the printer, Dong, bedridden with the flu, called her colleagues and discussed the matter. None of them could afford lawyers in a long court battle. "We weren't willing to take that risk," she said. She hung up from her colleagues and told *JAMA* to yank the article.

Boots had survived with their drug and their market share intact. But the company decided to make absolutely sure that Dong's data would never see the light of day.

During the protracted battle with Dong, Boots had been acquired by Knoll Pharmaceuticals, a New Jersey unit of the giant German drug company BASF. Dr. Gilbert H. Mayor, a former medical services director at Boots and now an executive with Knoll, took Dong's data, reinterpreted it using different statistical methods[4] to claim that Synthroid was, in fact, superior to generics, and then had his paper published in the *American Journal of Therapeutics,* where he was an associate editor. This tactic was double-barreled: not only did it provide Knoll with "clinical evidence" of its drug's superiority, it also served to thoroughly discredit Dong and her team.

But then, almost miraculously, the tide began to turn against Mayor and against Knoll.

First came a meticulously researched article by Ralph King Jr. that appeared in the *Wall Street Journal* in April 1996, detailing the entire episode and deeply embarrassing Knoll and BASF. The article prompted the FDA to look into the matter, and in November 1996 the FDA wrote to Knoll, charging that it had violated the Federal Food, Drug, and Cosmetics Act by misbranding Synthroid and concealing from FDA investigators the data it possessed from Dr. Dong.

Facing mounting bad publicity and increasing federal pressure, Knoll finally agreed to allow publication of Dong's original article. That paper appeared in the April 16, 1997, issue of *JAMA,* along with several remarkable letters. In one, Knoll executive Carter Eckert gives two reasons for Knoll's reversal. "First, we had gained a better understanding of the importance of supporting academic freedom and the peer review process," Eckert wrote, "and second, we were concerned that intense media speculation about the study's findings and conclusions was being regarded as fact."

Included in Dong's study was a calculation of the money that could be saved each year if doctors prescribed the equally effective generic versions of thyroid hormone over Synthroid: approximately $350 million. Using that figure, the cost to patients and society at large of the more than two-year suppression of Dong's paper was roughly $800 million.

Case Study 3: Pushing Prozac through the FDA

If there is a high priest of pharmacological Calvinism it is psychiatrist Peter Breggin. Breggin believes passionately that all drugs for depression are bad, and he says that in his twenty-five years of practice, he has never started a patient on antidepressants.[5] He believes that depression is "obviously" a psychological and spiritual condition and thus he thinks drugs can never do anyone any good because they don't address the "real" causes of depression.

His extreme positions make him a fringe critic of "biological psychiatry"—though by virtue of his willingness to be branded a zealot or worse, his is the loudest voice shouting from the edge. Although his denial of a biological dimension to mental illness leaves him vulnerable to charges of irrationality, some of his points about the drug industry are cogent and important.

Breggin's fury with drug companies has motivated him to undertake some painstaking investigations that more even-handed critics would never bother with. And one of these investigations produced findings well worth considering by anyone thinking about using the mind-altering products of the drug industry.

This particular investigation probed the way Eli Lilly conducted the testing required to get FDA approval of Prozac.

Because drug testing is inordinately expensive, and because U.S. taxpayers don't want to pay for such testing themselves, drug companies such as Lilly spend tens of millions of dollars to organize and conduct their own drug tests to produce data to support their case before the FDA. The FDA issues many rules and regulations that attempt to control the way these tests—called clinical trials—are conducted, to minimize manipulations that could make a drug appear more effective than it really is. Unfortunately there are always loopholes, and when a quarter-billion-dollar investment is on the line, those loopholes will be used to maximum advantage.

Breggin obtained FDA records and correspondence through the Freedom of Information Act and pieced together the following story of Lilly's strenuous efforts to get Prozac approved by the FDA.

Three separate sets of clinical studies, or protocols, were used by the FDA to decide Prozac's fate.

The first protocol was conducted at six separate sites by six principal investigators—all chosen by Lilly. Each of these studies compared the effectiveness of Prozac against a dummy pill, or placebo, and one of the traditional antidepressants, Imipramine. In only one of the six studies did Prozac appear to be clearly better than the placebo on most of the variables tested— variables such as self-reported mood changes, improvements in sleep and eating patterns, increased motivation or energy, etc. The other five studies either showed Prozac to be no better than the placebo, or better only on a few variables studied (such as improved energy, feelings of guilt, and ability to concentrate). Most of the studies, in contrast, showed that Imipramine was clearly superior to the placebo in alleviating depressive thoughts and feelings.

To extract some lemonade from these lemons, Lilly used the fairly common statistical technique of pooling the data from the six individual studies. This technique has a subtle but extremely important effect: it makes it easier to prove statistical significance in differences measured among the groups. In other words, if Prozac improved a patient's self-rated mood by, say, 3 percent compared to the placebo group in a pool of only 15 patients, the result would not be considered statistically significant—it could be due to random chance. But that same 3 percent improvement in a pool of 150 patients *does* reach statistical significance, because, by the laws of statistics, in a larger group of people it is less likely that the difference would be due to chance alone.

The bottom line is that by pooling all six studies, Lilly magnified the neutral or only slightly positive results to achieve an effect it could claim was statistically significant. Again, the technique of pooling, in itself, is not unethical—in fact, it's fairly routine. But in this case the technique was applied to studies that, individually, only weakly supported the company's claims.

Unfortunately for Lilly, this technique still failed to impress the FDA. "Imipramine was clearly more effective than placebo, whereas fluoxetine [the generic name for Prozac] was less consistently better than placebo," the FDA wrote in March 1985.

Lilly reworked the numbers again. The company discarded the results of one of the largest negative studies. And they reincluded patients who, while they were in the Prozac trials, were also being given other psychotropic drugs. This tactic muddies the view of Prozac's effectiveness. When two or more drugs are taken simultaneously, it becomes impossible to know whether the Prozac was responsible for mood improvement or whether one of the other drugs was responsible. Despite this unavoidable ambiguity, the FDA accepted the protocol as evidence supporting Prozac's effectiveness.

The second of the three protocols did show Prozac as more effective than the placebo on most measures— though not on one of the more important ones: how patients themselves rated how they felt. On this measure, Prozac was no better than the placebo. Still, only 25 patients completed this protocol, and only 11 of these were actually given Prozac.

The third protocol used by the FDA as the basis for Prozac's approval was the largest, being conducted at ten separate sites. Two types of patients were studied: those who were either "mildly" or "moderately" depressed. In the study of mildly depressed patients, Prozac did no better than the placebo. But the group of 171 moderately depressed patients who completed the trial did show some improvement on Prozac, including their own self-report of how they felt. However, this protocol had some fairly serious design flaws, including a high dropout rate of participants due to unpleasant side effects such as agitation, insomnia, and headache (up to 50% in some groups) and the use of a "placebo washout"—a fairly standard but questionable technique in which patients who respond to a placebo in a trial phase of the study are dropped and the study is begun again.

This "weeding out" of placebo-responders may lower the overall placebo response in the "real" trial—which would be good for the drug company because the goal is to show that patients on the drug do significantly better than those on placebo. The FDA, although it allowed the protocol as evidence on Prozac's behalf, concluded that the study was "seriously flawed" and determined that "It is not possible to arrive at a single, unequivocal interpretation of the results."

It was on the basis of these studies that Prozac was approved for sale in the United States in December 1987.

None of this means that Prozac is useless for some people with depression. Far from it. As we will see in the next chapter, Prozac *can* be helpful—sometimes even life-saving. The point here is simply that Prozac is less of a miracle drug than most people think and placebos—sugar pills—are much *more* powerful than most people think. In addition, Eli Lilly's effort to win FDA approval for Prozac illustrates how powerfully drug companies are motivated to get such approval and how much effort must sometimes be expended in getting approval for a drug that has shown only modest success in clinical trials.

Case Study 4: Miseducating the Public

It had all the appearances of a medically accurate, altruistic effort to educate the public about a misunderstood and underdiagnosed disease. It was a large, well-designed advertisement appearing in major newspapers across the country featuring a neuroanatomical drawing, two brain scan images, and a photograph of Abraham Lincoln. The ad was sponsored by the independent-sounding National Alliance for Research on Schizophrenia and Depression (NARSAD).[6] The title of the ad: "Depression. A flaw in chemistry, not character."

This ad was one of dozens appearing every year in popular media that purport to educate the public about a wide range of disorders. Often the ads are supported by patient advocacy groups such as NARSAD—organizations formed to lobby for increased awareness of and research into various types of medical disorders.

Such groups serve important and legitimate functions, but they also solicit and receive large amounts of money from drug companies. Often this money comes in the form of "unrestricted educational grants," meaning that a company donor cannot dictate how the money is used. For instance, the web site of the National Depressive and Manic-Depressive Association was created with funding provided by Glaxo-Wellcome, Inc., the maker of the antidepressant Wellbutrin. A "psychoeducational" program developed for the National Mental Health Association was produced with funding by Eli Lilly, Zeneca Pharmaceuticals, Abbott Labs, Pfizer, Wyeth-Ayerst, and four other drug companies. And for the past ten years, Lilly has donated money to NARSAD to support a scientific symposium to discuss research progress.

Even when such funding comes in the form of unrestricted grants, everyone involved in creating materials, designing programs, or organizing symposia understands the company's interests, and that understanding, even if subconscious, can color the eventual educational products.

The ad sponsored by NARSAD is a classic example.

The NARSAD ad contains several oversimplifications, some distortions, and one flagrant error. To begin with, it promotes the drug-company party line that depression "like diabetes" is a physical, chemical problem, not the complex expression of physical, psychological, and environmental variables it truly is. The "diabetes" metaphor is a favorite of drug companies because it implies that antidepressant drugs, like insulin, can be legitimately used on a lifetime basis to "correct" a genetically determined "chemical imbalance."

The ad goes on to flatly state that because depression is an "inherited disease," it may be "curable" instead of being merely "treatable." Given that the neurological underpinnings of depressive mood states are still only vaguely understood, and also given the unavoidable environmental influences on depression, talk of a "cure" for depression is, at best, hopelessly premature.

A blatant oversimplification of the nature of both happiness and depression comes in the caption beside a drawing of several neurons and their attendant synapses. "Here they are," the caption reads, "The keys to happiness. A few of the thousands of synapses that have the power to make any given day one of the most joyous in your life or the most despairing."

And another misrepresentation: the ad shows images of two brains: a "normal" brain and a "depressive" brain. Arrows point to dark spaces on both scans that represent the fluid-filled spaces called ventricles inside the brain. The ventricles of the "depressive" brain are significantly larger than those of the "normal" brain. The text beside the images says that according to recent medical research depression is caused "when an insufficient level of the neurotransmitter serotonin is passed through the synapses of the frontal lobe of the brain."

The errors here boggle the mind. Although some changes in ventricle size have been reported in the brains of some schizophrenics, no evidence connects ventricle size with depression. Furthermore, ventricle size has nothing whatever to do with "synapses" or serotonin. The ventricles pictured, moreover, are not in the "frontal lobes." Finally, as we've seen, it is simply not true that depression is "caused" by depleted serotonin levels. On the contrary, lower serotonin levels are probably "caused" by depression.

Nowhere in the ad are antidepressant drugs specifically mentioned. But the point of the ad is to create a context in which drugs appear as a perfectly logical solution to a problem. If the ad is accepted at face value, it becomes impossible not to view drugs as the only and best way of dealing with depression—which is exactly what the drug companies want.

Case Study 5: Dangerous Diet Pills

In the early summer of 1996, Mary Linnen was playing golf with her parents and the man she was going to marry in a few months. In midgame she noticed that her heart was fluttering and she couldn't catch her breath. True, she was overweight—at 5 feet, 5 inches and about 190 pounds, she was considerably heavier than the maximum "optimal" weight for a woman her height: 142 pounds. But this didn't feel normal to her—and she thought she knew what was causing it: the pills she had begun taking a few weeks earlier to help her lose 30 pounds by her wedding day.

And so, twenty-four days after she'd started, she quit taking the pill combination called "fen/phen," shorthand for "fenfluramine/phentermine," which some eighteen million other adults in this country were also using in the eternal quest to lose weight.

Oddly, her health only got worse after she quit. As summer turned to New England fall, she was in and out of the hospital with heart and lung ailments. Then her vision began to blur. And then on February 22, 1997, she died. She was thirty years old. An autopsy performed at Massachusetts General Hospital concluded that Linnen had died of "pulmonary hypertension associated with fen-fluramine and phentermine therapy."[7]

Months before Linnen had obtained her prescription in May 1996, a report was circulating among medical specialists about potential problems with fen/phen. That report, from the International Primary Pulmonary Hypertension Study Group, was finally published in the *New England*

Journal of Medicine on August 29, 1996—about the time Linnen was beginning to realize that her health problems weren't going away even though she had stopped taking the pills. That study found that the incidence of the potentially fatal lung disease was almost thirty times greater among people who were taking a diet drug closely related chemically to fen/phen—dexfenfluramine, sold as Redux.

The warning sounded by the report was muted by an editorial appearing in the same issue of the journal written by two prominent researchers, JoAnn Manson of Harvard Medical School and Gerald Faich of the University of Pennsylvania. Among other reasons to minimize the report from the international group, the doctors argued, was that the risk posed by the potential lung problems amounted to 14 deaths per million people using the drugs, while 280 people per million would die from complications of obesity itself.

The impact of the positive editorial more than outweighed any negative effects of the study report: on rumors of the editorial, the stock of Interneuron Pharmaceutical, Inc., the U.S. maker of Redux, shot up 13 percent the day before the article actually appeared.

Much to the journal's embarrassment, it was later revealed that Manson and Faich both had financial ties to the makers of Redux. Manson had been paid to testify on behalf of the company at the FDA hearings held to decide whether to approve the drug. Faich had served as a paid consultant for two companies, Servier, the company that markets Redux in Europe, and American Home Products, which markets the drug in the United States in collaboration with Interneuron.

If the authors' editorial was otherwise balanced and included all the known risks of using fen/phen and Redux, their conflicts of interest might be considered minor—simply a reminder that information from even the most prestigious medical journals can be tainted by self-interest. But, in fact, the editorial was incomplete, according to Dr. Elliot Valenstein at the University of Michigan in his book *Blaming the Brain.* The editorial did not review all known hazards of the pills and, in particular, it did not mention the serious problem that eventually led to both drugs being yanked from the market by companies suddenly nervous about hundreds of lawsuits.

More than two years before the editorial was written, a Belgian heart doctor named Mariane Ewalenko was trying to figure out why the valves in some of her patients had suddenly become leaky. She quizzed them on medications they were taking. Seven patients in a row said the same thing: diet pills. Specifically, either fen/phen or Redux, which went on sale in Europe much earlier than in the United States.

At a medical conference in February 1994, Dr. Ewalenko announced her findings. "This is very suspicious," she said. "Listen carefully to your patients for heart murmurs."

After that, more cases were found and reported in Belgium—at least thirty people who acquired heart-valve problems while taking the diet pills.

On April 30, 1996, with fen/phen already being consumed by millions of patients in the United States, the FDA approved the related drug Redux for sale. Nobody from the FDA and none of the medical experts appearing to testify for the drug said they had heard anything about the reports from Belgium according to a report in the *Wall Street Journal*.[8] And American Home Products, the company marketing the drug made by Interneuron, didn't mention the issue.

But they knew about it.

Redux went on sale and was an instant hit. In its first five months on the market, 1.2 million prescriptions were written, and sales were booming along at about $20 million per month.[9]

Although Redux was approved by the FDA only for the "morbidly obese," clinics and private weight loss centers promoted the drug widely and prescribed it to untold numbers of people only mildly overweight who sought the drug. "A very large proportion of people are using [Redux and similar drugs] for cosmetic weight loss," said Morton Maxwell, head of an obesity clinic at the University of California at Los Angeles.[10] "It's really scary."

In July 1997, the heart valve problem flared to life in the United States. Doctors from the Mayo Clinic in Rochester, Minnesota, reported finding twenty-four women using fen/phen with the same uncommon heart valve condition found years previously in Belgium. By December of that year, twenty-seven women had surgery to correct the valve problems. The surgery worked for twenty-four of the women, but three of them died from complications of the surgery.

When the Mayo Clinic findings were made public, a physician working for American Home Products was quoted as saying, "We'd never seen anything like this." Apparently he didn't know the scope of the company's information. Asked again by a *Wall Street Journal* reporter later that year, American Home admitted that it *had* known of the Belgian cases—twenty-five of them, in fact. And they knew of these cases *before* applying to the FDA for approval to market Redux. American Home says it passed on information about ten of the cases to the FDA, saying the rest were neither "serious nor unexpected."

But James Bilstad, director of the FDA's drug-evaluation office, says the agency received *no* reports of heart-valve problems—though he admits they might have been tucked into reports of "nonserious" cardiac side effects without being labeled specifically as heart-valve problems.

Responding to the Mayo Clinic findings, American Home issued a press release saying "the data from the Mayo Clinic are limited and therefore inconclusive."[11] Fenfluramine remained on the market, and millions of women continued to take it.

But the Mayo findings provoked the FDA to do its own investigation. A screening of 291 diet-pill patients from five sites indicated that about a third of those women had "silent" evidence of heart-valve damage— that is, damage that would not have been detected unless doctors were specifically looking for it because the damage did not provoke noticeable symptoms at that stage.

Suddenly the makers of both fen/phen and Redux were exposed to the potential of massive lawsuits by millions of people. Before the FDA could act to ban the drugs, the companies pulled the products from the market. Despite that action, more than eight hundred suits *have* been filed—including one still pending by the parents of Mary Linnen.

To defend itself against such claims, American Home funded a large-scale study of its own involving more than a thousand patients, some of whom took Redux and some of whom took a dummy pill. The results, announced at a meeting of the American College of Cardiology in Atlanta in March 1998, shows "no significant increase in the prevalence of clinically relevant heart valve [leakage] after two to three months of taking Redux."

Whether two to three months of exposure is adequate to determine the incidence of heart valve problems is just one of the questions raised by the study. A more global concern is the extent to which studies funded by a drug company can be trusted to be objective.

Several studies have shown that when drug companies sponsor a clinical trial the results are more likely to conclude that the company's drug had advantages over standard or traditional drugs.[12] In a specific example of this trend, a team of doctors in Toronto reviewed seventy research papers about a class of heart drugs called calcium channel blockers. The team ranked the papers as being either "supportive," neutral," or "opposed" to the drugs. They then determined whether the authors of the papers had any financial ties to the companies that made the drugs. They found that 96 percent of the authors who supported the calcium channel blockers had such ties, while only 37 percent of authors whose reports "opposed" the drugs had such ties. In only two of the seventy instances were the financial connections acknowledged in the articles.[13]

— ∽ —

These case studies are reminders that the drug industry is no less rapacious than other industries; that healthy skepticism is an appropriate attitude toward claims of drug effectiveness and safety; that drug companies wield enormous power to shape public opinion, either directly via advertising to consumers, or indirectly via advertising and sales pitches to doctors, or via financial contributions to mental health advocacy groups that may or may not acknowledge their funding sources.

These realities of the modern pharmaceutical industry mean that it's going to be difficult for average consumers to fairly evaluate the worth of the more perfect mood-altering drugs emerging from drug-company labs. These drugs will be launched with massive, slick, subtle, and effective marketing blitzes similar to that recently used to send Pfizer's impotence drug Viagra off on its stellar commercial career.[14] The only counterweight to such drug-company onslaughts is public education about the realities of the condition in question—an effort that is usually slow and ineffective because there are no profits to be made from the enterprise.

This is the context in which individuals must decide whether to use existing mood-altering drugs, and the better ones sure to come in the future. Vital to making such decisions is consideration of an aspect of mood management almost wholly missing from the information generally available: What mood, or moods, are people aiming for? In short, what is the goal of pharmacological mood management?

CHAPTER 6

Zen and the Art of Prozac

W<small>E HAVE SEEN THAT THE RAPID PACE OF DISCOVERY</small> in neuroscience and pharmacology makes the development of safer, more side-effect-free mood-altering drugs a virtual certainty. These drugs will enable people to manipulate the neural machinery of happiness, because happiness itself has as much to do with biology as with external variables such as education, wealth, and professional attainment. Research clearly suggests that we are born with a happiness set point that constrains our mood and emotional range.

Contrary to the prevailing disease model of depression, however, depressive moods and other negative affects such as anxiety, fear, and anger are not necessarily defects of nature or illnesses. They are products of millions of years of natural selection and are designed to provide us with warning signals that something is amiss in our lives. The machinery of mood is complex, and it can break in a huge variety of ways. But an overreliance on a strictly biological perspective on mood disorders can lead to mistaking a negative mood as a dysfunction when, in fact, it may represent a valid alarm being sounded by a healthy system.

The wise use of new mood-altering drugs is made more difficult by the skewed presentation of both the drugs themselves and the problems they are intended to address. The monumental profit to be made from such drugs creates pressure on all aspects of drug development, testing, marketing, and regulation—pressure that can lead to false or misleading claims about a drug's safety and efficacy, and an unbalanced description of the nature of mental illness.

One issue remains to be explored, and it is perhaps the most basic one facing everyone considering using a drug to enhance or correct their moods: What is the goal of such drug use? What mood, or moods, are people aiming at? Happiness? What, exactly, does that mean? How happy are we supposed to be? How happy *can* we be? Is there such a thing as an "optimal" mood? When should we be satisfied that we're feeling about as good, in general, as we can?

Until very recently, such questions, although of interest to philosophers, have had little relevance to ordinary folks because they were moot: What difference did it make when you couldn't do much to change your mood or happiness set point? But things have changed, and they're going to change even more in the near future with the advent of new, more effective drugs. These questions are thus taking on new urgency.

It wasn't until she went away to college that Lou Anne Jaeger fully realized just how crazy her family life had been.

The problems revolved around her father, a volatile man of great mood swings who was a prominent radio and television personality in his community. Throughout Lou Anne's childhood he cycled between periods of wild exuberance and dark, mean depressions.

"He abandoned us a couple of times," she says. "And he did certain really classical manic things. He'd take off with his secretary and go traveling in Europe until they ran out of money and then he'd come home."

Often the focus of her father's raging moods was Lou Anne's mother. Particularly when he drank—which was often—the scenes would turn ugly.

One of those scenes triggered Lou Anne's first full-blown episode of depression.

She was home from Colby College on Christmas break. Home after having months to ponder a family life she was now seeing as extremely dysfunctional. Her father could feel the shift.

"Up until that point I had never been verbally attacked," Lou Anne says. "I had never had him turn on me. Until that point my sister, and really my mother, shielded me. I think it was just that I was there, in the room, when he was verbally abusing my mother and I don't remember exactly what he said, but he just turned it on me for the first time. I think he was sensing the change in me, sensing that I had gotten to the point of recognizing that this was baloney. I didn't want to play his games anymore."

Lou Anne pauses a moment. It is January. A deep blanket of soft snow covers the low suburban hills where she lives. Her house smells of fresh paint because she just moved in two days ago with her children. We sit in the living room, which is empty except for our two chairs and a small wicker stand against one wall. On the stand is a small Buddha, some candles, and a dish for incense. Lou Anne has soft features and short-cropped hair that is beginning to go gray. Her gaze is steady as she recounts her first bout with depression.

Her father's verbal attack left her reeling, and she returned to Colby feeling miserable.

"I wanted to kill myself," she says. "I felt generally sick all the time. Just general malaise."

She visited the school doctor, who prescribed an old antidepressant, Elavil.

"I hated it," she says. "I think I slept eighteen hours a day when I started," she says. "It left me fogged, like I had taken too many antihistamines."

She was also referred to the school psychologist, but she found his views on depression—and psychology in general—unhelpful at best.

"This was a man who thought that the best way to treat homosexuality was through negative reinforcing shock therapy," Lou Anne says. "So his understanding of human compassion was limited, and he just had no clue what it was like to be a kid. No clue. So I went, but it was not productive."

After switching to a less sedating antidepressant, Lou Anne began a slow recovery. She finished at Colby, majoring in philosophy. But she never felt fully normal.

"I think I was pretty depressed throughout the entire time, but not enough to stop functioning," she says. "People have told me since that I was really a pain to be around because I was so negative."

Back in Rochester, New York, where she grew up, she worked at a department store and pursued opera in her spare time. While rehearsing for a production of *Die Fledermaus* she fell in love with a fellow actor. She says this was the first serious relationship in her life and that it was "disastrous." When it ended, depression overwhelmed her again. As her mood spiraled ominously downward, she doggedly continued working on psychological issues in her life with a therapist she liked—a young Ph.D. student at a local divinity school. Although not a formally religious person herself, Lou Anne found him supportive. But it seemed like the more she worked, the lower she sank.

"I made a suicide plan and I was going to do it," she says. "As a last desperate thing I called my therapist. And he's going on and on and trying to give me reasons why I shouldn't and I'm like 'right, there's no way he's going to tell me any reason not to.' Finally, in desperation, he said, 'I'm not supposed to say this to you, but I want you to know that I found tremendous help and strength in acknowledging Jesus Christ as my savior.' Well, I knew he wasn't supposed to say that, and I knew that if I ratted on him it would be his butt. And so I instantly realized that this guy really trusted me. And if he trusted me, well, all right, maybe it wasn't totally hopeless after all. That's one person who trusted me. And that kind of lifted the desire to do it."

Again she recovered. She met another opera performer, John, and they eloped in 1980. They had two children, Dietrich and Vanessa. It was just after Vanessa's birth that Lou Anne began therapy again.

"I presented it as needing to talk about my father—alcohol issues—because at that point the term 'adult child of an alcoholic' had been coined and I was exploring myself as one of those," she says.

But she also needed the therapy to help her deal with the slow disintegration of her marriage. Whenever the therapist would suggest a trial of antidepressant medication, Lou Anne would balk. Then during one session she broke down in the office and began sobbing. Her therapist gave it one last shot: "Are you sure you don't want to try some medication?" she asked.

Lou Anne relented. The medication the therapist chose was Prozac.

There was no mistaking when the drug began to work.

"I suddenly felt like I could take a deep breath," she says. "It just relieved the anxiety like that. I would not have ever described myself as being anxious. Never. But after starting I realized, 'Wow, have I been anxious. I've been incredibly tense.'"

Five months after she began taking Prozac, she and John separated.

"He had as much to do with our problems as I did," she says. "But he wasn't willing to work with it . . .

he refused to go into therapy. There was nothing else I could do."

The separation left her feeling liberated and buoyant. Things were looking up. She advanced in her career as a manager of computer programmers at a local hospital. And then, one day in 1995, a colleague at work invited her to visit the Rochester Zen Center, where he was a member. Several days later she walked up to the large wooden front door of the Zen Center, entered the foyer, and took off her shoes in the Buddhist tradition.

Through a large window, Lou Anne could see a serene interior courtyard with winding brick paths, neatly trained trees and shrubs, and a covered walkway that hugged the perimeter. A hub of Zen teaching since 1966, the Rochester Zen Center was founded by Roshi Philip Kapleau, an American who studied Zen in Japan and who wrote several seminal books introducing Zen practice to Western audiences.

Her friend gave Lou Anne a brief tour of the center, ending with the zendo, the heart of the center and the room in which most meditation practice takes place. The zendo was dim and quiet. A carved Buddha sat on a simple altar in the front of the room with an offering of fresh fruit in front of it. The air was still laced with the sandalwood incense used during ceremonies.

"I was practically reeling when I walked in," she says. "It was like being hit on the head in some way I can't even describe. There was just this tremendously strong sense of belonging."

She signed up for an introductory workshop and was soon meditating in earnest. She bought one of the long brown robes worn by members during sitting (zazen), and became acquainted with the routines and rituals of the center.

"Zazen helped me react to stimuli in a more simple, more centered way," she says. "I know when I haven't sat. It's like that quote from Jerry Garcia 'If I don't practice for one day, I know it. If I don't practice for two days, other people know it.'"

The more she sat, the more she wanted to get off Prozac, so she reduced her dose from 60 milligrams to 40 milligrams per day.

"I felt a difference, but it was okay," she says.

Then she dropped to 20 milligrams a day for about a month. And then she quit altogether.

"Six weeks later I was a mess," she says. "I was sobbing at work, breaking down, crying in front of my boss. Sleeping a lot. Irritable with the kids. Just no energy."

She plodded through the summer. In August she participated in a four-day sesshin—a period of intense meditation at the Zen Center. In previous sesshins she found clarity of mind, greater energy, and a keener sense of herself and her life situation. But this sesshin was a disaster.

"It was horrible," she says. "The sitting was terrifying. I was so filled with anxiety that just physically keeping myself from bolting out of the zendo was a conscious effort. Every round of sitting was like the first. Like 'O God, why am I here, why am I doing this?' There was never any letting go and settling into the practice."

But she stuck it out—and left the center with at least one very clear insight: she should resume Prozac.

In retrospect she says she fell victim to the notion that

it's better and more noble to live life's struggles without drugs. In her case, she thought that meditation alone would—or should—be enough.

"I thought zazen would somehow let me get past moods," she says. "I thought that somehow the more one sat, the less necessary the antidepressants would be. I thought that somehow being held up artificially was keeping me from moving deeper into Zen."

In fact, however, Lou Anne—and several other members of the Zen Center—have discovered just the opposite: *not* taking antidepressants has kept them from moving deeper into Zen. Only when they use their medications do they have the energy and the composure to fully engage in their practice and to experience the clarity of mind and deep insight that are characteristic of Zen.

"I feel normal now," Lou Anne says. "I have no doubt you can be enlightened and take Prozac."

Lou Anne's story illustrates many of the ideas threading through this book. Her depressive moods, for instance, were clearly not the result of a simple biological defect, nor were they purely the result of childhood trauma. Her suicidal depression, when it struck, was indeed an "illness," just as a heart attack is an "illness." But only in rare cases do either heart attacks or depressions result from a pure biological or genetic defect. In Lou Anne's case—as with the vast majority of people suffering from a mental "illness"—the dysfunction arose from the tightly coiled influences of *both* biology and psychology.

It's impossible at this time—and it may forever be impossible—to parse and quantify the roots of her depression. Was 25 percent of the problem due to faulty wiring and disordered genes? Or was it 50 percent? Or 75 percent? The fact that nature and nurture feed upon each other means that even when a given case of mental illness begins as exclusively a biological problem, or exclusively a reaction to psychological trauma, the problem quickly "infects" the other sphere, resulting in a problem with *both* roots. The trauma of abuse or neglect, for instance, inflicts physical damage on the developing brain and fragile neurons of a child. Conversely, a strictly genetic mutation that results in emotional hyper- or undersensitivity will soon produce changes in the behavior of caregivers that will leave psychological impressions.

Lou Anne suspects that her father suffers from some degree of manic-depression—a reasonable guess, given his classic behavior and mood patterns. Manic-depression, in turn, has been linked to a constellation of genes that are inherited in unpredictable ways.[1] Lou Anne may well have inherited some of those genes—and may have ended up with defects in the neural machinery that creates and maintains the happiness set point and the range of mood states on either side of the set point.

But Lou Anne's set point, her basic neural functioning, and her overall emotional development were also surely hit hard by the stress and the tension of her unpredictable family life and a father with a crippled capacity to form healthy relationships. Lou Anne's environment impacted her brain and its development, which, in turn, influenced how she responded to her environment, which created further changes on her brain and so on in the classic spiral feedback loop that characterizes all human development. In Lou Anne's case the forces of biology and upbringing conspired to drive the spiral downward: a neurochemistry perhaps slightly fragile at the start entered a world full of psychological hammers, which further weakened her neurochemistry, and so on.

Lou Anne's experience also puts flesh and blood on a related idea, that sometimes depression is the response of a *healthy* neurology or a *healthy* psychology to unhealthy, dysfunctional, or dangerous life events.

When she was verbally attacked by her father during Christmas break, Lou Anne felt devastated and depressed. Might this not have been, at least in part, a valid and appropriate response? Might it have been her psyche's way of trying to force introspection, self-evaluation, and, ultimately, healing? Similarly, was the depression that preceded the breakup of her marriage in part due to a subconscious awareness of serious incompatibilities between her and John? Did some part of her know there were unresolved issues and important differences that were preventing her from experiencing the intimacy and love she sought from the marriage?

Such questions reflect the complexity of real human moods and acknowledge the fact that the capacity for depressive moods, like the capacity for pain, has evolved for important, survival-related reasons. A given negative mood may, or may not, be related to relationship difficulties, undue stress, emotional denial or suppression, or any of a dozen other types of life problems. But the possible existence of such problems should never be discounted when evaluating a given negative mood. In fact, the temporary lifting of Mother Nature's rose-colored glasses during a period of depressed mood can provide a valuable, if painful, view of one's life and difficulties, as well as provide motivation to do something about it.

Lou Anne's story also demonstrates that pharmacological Calvinism is alive and well in the land. Her initial resistance to Prozac—and particularly her ill-fated attempt to wean herself off it—sprung not only from her previous bad experiences with antidepressants but also from a belief that she "should" be able to function without a drug. Like many people, Lou Anne felt that "natural" approaches such as therapy, meditation, good nutrition, exercise, and maintaining healthy interpersonal relationships should be enough to protect her from debilitating negative moods. And yet, for her, such practices were *not* enough. By the time she attempted to wean herself off Prozac she had gained considerable insight into her own psychology through decades of psychotherapy and, more recently, Zen meditation. She had dealt with her painful and complicated feelings for her parents, particularly her father, with whom she had restored a relationship after many years. And she was leading a relatively healthy lifestyle. But in the end she found her "natural" state unsatisfactory. Prozac provided a neurobiological supplement or correction that allowed her to live a richer, more satisfying life, much the way others use eyeglasses to correct their "naturally" poor eyesight, thus providing them access to the enriching world of print. As such, Lou Anne's story represents a transcendence of the narrow and outmoded confines of pharmacological Calvinism—a transcendence happening on a global level as Lou Anne's experience is repeated one life at a time.

All her life Lou Anne—like all of us—was searching for a better mood. She was aiming for some goal—call it happiness—a state free of depression, anxiety, fear, and other negative emotions and moods, and rich with pleasure, satisfaction, good humor, and peace. This was what William James was getting at a century ago when he said that everyone's secret motive at all times is "how to gain, how to keep, and how to recover happiness."

Lou Anne laughs now at her simple idea that Zen would somehow allow her to be happy by getting her "beyond moods" to some blissful state without the usual daily oscillations. She now understands a paradox about human happiness and human mood—a paradox that bears directly on a question the lies at the very heart of the many swirling debates about the use of new drugs for mood management. That question is: What *is* optimal mood? What is the goal toward which our efforts should be directed? What mood, or moods, are we trying to achieve with our drugs, or our meditation, or our diets, exercise, and lifestyles?

The Zen answer to the question is not, as is sometimes believed, that moods should be "conquered" such that a person lives in an ever-present state of serenity, detachment, and calm. This answer, and the paradox behind it, are illustrated by a story from another Zen student, the writer Lawrence Shainberg. In his book *Ambivalent Zen,* Shainberg recalls sitting one time with his teacher, or Roshi, as he made green tea.

"So, Roshi, how are you today?" Shainberg said.

"Fine! Fine!" Roshi replied, as he did every time Shainberg asked him.

On this particular day Shainberg found this seemingly automatic reply irritating.

"Come on, Roshi," Shainberg said. "You always say that. Nobody's fine all the time. Don't you ever have bad days?"

"Bad days?" the Roshi answered, "Sure! On bad days I fine. On good days I fine."

The idea, of course, is that one can be "fine" all the time despite "bad days." The trick is accepting the inevitability of "bad days"—which could be extended to the inevitability of negative mood states in general, including anger, anxiety, sadness, fear, and depressive moods—and not complicating matters by trying to deny, avoid, repress, or becoming attached to such moods. The optimal mood state, at least from this Zen perspective, is *not* uninterrupted bliss but a state in which a range of moods can be experienced with a minimum of needless pain and suffering.

This vision of an optimal mood is consistent with the dictates of Darwinian psychiatry, which emphasizes the importance of positive *and* negative moods and the necessity of maintaining a healthy capacity for the full range of human emotional responses. When so-called negative moods are experienced fully, without repression or denial, and when they lead to appropriate changes in behavior, they can enhance overall well-being rather than eroding it. Darwinian psychiatrists would thus probably agree with Zen masters who suggest that being truly happy requires at least an occasional—and perhaps a regular— experience of negative moods. And the fundamental reason for this unavoidable situation is that life itself is an unpredictable roller coaster of positive and negative events that if they are to be dealt with in a healthy, robust way, must be met with correspondingly unpredictable mood states.

The naturalness of this state of affairs was pointed out quite some time ago by the Chinese sage Lao Tzu. In the short book he is said to have written more than twenty-five hundred years ago just prior to heading into the wilderness, never to be heard of again, he wrote the following:

> Under heaven all can see beauty as beauty only
>   because there is ugliness.
> All can know good as good only because there is evil.
> Therefore having and not having arise together.
> Difficult and easy complement each other.
> Long and short contrast each other.
> High and low rest upon each other.
> Voice and sound harmonize each other.
> Front and back follow one another.[2]

In other words, polarity, including the polarities of mood, is an essential feature of the universe, according to Lao Tzu. Things do not exist without a context, a background, a contrasting field. Thus, if one were able to achieve, either by drugs or some superhuman force of will, a state of perpetual bliss, that state would inevitably disintegrate without the contrast of negative mood states, without which the very experience of bliss loses meaning. Eternal happiness, therefore, isn't just practically impossible, it's theoretically impossible as well, just as impossible as a one-sided coin or light without darkness.

As natural and essentially obvious as this situation is, it complicates the task of using more perfect mood-altering drugs by ordinary people. Such drugs must work well, but not *too* well. They must not eliminate the capacity for *all* depressive mood states—that would be both unnatural and ultimately unhelpful for the user. The same holds true for antianxiety drugs, or future drugs that will make the fearful bold, the shy extroverted, and the hostile placid. In every case a simple drug will not do. In every case the goal is not the wholesale elimination of a negative mood or an emotional trait, but the far more difficult goal of endowing the user with a limited but useful range of mood. If the direction of neuroscience and pharmacology continues its present course, such goals will be achieved eventually by the discovery of drugs with unique, subtle, and precisely tailored effects.

The availability of such drugs will present users with a similar challenge: they will need to use mood-enhancing or mood-shifting drugs carefully and with the proper expectations. As is the case today, two types of mood-altering drugs will probably be available: drugs with immediate, short-term effects for temporarily shifting mood in one direction or the other, and drugs with long-term effects that serve to shift the entire spectrum of mood one way or the other.

For instance, alcohol and caffeine today are used by millions of people to temporarily reduce sensations of anxiety or stress or to boost energy and motivation. Like taking aspirin for an occasional headache, such limited use of these drugs can work—and they can work with a minimum of side effects or further problems if used carefully.[3]

Also available today are longer-acting drugs such as Prozac, which appear to shift the entire happiness set point in a positive direction, providing users with a more effective emotional palette than the one they were born with or acquired over the years.

The two types of drugs are commonly used together—long-acting drugs to shift the spectrum, and short-term, fast-acting drugs to make occasional adjustments of mood to better cope with or relate to life experiences. In the future, improved versions of both types of drug will undoubtedly be available, and they will undoubtedly also be used both alone and in concert.

One of the few academics to spend considerable time researching the question of optimal mood and the best ways to achieve it is Robert Thayer, professor of psychology at California State University at Long Beach.

Thayer has found that human moods are supported by two fundamental conditions or variables: energy and tension.[4] When energy is high we tend to be active, alert, and engaged. Low energy leaves us feeling tired, depleted, and relaxed. Similarly, tension spans a continuum from high stress and anxiety to complete calm and relaxation. These twin variables operate independently of each other so that various combinations of energy and tension can exist in a given day.

Thayer describes four basic combinations of energy and tension that have cropped up repeatedly in experiments he has conducted: tense energy; calm tiredness; tense tiredness; and calm energy.

Tense energy is commonly experienced in work environments. Energy is high but so is stress—from deadlines, interpersonal conflicts, a rapid-fire work pace, or simply a strenuous load of work to complete. At moderate levels, tense energy can facilitate productivity, particularly for relatively simple or repetitive tasks. And some people consciously or unconsciously use drugs, primarily nicotine or caffeine, to induce tense energy.

Calm tiredness is the opposite of tense energy: the body is depleted of energy and there is a slow, sluggish feel to the mind and mood. This feeling is not particularly unpleasant when it can be indulged in without other demands—at the end of the day with feet up, for instance. The state can even be mildly pleasant when it represents the culmination of satisfying labor or intellectual achievement.

Problems arise when tension and stress are present without energy: tense tiredness. In observations of thousands of people over several decades, Thayer has found that this combination of mood-related variables is almost universally described as unpleasant. In this state, many people report being in a "bad" mood: feeling cross, hostile, irritable, short-tempered, impatient, pessimistic, and self-doubting. Not surprisingly, this mood is most often experienced toward the end of the day, when body reserves of energy are depleted and a day's worth of events and stress have accumulated.

In contrast, the mood most often described as "good" and most often reported as being the state most desired, is calm energy. In this state people's outlook tends to be positive—they report being satisfied, optimistic, and happy.

With calm energy, work is productive and is engaged in with focus, attention, and poise. This state is similar to one popularly called being in "flow."[5]

In general, Thayer says, calm energy is the most optimal mood to be in. And yet his research shows that it is impossible to achieve calm energy all the time—and it isn't even desirable all the time. Sometimes a modest state of tense energy can be exhilarating and useful, for instance, and a calm-tired state can be pleasurable when it can be enjoyed without pressing physical or emotional demands.

Thayer suggests, therefore, that there is no single "optimal mood." Instead, there are "optimal moods"—a range of moods well matched for particular activities and times of day. The mood that works best for sexual relations, for example, is not necessarily the same mood most useful for cleaning the garage or dealing with small children. Calm energy may be the most generally desired condition, but there will be times when other combinations of the two basic mood variables are more satisfying or appropriate.

In his book *The Origin of Everyday Moods,* Thayer paints a picture of life lived when optimal moods are experienced with smooth transitions between one and the other: "We have energy at our disposal at the high times of day and untroubled tiredness when rest and sleep are required. During our active hours, calm energy predominates, which leads us to full involvement in whatever we are doing. We are not distracted by tension-related demands; rather, each activity receives our full attention. In this calm-energetic mood, the state of our bodies and all our thoughts make us feel good. In this optimal mood, when it is time for rest and sleep, our relaxation is complete. We have no urgent thoughts of things left undone, of future problems that have not yet materialized. As we gently sink into deep sleep, we feel calm and tired from the activities of the day and pleasure as our cheek hits the pillow."

Echoing the perspective of Zen, Darwinian psychology, and Taoism, Thayer suggests that happiness is not the same as being happy all the time. Rather, it is a state of being in which a person experiences the full range of human emotions in mood states that are appropriate for the moment and free of distracting stress or insufficient energy.

Thayer is skeptical of the utility of drugs to facilitate the acquisition of optimal moods even though he acknowledges that his own research shows that inborn, genetically determined trait differences make it easier or harder for a given individual to obtain the generally optimal state of calm energy.

"Undoubtedly some people are very reactive and start out therefore at a lower point in that regard and need to come a lot further to achieve that optimal place," he told me. "That's not to say that such people should give up or shouldn't attempt to do it. There might be important advantages in such an effort. But I would say, yes, definitely some people start out at a different level in that respect."

If this unequal playing field is the unavoidable result of genetic variation, and if one's capacity to achieve optimal mood thus has a strong biological component to it (which, as we've seen, copious evidence suggests is true), then why should such people not turn to pharmaceutical technologies as potential remedies to supplement or facilitate their own efforts?

Although he agrees that medications can be an important part of treating serious depression, Thayer doesn't think drugs should be widely used for mood adjustment by "normal" people. He, like many people, has a global distrust of drugs and a particular distrust of drug company claims for the long-term safety and efficacy of mood-altering drugs.

"You have tremendous forces arrayed toward the use of drugs," he says. "The medical and pharmacological lobbies are all pushing us in that direction and then the media pick up on it and promote the idea of 'Why struggle with something that's more difficult when you can do something that's easier?' So I see us definitely moving in that direction, but whether that's good or not is another matter. I don't think that it's good, myself."

Thayer also says he has an "abiding trust" in evolution and "nature's way," which leads him to favor nondrug methods for achieving optimal mood.

He has a valid point. As we've seen, nature has apparently favored the natural selection among humans of a slightly-higher-than-neutral happiness set point. It is apparently in our genes' best interests that we experience a range of moods that oscillate around a set point that leaves us, on the whole, somewhat more optimistic, somewhat more cheerful and outgoing, and somewhat more happy than might be expected of mortal animals cavorting on a tiny planet lost in the vastness of the cosmos. If, on average, nature has designed people to be happy, then it would make a great deal of sense to arrange one's lifestyle to make it easy for nature to take its course. Thayer's prescriptions for getting enough sleep, maintaining a healthy diet, reducing stress, doing regular exercise, and planning work to coincide with one's natural energy cycles thus make eminent sense.[6]

Unfortunately, there are also many reasons to suggest that some individuals may, though bad genes or bad luck, have "natures" that are *not* ideal, *not* optimal, and *not* particularly enjoyable or satisfying. It is simply not true that "nature" really cares whether an individual is happy. We are not designed to be happy, except to the extent that our happiness increases our chances for survival and reproduction. And, in this regard, nature has apparently found it perfectly suitable to design creatures who are minimally happy—just happy enough to keep motivated, but not necessarily happy enough to really satisfy an aware, intelligent being pondering his or her own finite life span.

In addition to that general aspect of human nature, there is the incontrovertible fact of human variation—of people who are born with or have acquired the mood equivalent of poor eyesight or deafness. Drug interventions for such people may provide the buoyancy of outlook, the vim and vigor, the laughter and lightness that other people take for granted.

The prospect of millions of people using drugs to correct their mood "astigmatism" strikes some people as outlandish or even immoral. But people already use drugs this way—and have for thousands of years. It's just that the drugs in question—alcohol, caffeine, and nicotine—

are not generally recognized as the drugs they are. And despite the serious issues raised in the previous chapter about drug industry tactics, the risks of unknown long-term side effects, the potential for abuse by ill-informed users, and the dangers of subtle changes to human consciousness, the potential benefits of more perfect mood-altering drugs are undeniable.

Just as hearing aids and eyeglasses allow millions of people to experience richer, more meaningful, and more satisfying lives, just as insulin frees diabetics from painful or lethal complications, and just as analgesics provide enormous relief from unnecessary pain, so better drugs for manipulating our moods could lead to a healthier, happier society—if they are used wisely and with an appreciation for the holistic nature of human moods and with a respect for the essential utility of negative mood states in general.

If Lou Anne's father had taken medication to stabilize his moods, reduce his vulnerability to alcohol abuse, and provide him with a much higher degree of emotional resiliency, what scars might Lou Anne have been spared? How much child abuse, spousal abuse, and other crimes arising from mental dysfunction might be avoided with an enlightened use of appropriate drugs and counseling? Estimates for the direct and indirect costs of depression to society range up to $43 *billion* every year—but, of course, the cost in terms of pain, suffering, and lost opportunities for full and vibrant lives cannot be calculated.[7]

Whether the more perfect drugs now in development in drug company laboratories around the world will, indeed, be used wisely, with appropriate respect for the nonbiological dimensions of mental illness, is an open question. Clearly, many forces are arrayed against such use: the human desire for quick and easy fixes; the profits to be made from drugs as opposed to nondrug treatments; the comfort provided to patients and their families by disease models of mental illness; and the cost-saving preferences of health organizations and insurance companies.

Standing against these formidable forces is a fact of human nature that, if it does not provide utter comfort, at least provides a ray of hope that, in the end, mood-altering drugs will be used in a reasonable, appropriate, and humane way: human beings, and nature itself, are utterly and fundamentally pragmatic. If something works to achieve a desired end, it will be used. If it does not work, it will be dropped.

The human craving for happiness is the sum of innate drives widely considered to be practically unstoppable: the drives for sex, for pleasure, for love, and for knowledge, to name only a few. Humans have always tried whatever means at their disposal to better their chances of being happy, and have always avoided things that appear to diminish those chances—and that includes the use of drugs.

In the 1950s, to cite a recent example, the use of amphetamines soared. They were sold and marketed by drug companies for a huge range of problems, including simple tiredness. The ad campaigns for these drugs were just as biased, just as unbalanced, and just as manipulative as ads used today to sell antidepressants. Millions of people tried the drugs—and their easy availability did lead to a rise in the number of people addicted to amphetamines. And yet the use of amphetamines was also self-limiting. The crash that followed the high and the difficulty in using the drugs in a controlled way led most people to simply stop using them. It's true that stricter laws helped reduce use, but because it is relatively easy to manufacture, amphetamines were—and still are—relatively easy to obtain.

The point is that the biggest factor accounting for the lack of widespread use of amphetamines is that they simply don't work over the long term.

The example of alcohol is even more pertinent because access to it is almost completely unrestricted. If alcohol did not exist and was suddenly discovered in some clandestine drug laboratory, it would be immediately outlawed as the enormously hazardous, potentially addictive poison it really is. If anything, alcohol is more dangerous and more insidious than amphetamines, marijuana, LSD, and many other drugs proscribed by law today. And yet, despite alcohol's availability, society has not collapsed. Most people are not alcoholics. Most people do not trap themselves in patterns of behavior that constrict their opportunities for happiness. Instead, most people regulate their use based on an assessment of whether the drug is helping or hurting them in the long run.

So it is with antidepressants. Today millions of people have tried Prozac or Paxil or Serzone or Wellbutrin and, after a period of experimentation, have dropped the drugs because they found the experience unpleasant or unhelpful. The addictive potential of these drugs, in fact, is orders of magnitude smaller than the addictive potential of cigarettes or alcohol. And so, as more perfect drugs are developed, people will try them out and determine for themselves whether they are working. If they work, they'll be used—and if they work well, perhaps they will be used as widely and as regularly as people used soma in Aldous Huxley's *Brave New World.* If they don't work, however, if they interfere with the attainment of happiness by disconnecting people from reality, by inducing dependency, or by causing uncomfortable or dangerous side effects, then the drugs will be dropped. Dropped gradually, perhaps. Dropped with some difficulty, perhaps, particularly if they've been used for a long time. But dropped eventually, and no amount of drug industry propaganda, no amount of media or peer pressure, not even the human tendency to laziness will prevent it. Such is the power of the human craving for happiness.

Epilogue

— ∽ —

THE SCIENCE OF HAPPINESS GREW OUT OF MY CURIOSITY about the ways in which new drugs are changing the eternal pursuit of happiness. That curiosity was rooted in my own experiences with mood-altering drugs and with my own quest to obtain an optimal mood.

When I began writing this book the only drugs I used in my mood-regulating experiments were the ones most people use: alcohol and caffeine. But, somewhat to my own surprise and coincident with the writing of this book, I stepped into the Brave New World I was writing about—a world in which basically "normal" people such as myself use drugs in an informed and deliberate attempt to avoid dysfunctional and unpleasant moods and to enhance well-being. I thus became both a reporter on and a participant in the new pharmacology.

I am providing a glimpse into this personal journey for two reasons. First, I believe readers have a right to know about experiences any author has that might color his or her perception and reporting of the issues at hand. Second, my story might be of interest to readers as a microcosm of issues explored in this book and as a look at the way the issues play out in real life—or, at least, in one real life: mine.

I've been interested in the relationship between the brain and moods all of my adult life. As an inveterate journal writer I've recorded my numerous attempts to improve my mood by various manipulations—some directly pharmacological, others less so. My fundamental attitude hasn't changed much from some thoughts I jotted down in rather portentous cadences on April 8, 1981:

"I can't help thinking that so much of our behavior is governed and initially determined by the chemical makeup of our brains, that once the chemicals responsible for memory and the complex functioning of the brain are clearly understood, that a method may be found to accurately determine the optimum amount of each chemical and then procedures developed to administer the needed chemicals to the brains of those either deficient or in excess of the optimum amount."

I was referring, of course, to myself when I wrote of people with a "deficit" of brain "chemicals" required for "optimal mood." At that point I was a cub reporter working for a good weekly newspaper in Rochester, New York. I didn't have any training yet in neuroscience or pharmacology—I'm not sure I even knew the word "neurotrans-mitter" at that point. What I knew for certain was that sleep, diet, exercise, alcohol, and caffeine altered my mood in frustratingly unpredictable ways. I tried con-stantly to optimize these variables. I would try abstaining from caffeine, then try low doses, then high doses. Then I'd abstain again. I'd do the same for alcohol, trying dif-ferent combinations of the two drugs. I tried vegetari-anism. I cut down on sugar. I tried increasing exercise, decreasing exercise, increasing sleep, decreasing sleep. I studied Zen, and I meditated in the Zen style.

These efforts often provided important benefits, such as improved cardiovascular performance or a deeper insight into my own psychology. But no matter what I tried, my mood inevitably soured. It seemed impossible for me to maintain for long the energetic, outgoing, poised, lighthearted mood I craved. Seemingly at random I would find myself mildly depressed, lethargic, pes-simistic, and cross.

These bleak moods never blossomed into full-blown clinical depression, which is a realm of despair, pain, and abject dysfunction that I am most grateful I have never experienced. My mood "disorder" is mild—some might even say trivial—compared to clinical depression. I never lost a day of work because I felt down. I never lost my appetite or my ability to sleep. I didn't lose my friendships or isolate myself pathologically. It's just that when I would review my journal I would repeatedly see that I seemed to spend more time in a bleak or simply neutral mood than in a frankly happy mood.

In addition to a more or less chronic sense of being

slightly shy of "good-humored," there are infrequent times when my mood takes a distinctly abrupt turn for the worse. I call these quick eclipses "microbursts" because of their severity and brevity—they usually last no longer than forty-eight hours or so.

Caught in a microburst, I feel emotionally flat, tight, edgy, and hostile. Normally slow to anger, I become impatient and irritable. I find fault with practically everyone around me. I fume at people who don't think quickly enough or get to the point of a conversation fast enough. In the middle of a microburst I am also painfully aware of my own mortality. I feel as though a veil lifts from my eyes—perhaps that rosy gauze provided by nature to encourage us to continue living and, more importantly from our genes' point of view, procreating. Whatever. In a microburst I am convinced that life is fundamentally meaningless and that everybody's hopes and dreams amount to nothing in the cosmic scheme of things. Since I lack even a shred of belief in an afterlife, I am vulnerable to the depressing view that when we die, we die, and that a hundred years after our death, or two hundred or a thousand or ten thousand, depending on the impact we happen to have on those around us—not a trace of us will survive.

This, in any case, is how things appear when I'm nipped by the Black Dog—Winston Churchill's name for the depression that visited him throughout his life.

Unlike Churchill, however, my Black Dog lopes away from me as quickly and mysteriously as he appears. Despite the seeming certainty of my dark beliefs and the apparent clarity of my vision, I usually wake up a day or two after the onset of a microburst and feel better. My former preoccupation with death suddenly doesn't interest me. There is too much fun to be had. Too many people to love. There are children to hug, stars to marvel at, and good wine to enjoy in the company of dear friends.

And as I have observed myself over time, I have noticed that sometimes my microbursts are not as random as they at first appear. Sometimes they occur during a stressful or difficult time in my life. My problem is that I often don't realize I am stressed or that I am *in* a difficult time of my life until things reach a crisis. In short, I have come to realize that my bouts of blackness may have as much to do with my surpassing emotional ignorance as with some basic neurological or "chemical" deficit.

For instance, before I was married, I had several relationships with women that would flame brightly and then rapidly fizzle. But typically I was profoundly myopic when it came to realizing the fire was out. Rather than acknowledge a problem and either work on it or move on, I would plod along, convincing myself that things weren't really so bad, and whistling merrily in the conviction that things would improve with time. Such relationships bred microbursts the way Kansas breeds tornadoes.

The inevitable emotional storms—and attendant depressive bout—often provided the raw emotional energy I needed to shake me from my stupor and get me to do something.

The difficulty was that for every time a microburst was a helpful siren of an emotional emergency, there would be another time when it was a flagrant false alarm. For instance, in the grip of one microburst I became convinced that I had married the wrong woman. The incompatibility between my wife and me seemed so stark and obvious that I told her I wanted a divorce. Fortunately for me, my wife has a great deal more common sense than I do. Rather than viewing my pronouncement as an indication that she'd married a lunatic, she correctly surmised that I was in the midst of one of my "fits"—her term for microbursts. She insisted on talking about it—what a concept—and, though it took a much longer time than might seem reasonable, I eventually saw that I just might be overreacting.

Seven good years and two beautiful children later, I'm convinced that this episode—and many others like it—was the result not of a healthy emotional warning system at work but of a mood-regulation machinery with the neural equivalent of a sticky brake pedal: my mood lurches and bucks at times rather than shifting smoothly from a high to a low. And the sticky brake pedal effect can exacerbate the mood-upsetting influences of sleep deprivation, barometric pressure, lack of exercise, stress, excess caffeine or alcohol, or any of a dozen other environmental variables.

The maddening irregularity of my microbursts has propelled my decades-long search for some psychological or pharmacological inoculation to them.

Years ago, for instance, my wife and I established a relationship with a good therapist—someone to whom we have turned to help us through the inevitable difficulties of marriage. I also continue to meditate whenever I can—an effort that has yielded much insight over the years and one that reminds me that the logical, rational aspects of my temperament are not the only—or most important—aspects. And I also continue to keep a journal, which has been an invaluable tool for self-reflection over the years.

These efforts have been necessary—but insufficient—elements in my quest to avoid microbursts and obtain the optimal mood I seek. In addition to these, I have long sought a magic drug "bullet" to kill my microburst demon quickly, safely, and effectively.

Maintaining a steady intake of caffeine seems to help things—at least for a while. Unfortunately, caffeine is notoriously difficult to regulate, even when you've written a book about it and know its tricks. And so I often find myself repeating a pattern of use: slow escalation of caffeine use; the onset of unpleasant side effects such as excess muscle tension, achiness, and restless sleep; and a compensating increase in alcohol consumption to dull the buzz at the end of the day. When the side effects are high and the mood improvement I extract from the caffeine is low, I begin a slow withdrawal. Then, after a period of abstinence, some project or other would require a burst of energy, I'd cave in, pull a shot or two of espresso on my home machine, and I'd be off on the cycle again.

It was in the early phases of writing this book that I got fed up with this pattern. It seemed so clumsy. Alcohol, in particular, seemed like such a basically poisonous and unhealthy drug that I longed for something that would give me the caffeine "goodies" without requiring an alcohol counterweight. In short, I wanted a more perfect drug, a better drug, a drug that would complement my other mood-management activities such as exercise, meditation, and good nutrition. Not a somalike happy pill, but a *true* happy pill—chemical "eyeglasses" for my "near-sighted" brain.

I decided it was time to try some newer molecules. But I paused. The ghost of pharmacological Calvinism whispered that I hadn't given the "natural" approaches enough of a chance. Maybe what I needed wasn't a better drug, but no drugs.

I listened. Made sense. And so for about four months I lived a very wholesome life. I quit caffeine and drank only celebratory alcohol. I rode my bicycle every day, ate well, and got enough sleep.

And, at first, I felt great.

I felt calmer, I slept deeply, and a wry sense of humor emerged from time to time that seemed absent when I was "speeding" on caffeine. But slowly the calm began to feel more like lethargy. Despite sleeping well, I felt tired and unproductive in the afternoon. And even with a midday nap, I would start to yawn at about nine-thirty in the evening and be snoring at ten—which didn't leave much time for socializing, much less writing another book. But, more importantly, microbursts became more frequent.

One day I felt a rising sense of tension, irritation, and moodiness. I had no particular reason to be sad. I enjoyed my work, I loved my wife and daughters, I was about to move into a new home, and I was in great health. And yet, as I drove on the highway that evening, I felt more and more vexed and cross. And as I eased off the road and up an exit ramp, a black thought bubbled up from some muck in my brain: "I could just kill myself."

Even as the thought surfaced, another part of me said "How absurd," because I didn't really want to kill myself.

Not by a long shot. And yet, there it was. Some apparently sizable part of my marbled personality was shockingly indifferent to everything in my life—including life itself. I drove on, less concerned with suicide itself than with the fact that my brain somehow generated the thought of suicide. If this was being "natural," I decided, then to hell with it. It occurred to me then that living with my "natural" brain made about as much sense as walking around "naturally" naked.

About a week later, I sat in a small office facing a female psychotherapist who wore a colorful, decidedly unclinical outfit. (Our "family" therapist wasn't on my health plan—and I couldn't afford private consultation.) I really didn't want to see her. Therapists—as opposed to psychiatrists—can't prescribe drugs, and drugs were what I had my sights set on. But I thought it would be prudent—not to mention politically correct—to be "checked out" for psychological issues before launching my pharmaceutical experiments. And so I sat down and told her my story—the long years of experimentation, the microbursts, my desire for new drugs, and my belief that drugs alone are seldom the answer. She listened, took notes, and watched me with, I thought, a cautious gaze.

I was aware that I was an almost pathologically self-aware patient. I wouldn't have blamed her for being suspicious of that self-awareness and my facile use of the psychotherapeutic and pharmacological lingo I'd picked up from my research. But she was gentle with any doubts she might have had, reserving obvious suspicion for my microbursts.

"I've found," she said cautiously, "that many times people think their depressions are completely unrelated to their lives when, in fact, they almost always have something to do with important personal relationships. Tell me about your relationship with your wife."

A small pang of fear flared. My wife and I have a pretty healthy, normal relationship—better than many, but hardly perfect. There are issues that simmer below the hustle and bustle of daily life—issues we don't have the time or the energy to properly address, what with a new baby, a new house, full-time jobs, and courses to teach. And so the therapist had her finger on a somewhat tender spot and was pressing lightly there to see whether that spot might account for some of my symptoms.

All I could do was admit that things weren't always wonderful—that we fought sometimes and hated each other in flashes of irrational temper, but that despite everything we also loved each other, liked each other most of the time, and truly cared for each other and the work each of us pursued. The point, I argued, was that I thought our relationship was at times made more difficult by my descents into a biochemical funk that might profitably be avoided with a judicious application of modern pharmacology.

Somewhat to my surprise, she agreed with me. She said she had seen other people do very well on antidepressants—especially people like me with mild symptoms. And then, to my vast relief, she mentioned the "D" word—"dysthymia"—the chronic condition of low mood that has served in the past decade to immeasurably expand the umbrella of "mental illness" to include people like me who used to be considered "normal." Dysthymia was my ticket to drugs. The labeling would make everyone happy. My HMO would have the diagnostic code for billing, the psychiatrist to whom I would be referred would have a label to hang his hat on, and I could use the word to conceptualize my own difficulty. Reducing my highly idiosyncratic and frankly unusual mood irregularity to a common clinical syndrome was a relief in other ways.

As much as I value psychotherapy, part of me breathed a sigh of relief when she mentioned dysthymia. That word meant that the basic problem wasn't that I needed to learn better ways to communicate with my wife or, far worse, that the problem was some fatal flaw in my relationship that I had been denying all this time and for which divorce was the only remedy. Instead of long, hard work learning new skills and hashing through emotional minefields with my wife, the laying on of the dysthymia label promised the ultimate easy fix: a pill.

Two weeks later, a middle-aged male psychiatrist looked over my record on his computer screen. "Dysthymic," he muttered to himself. Then he turned to me, and I gave him the same story I gave to the therapist. Except it was abbreviated because I noticed him looking at his watch from time to time. The therapist had let me ramble for an hour and a half and never seemed rushed. After about twenty minutes, the psychiatrist was looking impatient.

"Well," he said, "I'd recommend Prozac."

I was afraid he'd say that. One of the projects I had recently completed was a documentary for the PBS sci-

ence program *NOVA* on erectile dysfunction—impotence.
For that I'd talked to a lot of doctors and a lot of patients
and I knew that the true incidence of sexual dysfunction
among people taking SSRIs such as Prozac was much
higher than reported in the literature—and certainly
higher than that reported by Eli Lilly.

"I don't want Prozac," I said. "I've read the literature.
I like my sex life, thank you. I was thinking of Wellbutrin."

I was nervous. Even in this age, when patients are
encouraged to be knowledgeable and assertive, an aura of
infallibility and superior knowledge surrounds a doctor's
white coat—and he was the one wearing the coat, not I.
Still, I wasn't so desperate that I was going to cede my
ground without a fight. I wanted Wellbutrin—and not just
because it left one's orgasms alone. Wellbutrin appears to
work at least in part by raising the levels of dopamine in
the brain. Amphetamine also raises dopamine. Cocaine
raises dopamine. Even caffeine raises dopamine, though
by a roundabout manner and to a much smaller degree
than its more powerful brethren. So Wellbutrin sounded
good to me. But would the good doctor bite?

The doctor shrugged. I could tell he didn't like being
second-guessed. But neither did he seem to care much
one way or the other.

"It's your decision," he said. "If you want to try Wellbutrin, we'll try Wellbutrin."

Two days later, just after breakfast, I opened the
orange plastic bottle, took out one of the little blue pills
and popped it into my mouth. Of course, I felt nothing.

An hour later I still felt nothing. I knew that any therapeutic effects would take weeks to kick in, but side effects

often occur very quickly. If I had felt some mild side effect at least I would know that something was happening. But day after day passed and, despite an almost obsessive self-awareness, I could detect no tangible difference in my mood, in the way I responded to the stresses and pleasure of my life, in my outlook or temperament.

The experience of taking a strong drug with no detectable effects was odd. Like most people, I'm used to drugs that work quickly. There is something comforting about slugging back a shot of espresso or a couple shots of whiskey and, within minutes, feeling the effect. There's a sense of control that comes with such rapid feedback. But this Wellbutrin was strange.

I knew it was doing something in my brain. At the very least, the drug was binding to reuptake pumps, and perhaps to the postsynaptic receptors themselves. The latest research suggests that other alterations were happening: genes were being switched on, and perhaps neuronal growth factors were being produced, causing my brain cells to sprout new dendrites.

And yet I felt unchanged. It was spooky.

About a week into the experiment, I noticed something that surprised me. I was paying a keen attention to women—to their bodies. It was a subtle effect, but after a day or two, I decided that my slightly revved-up libido wasn't just a figment of an overactive imagination. Then, about a week later, I noticed something else. As part of the experiment, I had reduced my caffeine intake and practically quit drinking any alcohol. At first this required a mild effort, since I've always enjoyed coffee and alcoholic drinks. But as the weeks wore on, I noticed that I lost interest in alcohol and caffeine. My morning espresso started to taste distinctly bitter and harsh. My evening scotch started to remind me of gasoline. It was as if I no longer cared as much about the drugs these beverages contained, and with that motivation gone, I was free to realize that they weren't the delicious, subtly flavored drinks I had convinced myself they were.

This effect of Wellbutrin is well known, though it isn't experienced by everyone who uses it. It's the basis, in fact, for the use of the drug (under the trade name Zyban) as an aid to people trying to quit smoking.

Still, I felt nothing in the way of a general improvement in mood or energy. I felt basically fine . . . still somewhat sluggish, but basically fine.

I reported this to my psychiatrist, and he agreed to raise my dose to the more typical level of 300 milligrams a day.

Despite high hopes, I continued to feel nothing. The side effects seemed unchanged. I kept at it for five weeks—long enough, I figured, for any possible long-term neuronal changes to solidify and make themselves known.

After a final week in which I unilaterally upped the daily dose to 350 milligrams, I decided to call it quits. I went back to the doctor. He listened and suggested that maybe depression wasn't the problem—and thus an antidepressant wasn't the answer. Perhaps it was simply an energy thing. Maybe that was why I liked caffeine so much. It seemed like a reasonable hypothesis, though I was surprised by his suggested remedy: Ritalin.

Ritalin is a close chemical cousin of amphetamine, and it's used most often by children and adults to correct supposed attention deficit problems. I was familiar with Ritalin, with its chemical structure and mechanism of action in the brain. And since I'd had some pleasant experiences with real amphetamine in the past, I thought this would be a very interesting experiment indeed.

Again, however, I was disappointed. I took two of the tiny yellow dotlike 5-milligram pills, per the doctor's suggestion. I barely felt a thing. The next day I took three. I felt a mild stimulation similar to that obtained by a good cup of coffee. "Huh," I said to myself. "What's the big deal?" That day I tried another two pills in the afternoon—and promptly felt an overwhelming urge to take a nap. This was definitely not working out.

So-called paradoxical responses such as my sleepiness in response to Ritalin are not uncommon. Some people experience this with high doses of caffeine, in fact.

In the weeks that followed I toyed with different doses at different times of the day. I found that taking five pills gave me a definite lift for a few hours—again, similar to what I used to get with caffeine. But the energy would inevitably fade, leaving me with the choice of taking yet more yellow pills or taking a nap to let my circuits revive on their own. Most often I took the nap, but, of course, what I wanted was to eliminate naps.

So it was back to the good doctor once again. He was getting a little frustrated. "Your symptoms are so vague," he said, his voice edged with irritation. "It's hard to know what to do next."

Of course my symptoms were vague. The doctor and I were groping our way through the fog-shrouded territory that lies between what has long been considered "normal" and what is now being seen as "treatable." My symptoms were subtle—though real enough to prod me toward further experimentation. And the subtlety of the symptoms made it that much harder for either of us to determine whether the drugs I was trying were having any effect. And here lies a crucial point: the future of mood pharmacology lies in subtle drugs, not drugs with obvious effects such as alcohol and caffeine. To be effective over long periods of time, mind-altering drugs *have* to be somewhat subtle—if they exert their effects too rapidly or too strongly, a host of compensatory brain mechanisms kick in that reduce the effects of the drug and force the user to take more and more to achieve the original effect. The subtlety of today's drugs is one of their chief virtues. But this makes them more difficult to use because it's harder for a user to detect their presence—particularly users such as myself, who don't have such flagrant dysfunction. This leads to a pattern of use similar to the one I was about to embark on.

Faced with the failure of Ritalin, my doctor returned to his original suggestion, Prozac, because it's known as an "activating" antidepressant, meaning it gives some people a caffeinelike jolt of energy. He downplayed the risk of sexual side effects. "We can deal with those if they happen," he said, meaning that I could use another drug, such as Viagra or Yohimbine, to give back what the first drug took away.

To say I wasn't excited by this prospect is an understatement, but I started a course of Prozac anyway, out of both curiosity and an honest hope that perhaps he was right.

After six weeks I noted some possible effects in my journal. It seemed that I was, in fact, in a pretty good mood lately, and I certainly wasn't having any microbursts of depressive moods. I seemed to have a sense of humor again, and a certain resilience to the usual stresses of parenthood. I wasn't troubled by side effects, and I didn't detect any sexual difficulties either.

To somebody who had been truly depressed, what I was feeling probably would have felt marvelous indeed. After all, I functioned well at work (though I still didn't have as much energy as I wanted); I enjoyed life, particularly my children; and I wasn't unduly anxious or troubled—certainly not by the existential realities of life.

But to me, this state of affairs felt awfully close to normal—so close that I just couldn't tell whether the drug was doing anything. And I was a bit queasy about taking a powerful drug such as Prozac for such a seemingly small benefit—serotonin is involved in many bodily processes, particularly those connected with the cardiovascular system, and although all studies show Prozac and other SSRIs to be safe in long-term use, I didn't feel comfortable exposing my body to a powerful drug unless I really needed it.

And so I never refilled the prescription. I decided to simply quit and see what happened. I figured that would be one way to judge whether the drug really was having any effect.

Stopping any drug cold turkey is not recommended— even for a drug as benign as caffeine. But Prozac has an extraordinarily long half-life, which means it takes many days for the drug to be eliminated from the system. And so, unlike other drugs, such as alcohol, caffeine, nicotine, and many prescription drugs, going "cold turkey" with Prozac is a gentler experience than it might be, particularly for people who are basically normal to begin with and who are on a low dose.

I was surprised by what I felt as the Prozac slowly drained from my system. Indeed, I could tell a difference. Again, it was subtle, but real. As the Prozac departed, I could feel a certain edginess and hardness in my personality return—as though some protective foam cushion were being slowly removed, leaving a leaner, bonier mental self behind. With the removal of this padding, I found that I started seeing the dark sides of things more clearly. My cynicism returned—a rather self-righteous distrust of official pronouncements, for instance, and a suspicion of altruistic remarks or behaviors. I saw hypocrisy more easily.

"Well, hello there," I wrote in one journal entry. "Restless, caustic, edgy ol' me. Little tense. Little nervous. Can't exactly relax. Don't exactly want to."

For some time I didn't mind returning to this state. It was actually rather useful in some stages of writing. And in the months following my trial with Prozac I tried, again, to modify my lifestyle to lower stress, increase energy, and slow down—all with an eye to doing what I could without drugs to improve my overall mood.

But about two months after I finished the final draft of this book I again began to feel unbalanced in some difficult-to-describe way.

"My mind seems to have this peculiarly maladaptive habit of focusing on the grim realities of life, rather than being satisfied to live in the bright and lively bubble of the years I have on this earth," I wrote in my journal. I felt very much like Leo Tolstoy, who, in his *Confessions*, describes a time in his life when he was "surrounded on all sides by what is considered complete happiness"— health, a beloved wife, lovely children, and respect from all quarters. And yet he felt rotten in his core.

"I could not attribute a rational meaning to a single act, let alone to my whole life," he wrote. "I simply felt astonished that I had failed to realize this from the beginning. It had been common knowledge for such a long time. Today or tomorrow sickness and death will come (and they had already arrived) to those dear to me, and to myself, and nothing will remain other than the stench and the worms. Sooner or later my deeds, whatever they may have been, will be forgotten and will no longer exist. What is all the fuss about then?"

Returning again to the good doctor, he suggested a new drug—Celexa—which had been used widely in Europe but had only recently been approved for use in the United States. He said some of his patients were having good luck with it and that it appeared to have very few sexual side effects.

That was almost six months ago now. This time I have refilled my prescriptions as they have expired. Several times I've thought about stopping, again because everything feels so normal. My mood fluctuates in response to events around me. I can get angry, annoyed, and blue. Life is hardly uninterrupted bliss. And if it were not for my previous trials with other drugs, I might well think the drug I was taking was doing nothing, nothing at all.

But I think I know better now. And I may have succeeded in my quest. I may have actually nudged up my
happiness set point—enough for me to participate more
fully in life, but not so much as to render me insensible
to life events, to the slings and arrows of outrageous fortune. Almost miraculously, a single small white pill taken
every day seems to have balanced my mood machinery
such that I can look my fate squarely in the eye—hold my
own mortality and the existential uncertainties of life
firmly in mind—and not flinch, quail, or despair.

Watching me take my daily dose the other day, my
wife asked, "So are you going to take that for the rest of
your life?" It's a fair question and not one I take lightly.
There are no long-term studies of the health risks of taking Celexa or other newer antidepressants—everyone
who uses them is, in effect, participating in a massive
experiment. And yet animal research and the experience
of thirty years with other antidepresants is encouraging—
and I consider the risk of ill effects quite acceptable. And
I strongly suspect that using high doses of caffeine and
alcohol as alternative drugs for long-term mood regulation would have much harsher physical and mental consequences than any produced by Celexa.

And so I'll continue for now. I'll keep using these
pharmaceutical "eyeglasses" to correct my mood astigmatism. I'll keep up with the news from the drug companies. I'll remain connected with both my therapist and my
psychiatrist. I'll certainly continue to exercise, meditate,
deal with relationship issues, and follow other common-
sense guidelines for a balanced lifestyle. And despite my
profound skepticism toward the claims and tactics of drug

companies, I will wish them well in their chase of more perfect drugs, hoping that in a better, clearer understanding of human mood will come pharmacological tools that are safe, effective, and useful to everyone seeking to live a long, healthy, happy life.

Notes

CHAPTER 1
Prozac: The Next Generation

1. "New Ranking on Drug Sales in U.S. in '97," *New York Times* (February 27, 1998): D3.
2. A generic drugmaker, Barr Laboratories, has mounted repeated legal challenges to Lilly's patent rights in an attempt to distribute generic fluoxetine well in advance of the 2003 patent expiration. In a January 1999 out-of-court settlement, Lilly agreed to pay Barr $4 million to ensure that Barr doesn't break Lilly's monopoly before the patent expiration.
3. For a fuller description of Huxley's concerns, see *Aldous Huxley, A Biography* by Sybille Bedford. (New York: Alfred A. Knopf, 1973).
4. Aldous Huxley, *Brave New World Revisited* (New York: Harper & Brothers, 1958), pp. 90–91.
5. The data come from an annual survey of pharmaceutical sales conducted by I.M.S. America, a health care information company; in the 1997 ranking, Prozac was second, with U.S. sales of $1.94 billion; Zoloft was fifth, with U.S. sales of $1.2 billion; and Paxil was seventh, with U.S. sales of $949 million (*New York Times,* February 27, 1998).
6. "Use of Antidepression Medicine for Young Patients Has Soared," *New York Times* (August 10, 1997), p. A1.
7. R. M. A. Hirshfeld et al., "The National Depressive and Manic-Depressive Association Consensus Statement on the Undertreatment of Depression," *Journal of the American Medical Association* 277, no. 4 (1997): 333.
8. One of the best popular books about manic-depression is *Touched by Fire* by Kay Jamison, a researcher who has manic-depression.
9. A small percentage of users experience a short-lived burst of energy that resembles an amphetamine high in the first week or

so of taking an antidepressant, but this heightened mood fades quickly.

10. Some of these side effects are much more common than initially reported, particularly sexual dysfunction. Although measuring sexual dysfunction is tricky business, the rate of erectile dysfunction (impotence), reduced libido, or reduced ability to experience orgasm reported in recent studies of the effects of selective serotonin reuptake inhibitors varies between roughly 30 percent and 55 percent. The rate of sexual dysfunction for those taking Prozac and other selective serotonin reuptake inhibitors is certainly higher than the 2 percent that companies such as Lilly initially claimed. For more detailed information see M. E. Thase et al, "Effect of Antidepressant Treatment on Sexual Function in Depressed Men," *Psychopharmacology Bulletin* 30 (1994): 83; J. H. Hsu and W. W. Shen, "Male Sexual Side Effects Associated with Antidepressants: A Descriptive Clinical Study of 32 Patients," *International Journal of Psychiatric Medicine* 25 (1995): 191–201; and W. W. Shen and J. H. Hsu, "Female Sexual Side Effects Associated with Selective Serotonin Reuptake Inhibitors: A Descriptive Clinical Study of 33 Patients," *International Journal of Psychiatric Medicine* 25 (1995): 239–248.

11. R. Shelton et al., "The Study of Olanzapine Plus Fluoxetine in Treatment-Resistant Major Depressive Disorder Without Psychotic Features," paper presented at the thirty-eighth annual New Clinical Drug Evaluation Unit meeting, Boca Raton, Florida (June 10–13, 1998).

12. See Mark S. Kramer et al., "Distinct Mechanism for Antidepressant Activity by Blockade of Central Substance P Receptors," *Science* 281 (September 11, 1998): 1640–1645.

13. The full quote is "The unleashed power of the atom has changed everything save our modes of thinking and we thus drift toward unparalleled catastrophe." Einstein made the comment in a telegram on May 24, 1946, that was published in the *New York Times* on May 25, 1946.

14. Stephen Braun, *Buzz: The Science and Lore of Alcohol and Caffeine*, (New York: Oxford University Press, 1996). Reprinted in paperback by Viking Penguin, 1997.

CHAPTER 2
Set Point

1. This study is but one reviewed in Meyers's book *The Pursuit of Happiness: What Makes a Person Happy—and Why* (New York: William Morrow, 1992).

2. For details, see two studies: Alex Michalos, *Global Report on Student Well-Being:* vol. 1, *Life Satisfaction and Happiness* (New York: Springer-Verlag, 1991); and Ronald Inglehart, *Culture Shift in Advanced Industrial Society* (Princeton, N.J.: Princeton University Press, 1990).

3. What *did* explain some of the differences in overall happiness levels was not money, but how long a nation had enjoyed a stable democracy. "The thirteen nations that have maintained democratic institutions continuously since 1920 *all* enjoy higher life satisfaction levels than do the eleven nations whose democracies developed after World War II or have not yet fully emerged," writes Meyers in *The Pursuit of Happiness.* Democracy, of course, is associated with many things that might facilitate happiness—personal freedom, the empowerment of voting, and a lack of stress from political upheaval being primary among them.

4. See an article by Ed Diener et al., "The Relationship Between Income and Subjective Well-being: Relative or Absolute? *Social Indicators Research* 28 (1993): 195–223.

5. Philip Brickman, Dan Coates, and Ronnie Janoff-Bulman, "Lottery Winners and Accident Victims: Is Happiness Relative?" *Journal of Personality and Social Psychology* 36, no. 8 (1978): 917–927.

6. G. R. Lee, K. Seccombe, and C. L. Shehan, "Marital Status and Personal Happiness: An Analysis of Trend Data," *Journal of Marriage and the Family* 53 (1991): 839–844.

7. Paul T. Costa Jr., Robert R. McCrae, and Alan B. Zonderman, "Environmental and Dispositional Influences on Well-being: Longitudinal Follow-up of an American National Sample," *British Journal of Psychology* 78 (1987): 299–306.

8. This quote from Diener was reported by Daniel Goleman in his article in *The New York Times* (July 21, 1996): E2.

9. These studies are reviewed in more detail in David Meyers's book *The Pursuit of Happiness: What Makes a Person Happy—and Why.*

10. C. Layne, "Painful Truths about Depressives' Cognitions," *Journal of Clinical Psychology* 39 (1983): 848–853.

11. David Lykken and Auke Tellegen, "Happiness Is a Stochastic Phenomenon," *Psychological Science* 7, no. 3 (1996): 186–189.

CHAPTER 3

The Machinery of Mood

1. The quote is from *The Three-Pound Universe* by J. Hooper and D. Teresi (New York: Dell, 1987), p. 31.

2. Some of the lag time seen with current antidepressants is probably due to the fact that neurons respond to the raised levels of neurotransmitters by decreasing the amount of serotonin or norepinephrine or dopamine released into the synapse. This self-regulation is mediated by "auto receptors," which are receptors on the *sending* neuron that sense when neurotransmitter levels in the synapse are unusually high and tell the sending cell to reduce neurotransmitter output as a result. Some attempts are being made to block these autoreceptors and thus speed up the action of existing antidepressants, but thus far efforts have not been successful, leading to speculation that there are other, probably more important, reasons for the lag time.

3. Evidence has recently been found that some neurons in the hippocampus section of the brain—a section involved in the transfer of memories from short-term storage to long-term storage—do reproduce. See "New Leads to Brain Neuron Regeneration, *Science* 282 (November 6, 1998): 1018. But the general principle that neurons do not replicate the way other body cells do remains true.

4. The quote is from James H. Austin, M.D., *Zen and the Brain* (Cambridge, Mass.: MIT Press, 1998), pp. 256–257.

CHAPTER 4
Listening to Depression

1. Michael McGuire and Alfonso Troisi, *Darwinian Psychiatry* (New York: Oxford University Press, 1998).

2. These ideas are more fully explored by Nesse in "Evolutionary Explanations of Emotions," *Human Nature,* no. 3 (1990): 261–289. See also "What Good Is Feeling Bad? The Evolutionary Benefits of Psychic Pain," *The Sciences* (November–December 1991): 30–37.

3. Not only has nature endowed us with emotional responses that can be more intense and long-lasting than is needed these days, she has also designed us to have more negative emotional responses than positive—about twice as many by one count.

"The idea is that there are more different kinds of bad things that can happen to us than good things that can happen to us," Nesse says. "You can fall off a cliff or eat some poison or get excluded from your group or cut your finger off or have your mate leave you or have your mate be unfaithful to you or have your kid die or something, which are all different nasty things that can happen to you. How many good things can happen to you? You can have a good meal or have sex or have somebody care about you or have something good happen to your kid . . . it would be interesting to list them out specifically." Thus not only may we be saddled with a depressive response machinery that sometimes goes off too fast and sustains too long, but also we are prey to a host of other negative emotions that, when combined with a depressed response, may exacerbate and sustain a given episode of depression.

4. The cases of Ms. E, Mrs. N, and Mr. A and Mr. B are taken from *Darwinian Psychiatry,* pp. 161–163.
5. From Emmy Gut, *Productive and Unproductive Depression,* (New York: Basic Books, 1989), pp. 84–95.
6. From Peter Kramer, *Listening to Prozac,* (New York: Viking Penguin, 1993), pp. 1–10.
7. Elliot Valenstein, *Blaming the Brain,* (New York: The Free Press, 1998), p. 218.
8. Ibid., p. 197.

CHAPTER 5

Selling Happiness

1. For more details on this epic chapter in pharmacology see John C. Sheehan *The Enchanted Ring: The Untold Story of Penicillin* (Cambridge, Mass.: MIT Press, 1982).
2. C. Brook, editorial, "Growth Hormone: Panacea or Punishment for Short Stature?" *British Medical Journal* 315, no. 7110 (1997).
3. A more complete account of this episode can be found in Linda Marsa's book *Prescription for Profits: How the Pharmaceutical Industry Bankrolled the Unholy Marriage Between Science and Business* (New York: Charles Scribner's Sons, 1997).
4. These methods are detailed in a letter by Dr. Dong and her colleagues appearing in the April 16, 1997, issue of the *Journal of the American Medical Association,* pp. 1199–1201.
5. Breggin makes this statement on p. 229 of *Talking Back to Prozac,* a book he cowrote with Ginger Ross Breggin (New York: St. Martin's Press, 1994). The material that follows was drawn from the book.
6. NARSAD is an alliance of three major mental health support groups: the National Alliance for the Mentally Ill, the National Mental Health Association, and the National Depressive and Manic-Depressive Association.
7. Peter Howe, "In Wake of Lawsuit, Diet Doctors Defend Use of 'Fen/Phen,'" *Boston Globe* (May 7, 1997), p. B1.

8. Laura Johannes and Steve Stecklow, "Early Warning: Heart-Valve Problem That Felled Diet Pills Had Arisen Previously," *Wall Street Journal* (December 11, 1997): A1.

9. Robert Langreth and Laura Johannes, "Is Marketing of Diet Pill Too Aggressive?" *Wall Street Journal* (November 21, 1996): B1.

10. Ibid.

11. Gina Kolata, "The Fearful Price of Getting Thin" *New York Times* (July 13, 1997): E3.

12. See, for example, R. A. Davidson, "Sources of Funding and Outcome of Clinical Trials," *Journal of General Internal Medicine* 1 (1986): 155–158, and J. Lexchin, "Is There a Bias in Industry Supported Clinical Research?" *Canadian Journal of Clinical Pharmacology* 2 (1995): 15–18.

13. H. T. Stelfox et al., "Conflict of Interest in the Debate over Calcium-Channel Antagonists," *New England Journal of Medicine* 338 (1998): 101–106.

14. In fact, the launching and marketing of Viagra involve many parallels to the launching and marketing of new antidepressants. With Viagra, the drug company's task was to get men to view their impotence as a "physical" or a "medical" problem about which they shouldn't be embarrassed and for which Viagra is an appropriate cure. In reality, impotence is the paragon of a problem with entwined physical and psychological roots. Sexual function is enormously sensitive to psychological and emotional conditions—conditions a pill cannot alter. The emphasis that a pill such as Viagra places on a man's erection skews the view of human sexuality away from a complex interplay of emotional and physical factors and toward a view that sex is a mechanical act, with penile penetration as the goal. But, as is the case with depression, the psychological dimension of human sexuality is trivialized by the drug company while the biological dimension is exaggerated in a frenzied effort to boost sales.

CHAPTER 6

Zen and the Art of Prozac

1. For an excellent lay exploration of the genetic roots of manic-depression see Samuel Barondes, *Mood Genes* (New York: W. H. Freeman, 1998).

2. Translation of such an ancient text as the Tao Te Ching is as much art as science. Of the many translations available, I prefer the lovely 1972 interpretation by Gia-Fu Feng and Jane English

(New York: Vintage Books). This passage is from chapter 2 of that translation.

3. Of course, using alcohol and caffeine wisely is tricky because of the insidious ways in which both molecules can appropriate the brain's pleasure circuitry, and because the brain so readily adapts to the presence of almost all drugs—a process called tolerance—which results in the need for larger and larger doses to achieve the original effect. Tolerance can be avoided by limiting the amount of drug used and by giving the brain a chance to readjust between doses. The twenty-four-hour cycle in which most people use either alcohol or caffeine, in fact, provides this "resting" period, which is why many people can consume these drugs in a stable, steady way for decades on end.

4. His research is fully described in his two books *The Biopsychology of Mood and Arousal* (New York: Oxford University Press, 1989) and *The Origin of Everyday Moods* (New York: Oxford University Press, 1996).

5. The term "flow" was coined by Mihaly Csikszentmihalyi, a professor of psychology and education at the University of Chicago. Csikszentmihalyi says that "flow" is not the same as happiness. He defines "flow" as the peak experiences and the great joys that people feel when they are totally absorbed in a task that demands skill and commitment. "Flow" and such peak experiences can certainly leaven life and contribute to happiness, but they are not happiness itself, which is, as Meyers has pointed out, an enduring sense of well-being. For further information, see: M. Csikszentmihalyi, and I. S. Csikszentmihalyi, *Optimal Experience: Psychological Studies of Flow in Consciousness* (New York: Cambridge University Press, 1998) and M. Csikszentmihalyi, *Flow: The Psychology of Optimal Experience* (New York: HarperCollins, 1990).

6. For more details about Thayer's suggestions for ways to improve mood without drugs see his appendix "Beyond Stress Management" in *The Origin of Everyday Moods* (New York: Oxford University Press, 1996).

7. The estimate comes from "Depression: More—and Meaner—Than It Seems," *Harvard Mahoney Neuroscience Institute Letter* (Spring 1996), p. 1.

Index

Abbott Labs, 125
acetylcholine, 64
addictive potential, 159–60
alcohol, 24, 53, 56, 59, 150–51,
    156, 159, 160, 163, 167, 173
Ambivalent Zen (Shainberg),
    147–48
American Home Products, 128,
    130–31, 132
American Journal of Therapeutics,
    118
amine neurotransmitters, 61–64
amphetamines, 7, 15, 53,
    158–59, 172
amygdala, 71, 76
antidepressants, 159–60
    attitude and, 23
    effectiveness of, 11–13, 106,
        179–81
    first developed, 6
    marketing of, 22
    onset of action, 12
    personality shifting by, 59–61
    Prozac as most prescribed, 2, 7
    sales volume of, 7
    search for better, 19–20
    See also specific names and types
Austin, James, 75
axons, 57

BASF (drug company), 118
Bilstad, James, 131

biogenic amine theory, 61–62
biological psychiatry, 119
bipolar disorder. *See* manic-
    depression
Blaming the Brain (Valenstein),
    107–8, 129
Boots Company, 115–19
brain mechanisms, 55–76
Brave New World (Huxley), 4–7,
    10, 160
Breggin, Peter, 119–20

caffeine, 24, 56, 59, 150–51,
    156, 163, 167–168, 172, 173
calcium channel blockers, 132
Calvinism. *See* pharmacological
    Calvinism
Celexa, 7, 179–80
children
    antidepressant use, 7
    growth hormone use, 113–15
Churchill, Winston, 164
cocaine, 53, 172
Cole, Jonathan, 102
Confessions (Tolstoy), 179
cosmetic pharmacology, 59–60
Costa, Paul, 38

Darkness Visible (Styron), 106
Darwinian fitness, 10, 91, 100
Darwinian psychiatry, 87, 90,
    94–95, 101–2, 148, 154

WHAT WAS I THINKING?

THINGS I'VE LEARNED

SINCE I KNEW IT ALL

HOWARD BOOKS
A Division of Simon & Schuster

NEW YORK LONDON TORONTO SYDNEY

STEVE BROWN

To my beloved friend and mentor,

FRED SMITH,

whose life has so deeply affected mine

and whose wisdom and teaching are

such an important (albeit unspoken)

part of this book.

OUR PURPOSE AT HOWARD BOOKS IS TO:

- *Increase* faith in the hearts of growing Christians
- *Inspire* holiness in the lives of believers
- *Instill* hope in the hearts of struggling people everywhere

BECAUSE HE'S COMING AGAIN!

Published by Howard Books, a division of Simon & Schuster
1230 Avenue of the Americas, New York, NY 10020

What Was I Thinking? © 2006 by Steve Brown

Library of Congress Cataloging-in-Publication Data

Brown, Stephen W.
    What was I thinking? : things I've learned since I knew it all / Steve Brown.
        p. cm.
    Includes bibliographical references (p.   ).
    ISBN-13: 978-1-58229-570-1
    ISBN-10: 1-58229-570-0
    1. Theology, Doctrinal—Popular works. 2. Reformed Church—Doctrines. 3. Christian life. 4. Brown, Stephen W. I. Title.

    BT77.B86 2006
    230'.57—dc22

2006043590

10 9 8 7 6 5 4 3 2 1

For information regarding special discounts for bulk purchases, please contact Simon & Schuster Special Sales at 1-800-456-6798 or business@simonandschuster.com.

Edited by Between the Lines
Interior design by John Mark Luke Designs

CONTENTS

Contents

ACKNOWLEDGMENTS

THE DANGER IN thanking people who make a book possible is in leaving out the names of significant people who made this book possible or, on the other hand, including names of significant people who don't want to be associated with it.

Nevertheless, I must mention my wife, who makes all that I do better and continues to love me when it isn't.

And I must not forget . . .

Denny and Philis Boultinghouse, at Howard Books, who struggle to make me write and then make it better when I do.

Dawn Brandon and Tammy Bicket, whose skilled editing fixed what I wrote and possibly kept me out of jail.

My friends, the staff at Key Life, who continue to "hold up my arms" and do stuff for which I get the credit.

My friends and colleagues at Reformed Theological Seminary in Orlando, who struggle to keep me from being a heretic.

My friend Tom Wood, who found a quote that only he and God knew.

And finally, Robin DeMurga, through whose skilled writing and editing hands passes everything I write here and a thousand other places.

If you're on the list and didn't want to be . . . deal with it!

WHAT WAS I THINKING?

ONE TIME Mark Twain's wife got furious with him and did something she rarely, if ever, did. She started cursing. Twain started laughing, and that, of course, made her even angrier. She asked him what he thought was so funny.

"My dear," he said through gales of laughter, "you know the words, but you don't know the tune!"

Some things should be settled in a believer's life. The eternal verities of the faith should not be adjusted to fit the times, softened to fit the culture, or set aside to fit the changing whims of modern proclivities. Truth is truth because it is true, and it is true in every place and at every time. Real truth doesn't change.

There was a time when I thought that knowing the truth was enough. I defended it (still do), taught it (still do), and believed that if you got the truth right, everything else would be right.

I'm a lot older now, and some wiser. I was wrong. I got the words right, but I missed the tune.

This book is about the tune.

A number of years ago, a friend of mine left the denomination of which I'm a part. The doctrinal basis of my denomination is a confession of faith, the Westminster Confession of Faith, which contains many of the doctrines of the Reformation.

In our conversation, I asked my friend if he still believed that the Confession was true.

"Of course it's true," he replied. "It's just irrelevant."

Before we begin, let me state for the record that my theology is orthodox, evangelical, and Reformed. By that I mean that I believe the historic creeds of the Christian faith, I accept the Westminster Confession of Faith as representing the basic doctrines of the Christian faith, and I believe the Bible is true—all of it. Not only that. I believe that the Bible, the creeds, and the Confession are vitally important. They are important like the foundation of a building. They are like the words of a song.

I tell you this for two reasons. First, some of what I'm going to say in this book will make you wonder about my orthodox credentials. And second, I believe the very thing that points one to Christ (i.e., the foundational biblical truths) can also become death to us if, once we go to Christ, we stop there—in other words, if we then get a polemical gun and see our call from God as defending the orthodoxy that got us there.

I've been there, done that, have the T-shirt . . . and it almost killed me. Theology (no matter how orthodox), a belief statement (no matter how biblical), and propositions (no matter how exact and correct) are all useless if they don't lead us to the reality which is God and to the astonishment that ought to be a regular occurrence in the believer's life.

Of late I've looked at the words—those statements of faith—that I thought were enough and have come to the sobering realization that if we get the words right but can't sing the tune, we miss the grandeur of the song. I've looked at my years of ministry and teaching; I've read old sermons I've preached

and books I've written; I've thought of the people with whom I've worked and of the battles I've fought.

As I've revisited those places, I haven't been ashamed of the truth, but I have often said to myself, "What in the world was I thinking?"

This is a book written by an old guy who started out with the right words but has spent most of his life learning the tune. Along the way I've discovered that the Christian faith is far more radical and far less cerebral than I thought it was.

I would really like to go back and re-teach some of the things I've taught to the congregations I've served and at the conferences and seminars where I've spoken. I don't want to re-teach the words of the song. I got those right. I want to teach—as the song says— the world to sing.

Of course, I can't do that. I don't have that kind of time, and I'm not sure people would understand.

So I'm writing this book instead.

I don't know about you, but I'm tired of glib answers to hard questions, irrelevant "God words," and stark, cold foundations on which no house has ever been built. This book is not about the foundations (i.e., the words). If you're still struggling with the truth of the Christian faith, read another book.

In this book are my second thoughts on matters of first importance, with the hope of putting music to the words.

So, can you carry a tune?

A VOICE IN THE WIND I DO NOT KNOW;

A MEANING ON THE FACE OF THE HIGH HILLS

WHOSE UTTERANCE I CANNOT COMPREHEND,

A SOMETHING IS BEHIND THEM: THAT IS GOD.

GEORGE MACDONALD

GOD IS A LOT BIGGER THAN I THOUGHT HE WAS

From him and through him and to him are all things.
To him be glory forever. Amen.
ROMANS 11:36

TRUTH IS TRUTH—unchangeable and eternal. That is especially true with God. As I mentioned in the introduction, theology (no matter how orthodox), a belief statement (no matter how biblical), and propositions (no matter how exact and correct) are all useless unless they lead to the reality of God himself.

I started out with all the right words yet somehow missed the tune. I hadn't gone far enough.

What was I thinking? Perhaps I was thinking too much. Let me say it again: the Christian faith is far more radical and far less cerebral than I thought it was.

Sometimes I wish I knew as much as my students. There was a time when I thought I did.

It's said that the late Albert Schweitzer—the German theologian, musicologist, philosopher, and missionary (a Nobel laureate)—was working on a construction project, building a hospital. One of the nationals came by, and Schweitzer asked him to help. The young man refused on the grounds that he was an intellectual.

"I thought," Schweitzer said, turning back to his work, "that I was an intellectual once."

I thought I was one too.

I struggled for years with the eternal verities of the Christian faith. I had an undergraduate degree with a major in philosophy and religion, and I was working through some really hard stuff. I read more books than many people will ever read, asked more questions than many will ever ask, and pushed my epistemological presuppositions to the wall. After the struggle, I came to the Christian worldview from which I now live.

I thought I was at the end of my theological journey. Once the foundations were settled, I thought it was all settled.

I didn't know it then, but it wasn't settled at all.

There is no "settled" when it comes to God. For me, faith was cerebral. And having a relationship with God—the real God—is so much more than that. What *was* I thinking?

I often say to my students, when they are especially strident about a subject, "You haven't lived long enough, sinned big enough, or failed nearly enough to even have an opinion on that."

Well, I have lived long enough, sinned big enough, and failed enough. So I want to share with you what I know about God—which, frankly, isn't as much as I once thought it was.

A BIG GOD

An acquaintance of mine has two earned doctorates. During his academic work, he was an atheist; but as he approached his final dissertation, he had a number of important questions. "The first question on my list," he said, "is this: is there a God? If there is a God, then he's in charge. If there isn't a God, then I'm in charge."

Good point, that.

It is not the main point, however. The main point is what we come to through this line of questioning: If there is a God, and he is in charge, what does it mean? Where will it lead? What are the implications of that fact? Does it really matter? Given that he is infinite and I'm finite, does it even matter that he's in charge? Why should I—a mere mortal—care who is in charge? It may be fate, a system, or God, but someone else is in control, so it's all the same. God is in his heaven, and I am here on earth. There are matters, appropriately, about which I can do nothing, for which I have no plan, and on which I have no vote.

A friend of mine drew a cartoon of two ants standing next to the leg of an elephant. One ant says to the other ant, "Let me introduce you to my new friend. I really didn't want to be his friend, but when something that big insists, it is a good policy not to offer any resistance."

Back to our questions. If God is the elephant, what's an ant to do? Frankly, not much. Then again, a whole lot . . . we'll get to that later in this chapter and throughout the book.

The wise preacher who wrote the book of Ecclesiastes said this:

> I turned about and gave my heart up to despair over all the toil of my labors under the sun, because sometimes a person who has toiled with wisdom and knowledge and skill must leave everything to be enjoyed by someone who did not toil for it. This also is vanity and a great evil. What has a man from all the toil and striving of heart with which he toils beneath the sun? For all his days are full of sorrow, and his work is a

vexation. Even in the night his heart does not rest. This also is vanity. (2:20–23)

For those of you who think the Bible is an unrealistic book, put that in your pipe and smoke it. That, of course, isn't all the Bible says. But a good place to start is with this understanding of God's absolute sovereignty. We don't get a vote.

THE REAL GOD

I used to think I had God figured out. I put him into my theological box, nice and tidy. Now I realize that God simply doesn't fit in that box. God is not who I thought he was.

A business friend of mine is very good at what he does. In fact, Sam is quite rich, and he's rich because he's better at what he does than his competitors are. Before I knew my friend, I knew some of his competitors. One day, for some reason known only to himself, and before Sam was even an acquaintance, he invited me to lunch. Some of his competitors heard about the appointment and issued warnings: "He would sell his mother if he could make a buck," one told me. "You don't even want to be seen in a restaurant with that man. It will hurt your reputation," another said. "If I were you, I would turn down the invitation. There's no such thing as a free lunch," another advised.

Against this advice, I accepted the lunch invitation and, in fact, ended up having lunch with Sam on a fairly regular basis. We became friends. It worked because I didn't want anything from him, and he didn't want anything from me. We were both just looking for a friend. I quickly learned that Sam wasn't anything like what I'd been told about him.

As I've gotten older, I've discovered that God isn't altogether what I thought he was either. Some people have been misrepresenting him too. Don't get me wrong; these people don't know they're misrepresenting him. In fact, they think they're doing God and others a great service. Nonetheless, perhaps their perceptions don't get to the heart of who God is. So I want to, as it were, invite you to have lunch with him.

You might be surprised.

Perhaps people have told you that God is a "child abuser"—a Father who will cut off our legs if we get out of line. Or that he is eternally disappointed with us and that his disappointment was reflected in the cross. Perhaps they said there are certain people God loves and certain people he doesn't love. He has been portrayed in books, on broadcasts, and from pulpits as a religious God who wants everybody to be religious—or else. And then there were others who told us God is sort of like Santa who gives gifts, like a favorite uncle who affirmed and loved us, or like a grandfather who stayed up at night admiring us.

> AS I'VE GOTTEN OLDER, I'VE DISCOVERED THAT GOD ISN'T ALTOGETHER WHAT I THOUGHT HE WAS.

I did my fair share of misrepresenting God. I was quite secure in my worldview—I believed it, taught it, defended it, and wrote about it.

Then God—the God of the universe, the real God—came . . . and put me in my place.

A SCARY GOD

If you've never stood before God and been afraid, then you've probably never stood before the real God. (It doesn't end there—

with fear—but that is where it starts.) I used to think that God was nice and safe. Now I know that he is scary.

As long as I could keep God in church, in my theology books, and in my academic discussions, I could deal with him. But when the real God came, it felt like he shook the church, burned the books, and laughed at my academic discussions. I then realized that one doesn't "deal with" God. He deals with us.

The church where I'm a member is a bit different from most. Do you know what our elders gave my pastor for his birthday? They gave him a forty-five. Yeah, a gun. Don't ask me. Maybe it was for church discipline or something—be holy as God is holy . . . or our pastor will shoot you dead.

I have a book in my library titled *Bible in Pocket, Gun in Hand*. It's about the early circuit riders in America. Maybe our elders were reverting to an earlier and simpler time when things were clear: do it our way or pay the consequences.

Well, God doesn't wield a gun. But he isn't "safe" either.

The book of Job is a philosophical discussion about the problems of suffering, evil, and pain. These problems are debated in college dorm rooms everywhere; nobody has any answers, but it's fun to talk about the questions. The difference between the book of Job and a dorm-room debate is that with Job, the questions weren't just theory. His questions were of great existential importance because he was not an outsider talking about the philosophical problem of suffering. Job had lost his family, his possessions, his reputation, and his friends. He sat on an ash heap, scraping the scabs off his sores, and he had had it.

Don't let people use Job as an example of an especially spiritual person who took his suffering the way Christians are sup-

posed to take it: praising God. He did that, but only once. He said, "Though he slay me, I will hope in him" (13:15). After that, Job reverted to a normal human reaction—anger, bitterness, and self-pity. He was ticked, and he yelled at God.

When Job had told God what he really thought, God asked, essentially, "Are you finished?"

Then God started asking some very intimidating questions. Job, having encountered the real God, had an attack of sanity and said, "I had heard of you by the hearing of the ear, but now my eye sees you; therefore I despise myself, and repent in dust and ashes" (42:5–6).

God is scary . . . really scary. So be afraid . . . be very afraid.

Why do you think the Scriptures say no one has ever seen the face of God? Why do you think prophets hid their faces from God? Why do you think Elijah ran and Jeremiah wept? Why do you think Jacob almost died wrestling with an angel? Why do you think Paul said he was talking like a fool when he bragged? Why do you think most folks don't read the book of Revelation or, if they do, feel the need to soften it?

Because one does not trifle with a God who is big and scary.

In my saner moments I'm glad he's that way. Little gods do little things. They speak silly words, and while they might be less threatening, little gods don't give us meaning, demand anything of us, or inspire us.

A GOD IN CONTROL

I used to think (or at least hope) that I was the one in control. Now I know that God is the only one in control. I'm not. I'm helpless.

I'm big into control. I'm an adult child of an alcoholic, and

that means I have the perception that every time I've been out of control, I've gotten hurt. So I try to control everything in my life. My theology is an effort to get some kind of handle on God and control him. My religious profession is, I suppose, an effort to control God too. I pray and preach and teach about God to get some kind of handle on him.

This is slowly beginning to change for me. Over the years I've begun to loosen my grip. To be honest, I didn't have any choice in the matter. When you encounter the real God, you learn that he simply refuses to be controlled.

That was Paul's experience. In his letter to the Romans, Paul sounds like a helpless man—because that's exactly what he was. He wrote, "I do not understand my own actions. For I do not do what I want, but I do the very thing I hate. . . . Wretched man that I am! Who will deliver me from this body of death?" (Romans 7:15–24).

The psalmist cried out to God, "O LORD, God of my salvation; I cry out day and night before you. . . . Incline your ear to my cry! For my soul is full of troubles, and my life draws near to Sheol. . . . Your wrath lies heavy upon me, and you overwhelm me with all your waves" (Psalm 88:1–7).

If you've ever had kidney stones, what I'm going to say next won't surprise you.

YIKES!

I have women friends who've had both kidney stones and babies, and they actually say that the pain of having a kidney stone is worse than the pain of childbirth because at least when delivering a baby, you get a baby. With a kidney stone, all you get is that stupid stone.

At any rate, when I went through my experience with kidney stones, at first I didn't know what it was and thought I was going to die. As my wife took me to the hospital, I was thinking about my will. Who would get my computer? Was my insurance up to date? Whom would my wife marry after I was gone?

When I got to the hospital, they gave me a shot, and I felt wonderful. Then they gave me pills, and whenever the pain got bad, I just popped a pill. Then a surgeon—who seemed to me a very young surgeon, kind of like Doogie Howser—explained what he was going to do about getting the stone out. I said something like, "Oh no, you're not! I can live on these happy pills the rest of my life."

But I didn't have any choice. After a while the pills would begin to lose their potency. I could cuss and spit, but that wouldn't help get rid of the stone. In fact, there wasn't a thing I could do but go through with the surgery. So do you know what I did? I let go. I couldn't fix the problem, and I couldn't make the situation any better. All I could do was take the anesthetic, go to sleep, and let the surgeon do his work.

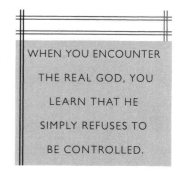

WHEN YOU ENCOUNTER THE REAL GOD, YOU LEARN THAT HE SIMPLY REFUSES TO BE CONTROLLED.

When the real God comes to us, he is like the surgeon. He is going to do what he is going to do, and I'm helpless to change or fix anything. I don't get a vote, and it drives me nuts. Not only that. I'm powerless to get him to stop because, as C. S. Lewis said, God is a *good* surgeon. He won't stop until he accomplishes whatever he has determined to accomplish.

I feel completely helpless.

That is appropriate.

I am.

I used to say that God and I were partners. We're not. He is God, and I am not. So sometimes the most important thing I can do is get out of the way.

A CONFUSING GOD

I used to think that I had God down. Now I realize that much of the time, all I am is confused.

Does God confuse you? Have you ever been sure that God told you to do something or promised something only to find out that you were wrong—terribly wrong? Have you ever pontificated about God only to find out that you didn't speak from Sinai, and you had to eat crow? Have you ever told someone that God told you to tell that person something and then found out that the person got into serious trouble because of your dumb remarks? Have you ever thought that you had seen God, only to find out that you were crazy? Have you ever answered questions about God not because you knew the answers but because you simply had a glib tongue or were trying to cover for your lack of answers?

I have.

In Romans 11:34 Paul asked a rhetorical question: "Who has known the mind of the Lord, or who has been his counselor?" The answer to that question is, of course, nobody. No one has understood God, and no one has ever helped him out with advice. "For my thoughts are not your thoughts, neither are your ways my ways, declares the LORD. For as the heavens are higher than the earth, so are my ways higher than your ways and my thoughts than your thoughts" (Isaiah 55:8–9).

I teach through a syndicated radio broadcast called *Key Life.* On part of Wednesday's program and on all of Friday's program (when my pastor, Pete Alwinson, joins me), I devote time to answering some of the thousands of questions we receive at Key Life Network. In addition, at almost all of the conferences and seminars this ministry conducts around the country, we include a segment during which I answer questions. I also spend considerable time at Reformed Theological Seminary answering questions from students.

I used to be anxious about those Q&A sessions. No more. I'm no longer anxious because I generally know more than those who are asking the questions. That isn't pride; it's just true. After all, I've been at this longer than most of them. (Would you go to a surgeon who doesn't know more than you do about surgery?)

More importantly, though, I'm comfortable with those Q&A sessions because I don't mind responding, "I don't know. I don't have the foggiest idea about how to answer your question, and I am, as a matter of fact, probably more confused than you are."

Do you remember the Y2K scare, when the "experts" predicted that all of civilization would come to a screeching halt because computers were programmed to work with two-digit numbers for years, like 98 or 99, and wouldn't be able to transition to using four digits, like 2000 or 2001?

I didn't buy into the mania. So when the great crash didn't happen, boy did I have fun on my next broadcast.

I love making fun of "experts" who are wrong. There is so much arrogance, so much self-righteousness, and so much self-aggrandizement in many experts that when they're wrong (and they often are), it's hard to resist pointing it out.

God does that to us sometimes, when we're acting like experts: "Who is this that darkens counsel by words without knowledge? Dress for action like a man; I will question you, and you make it known to me" (Job 38:2–3). In other words, what do we know about his plans or his ways? If we're honest, very little.

A few months ago I was the officiating minister at the funeral of a teenage boy who had committed suicide. I guess people expected me to explain how a good God could allow such a tragedy.

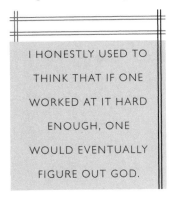

I HONESTLY USED TO THINK THAT IF ONE WORKED AT IT HARD ENOUGH, ONE WOULD EVENTUALLY FIGURE OUT GOD.

There was a time when I would have tried. But instead, I said, "I don't understand this. It makes me angry and confused. So if you're angry and confused, at least we can cry together."

Angry and confused. I'm not sure about the anger, but I do believe confusion is appropriate when standing before the real God.

I honestly used to think that if one worked at it hard enough, studied the Bible long enough, and talked to the right people often enough, one would eventually figure out God. I'm an old guy now, and I've been doing all three for a long time. And I was wrong.

GOD'S WEIRD CHOICES

I used to think that God liked only certain people—those who lived up to his standards. But I'm increasingly surprised by his choice of friends. And even more surprised that his choice includes me.

God makes what seem to me some very funny choices—

meaning, they're not necessarily the choices I would make. You see, I always thought God had a big house in which the people who did what he said could live, worship, and enjoy fellowship. On the outside were the people who didn't do what God said to do. I, of course, was on the inside, because I did what he said—or at least tried to. I figured my sincerity would give me a pass.

But I was wrong.

God said to Moses in Exodus 33:19, "I will make all my goodness pass before you and will proclaim before you my name 'The LORD.' And I will be gracious to whom I will be gracious, and will show mercy on whom I will show mercy." In other words, God will choose his own friends, thank you very much.

That has always bothered me.

I am probably as religious as any person you know. Maybe even more. I teach religion to religious students at a religious graduate school. I stand before a whole lot of people and say religious things. I write religious books, I teach religious seminars, and I do religious radio broadcasts.

I'm really religious.

What bugs me is when God chooses to love people who aren't religious or, at any rate, not as religious as I am. I'm beginning to learn that God makes, by my judgment, some weird choices. He loves people who drive me nuts, and he has mercy on people to whom I would not show mercy. He moves beyond religious institutions and befriends people with whom I would not be friends.

Whoopi Goldberg, who calls herself an atheist, is not one of my favorite people. But did you see her movie *Sister Act*? It's about a prostitute who hides from some thugs who want to kill

her. What makes it unique is that she hides in a Roman Catholic convent. She dresses like a nun and becomes the choir director, teaching the nuns to sing music that's more upbeat and fun than their usual convent fare.

OK, that's cool and a good story.

But what makes the story for me is this: Early in the film, the convent church is old and filled with old people who are very religious. Once the prostitute/nun starts leading the choir, however, the people on the outside (prostitutes, drug addicts, and other colorful characters) start coming into the church. In fact, they fill the church.

When I first saw that scene, I started crying. (I hardly cry at anything. I'm a guy, OK?) My wife, who was with me, gave me a look that said clearly, "Will you stop it? Are you a fruitcake? This is a comedy. Can't you see that everybody else in this theater is laughing, and you're crying? I think I'm going to sit somewhere else and pretend that I don't know you."

Nevertheless, I couldn't stop weeping. When the movie was over, I asked God about my peculiar reaction, and I felt him answer that it wasn't me—it was him. He was speaking through that scene.

I whined in response. *But Lord, Whoopi Goldberg? Why couldn't it have been through Billy Graham or the Pope?*

I didn't get an answer.

I have a recurring dream in which I'm finally home in heaven and am sitting at the Lord's table for the marriage supper of the Lamb. All kinds of people are there: those who were once homosexuals, pornographers, and gluttons. As I look around, I

also see former adulterers, liars, and thieves. There are one-time prostitutes and pimps, tax collectors and drunks. I'm generally pleased that some clergy persons are present, some leaders of the church, and even one or two television preachers. And, frankly, I'm shocked.

Then, in my dream, I hear a voice from the throne, and the words are addressed to me. The voice is God's, and he asks, "And what do you think you're doing here?"

I think maybe he was kidding, but I'm not sure. I usually wake up before I find out.

A LOVING GOD

I used to think God's love could be logically explained and measured. I now know that God's love runs far deeper than we can fathom.

There was a time when I was sure I could explain and defend God. I've found out, though, that he is beyond explanation—and not in need of defense. He was doing fine before I came along, and he will do fine long after I'm gone. Yet for some reason, this big, scary, and confusing God who chooses unlikely friends has chosen to love me. And I see his love in everything, without exception. The question is not, "Where is God's love?" The question is, "Where *isn't* God's love?"

Frankly, the love thing makes me even more confused about God. I could understand a monster God, a God who was justly angry at his creatures who have messed things up so terribly—or even a God who was on vacation. But a God who loves people who don't deserve love?

It's true. "God so loved the world, that he gave his only Son" (John 3:16).

Charles Spurgeon said that if we can't trace God's hand, we should trust his heart. I feel like I've been doing a lot of heart-trusting as of late. Every time I have a question about God (and I have a lot), every time I'm confused (and I'm confused a lot), and every time I feel helpless (and I feel helpless a lot), I have to trust God's heart. Because I can't trace his hand.

Brian McLaren has written, among other books, three semi-fictional works about "Pastor Dan" and his postmodern friend and mentor. The third book is titled *The Last Word and the Word after That: A Tale of Faith, Doubt, and a New Kind of Christianity.* While I don't agree with everything Dr. McLaren wrote, I am in agreement with his belief that our real problem in the church is that we start with the doctrine of hell rather than with the doctrine of God's character.

What is God like? That's the first question. How we answer it—how we understand God's character—determines how we deal with all other questions. I'm confused about a lot of stuff, but if I begin at one truth that is clearly taught in Scripture, demonstrated in the incarnation of Christ, and experienced in my own life—that God isn't just loving, and he doesn't just act in loving ways, but he *is* love (see 1 John 4:16)—then it helps me put everything else into proper perspective.

Perhaps you've heard the song that says, "God is good. He is good all the time." Well, he is. I don't know if I fully understand that. I have a lot of questions about it. But the bottom line is, God's is the heart I trust. And trusting his heart of love, I've

discovered a supernatural peace and meaning that could not have come from my questions.

After Jesus's resurrection, he appeared on the shore of the Sea of Tiberias and fixed breakfast for his astonished disciples. During that encounter (see John 21), Jesus asked Peter if Peter loved him—and he asked Peter that same question three times. I suppose Jesus was giving Peter the opportunity to speak his love three times, once for each earlier betrayal.

It was a good question.

My question, in the face of uncertainties, fear, helplessness, and confusion, is the same as Jesus's question—only reversed. "Jesus, are you sure you love us? Sometimes it seems you don't treat your friends very well, and we wonder. Are you there? Do you care? Are you angry?"

And then, very hesitantly, "Do you . . . uh . . . love me?"

The answer is always a clear yes, and I find it throughout the Bible and throughout my life. I've gotten the answer in the way I've been forgiven. I've experienced God's love in the laughter of my grandchildren and in the beauty of a sunset. I've seen it in the tears of a friend who was weeping over my sin and in the sermon by which my pastor reminded me that God had not gone away on vacation. I've seen God's love for me in the church, made up of imperfect people who have stopped playing games, and in books that helped me know his truth and grace.

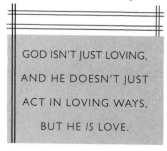

GOD ISN'T JUST LOVING, AND HE DOESN'T JUST ACT IN LOVING WAYS, BUT HE *IS* LOVE.

But I've also experienced God's love when I've seen Jesus in

the faces of devastated families who've lost a child. I've met God and experienced his love by the bedsides of people who are dying of cancer, and I've seen it in the eyes of people who have tried and failed over and over again.

And always God's tears mingle with ours. I know because I know him in his tears and in his love. God *is* love.

I used to think that understanding him was the main thing. It isn't. The main thing is being loved by him. And that I know.

IS IT ANY WONDER THAT TO THIS DAY THIS GALILEAN
IS TOO MUCH FOR OUR SMALL HEARTS?

H. G. WELLS

Jesus Is a Lot More Radical Than I Thought He Was

The law was given through Moses; grace and truth came through Jesus Christ. No one has ever seen God; the only God, who is at the Father's side, he has made him known.

JOHN 1:17–18

I HAVE A confession to make: I've had to change what I thought about Jesus.

Perhaps the most salient fact about Jesus is that he surprises us. Well, *surprise* may not be the right word. He offends, amazes, shocks, and confuses us. And he refuses to fit into the mold we've designed for him.

And Jesus surprised—and offended, amazed, shocked, and confused—me.

Did you hear about the man who was given a tour of the various levels of hell? The first level was horrible, and he asked his tour guide what the people held there had done. The guide said, "Those are Baptists who danced."

The second level of hell was even worse. To the man's query, the guide responded, "These were the Episcopalians who spent their capital."

When they got to the third level, it was a lot worse. The man

asked the tour director what those people had done. "They're Pentecostals who refused to raise their hands," he replied.

Finally they reached the deepest level of hell. The people there were in utter agony. "Good heavens," the man said. "What did these people do?"

"They're Presbyterians," said the tour director, "who smiled, said, 'Praise the Lord!' in a formal worship service, and used the wrong fork at dinner."

That joke wasn't funny to me for the longest time. Do you know why?

I had made Jesus into a Presbyterian! Is that crazy or what?

Don't get me wrong . . . I thought he should be. In fact, for years I tried to force him into that mold—nice, proper, and if he had lived in the twenty-first century, an owner of blue-chip stocks. I always thought Jesus would be comfortable in most Presbyterian churches and would subscribe to the Westminster Confession of Faith. If his incarnation had taken place in modern times, I was quite certain he would be a Republican.

What was I thinking?

All that was before I understood the real Jesus. He didn't frighten me as much as God the Father did, but he did confuse me.

Jesus simply doesn't fit into our mold. If Jesus were just a man, that wouldn't be a big deal. It's not so surprising when people do weird things. I can deal with a psychotic megalomaniac or, perhaps, a neurotic religious nut. But when Jesus offends, amazes, shocks, and confuses us, that's another matter altogether, because he isn't just a man. He's God.

Jesus actually claimed godhood. That would be sick if not

for the evidence of crutches thrown jubilantly into the air and of empty caskets. At the reports of a dead man getting up and walking around, I decided I should listen to what was said by the one who had raised him.

And that man said he is God.

In chapter one I made reference to Albert Schweitzer. He's a hero to me not so much because of what he did but because of what he wrote. In fact, if Schweitzer had never written anything but what follows, taken from his book *The Quest of the Historical Jesus*, it would be enough:

> He [Jesus] comes to us as One unknown, without a name, as of old, by the lake side, He came to those men who knew Him not. He speaks to us the same word, "Follow thou me!" and sets us to the tasks which He has to fulfill for our time. He commands. And to those who obey Him, whether they be wise or simple, He will reveal Himself in the toils, the conflicts, the sufferings which they shall pass through in His fellowship, and as an ineffable mystery, they shall learn in their own experience Who He is.[1]

If you want evidence of the truth in Schweitzer's words, I'm it.

It's not that I've always obeyed Jesus, but I've followed him for a long time, and I'm still here. I'm bloodied, sinful, and afraid . . . but I'm still here. The longer I follow Jesus, the more I learn about him—and the more I've had to change what I think about him.

Jesus as God

The problem was, I had made Jesus into a doctrine, and while there are important truths *about* him, those facts aren't who he is.

Most Christians, myself included, have quite rightly looked at the incarnation of God in Christ as foundational to the theological superstructure of our faith. It's one of those "but of course" doctrines we've simply accepted. But perhaps we accepted it too quickly.

Did you know that almost all Christian heresies, as defined by the church, are Christological heresies? In other words, the central place where people get it wrong, according to the historic church councils, is in the definition of who Jesus is and what he did.

I can understand that.

The incarnation of God in Christ is a crazy doctrine. If you don't find it difficult to believe or, if you do believe it, to apply, then you simply haven't understood how radical the coming of Jesus was. Much of my life, I've tried to make the incarnation of Christ palatable to the rational minds of the people to whom I believe God has sent me. I've softened it, repackaged it, and even tried to redefine it. The reason is this: I knew that if I were not a believer, this is the place where I would stumble.

> THE DOCTRINE OF THE INCARNATION OF GOD IN CHRIST IS THE "EATING A FROG," AS IT WERE, ASPECT OF THE CHRISTIAN WORLDVIEW.

If I weren't a Christian and you were, I would understand your beliefs about God's existence (only a fool, the Bible says, subscribes to atheism), immortality (I'm not really that happy about dying and could use a little hope), and ethics (they keep stealing my car, and somebody has to say that's wrong). If I weren't a Christian, I would probably even have a secret hope that you were right.

But when you started talking about Jesus being God, I think I'd draw the line there and start to wonder about your sanity.

It's the "eating a frog" syndrome.

Let me explain. Have you ever talked to someone in a rational and calm way, and then that person goes off the deep end, saying something so wild that you think you misunderstood the entire conversation? Have you ever been absolutely shocked by the actions of some of your friends, or maybe even of your own? If you've had this experience, you'll probably understand why I liken it to what I call the "eating a frog" syndrome. It's as if everything was fine, and then, in the very middle of "fine," a frog hopped across the floor—and the other person scooped up the frog and ate it. It's bizarre. It seems crazy.

When you find out that your preacher is gay after all that time of his preaching against homosexuality, or that your philosophy professor is a member of a Wicca coven, or that your neighbor who loves kittens is a serial killer, or that your very respectable father is married to two women other than your mother . . . I call that "eating a frog."

The doctrine of the incarnation of God in Christ is crazy—like eating the frog—but in a far different way. It's a surprise, it's astounding, it creates all kinds of questions, and it keeps us awake at night.

The doctrine of the incarnation of God in Christ is the "eating a frog," as it were, aspect of the Christian worldview. I didn't see that for years.

The book of John says, "In the beginning was the Word . . . and the Word was God. . . . And the Word became flesh and dwelt among us" (1:1–14). The writer of Hebrews said, "Long ago, at

many times and in many ways, God spoke to our fathers by the prophets, but in these last days he has spoken to us by his Son, whom he appointed the heir of all things, through whom also he created the world. He is the radiance of the glory of God and the exact imprint of his nature, and he upholds the universe by the word of his power" (1:1–3).

The apostle John, who was there when the Gospels' story unfolded, was confident of the truth of Christ's eternal nature and identity as God because of his personal experience with Jesus: "That which was from the beginning, which we have heard, which we have seen with our eyes, which we looked upon and have touched with our hands, concerning the word of life—the life was made manifest, and we have seen it, and testify to it and proclaim to you the eternal life, which was with the Father and was made manifest to us—that which we have seen and heard we proclaim also to you, so that you too may have fellowship with us" (1 John 1:1–3).

The God who is omnipresent (all-present), omnipotent (all-powerful), and omniscient (all-knowing); the God who is the creator, sustainer, and ruler of all that is, became a baby. It's true, but it's weird.

I have just articulated to you the central doctrine of the Christian faith. For much of my teaching and preaching career, I've stopped there.

I didn't go far enough.

Jesus not only is God; he also was a man.

JESUS AS MAN

Let me tell you something quite radical: Jesus wasn't playing games. He didn't say, "Yeah, I'm a man (wink, wink)," knowing

that he really was just God in a man suit.

He really was a man.

Most Christians don't have any problem with the God part. It's the man part that drives us nuts. We want Jesus to wear a costume of humanity, but we aren't willing to see his humanity as anything more than a costume. We like the idea of Jesus walking on water, but we have difficulty with his loneliness and his fear. We don't mind the raising of the dead, but we have difficulty with the dirt under the fingernails.

The Bible gives two accounts of the temptation of Jesus. One is in Matthew 4 and the other in Luke 4. A lot of things can be said about Satan's tempting Jesus, but it seems to me that a part of the temptation was Jesus's own question about who he was.

When Jesus talked about the end of all things, he said that he didn't know when it would be. Do you know why he said that? He said it because he really didn't know. When Jesus faced his death, he asked God to prevent it. Do you know why he asked this? He asked because he wanted a way out of that suffering. When Jesus prayed in the garden before his death, the text says that his sweat was like drops of blood. Do you know why? It was because Jesus was really scared.

A major purpose of the incarnation was identification: God identified with us.

I've always talked about the Cross as Christ's self-sacrifice for our sins; I still do. I believe that God showed his love by coming to us in an unfathomable act of condescension. I have always believed that Christians have been declared righteous and justified and that the declaration is legal and settled. I still believe that.

But what I learned by walking with Jesus all this time is his

pain. I've learned that he identified with us so totally and so completely that the Scripture says, "We do not have a high priest who is unable to sympathize with our weaknesses, but one who in every respect has been tempted as we are" (Hebrews 4:15). In other words, he didn't play games. When God entered time and space and became human, he really became human.

One of the ancient Christian heresies was called Docetism. It's the view that matter is evil and that God would never condescend to enter an evil human body. The word *Docetism* is derived from the Greek word *dokein*, meaning "to seem." Thus the incarnation was not real. It just seemed real. But that's not what the Bible tells us, and it's not what I believe.

When I go through self-doubt, when I'm afraid, and when I want to avoid the difficult path ahead of me, I tell Jesus, and he says, "I know. Been there, done that." He knows our sufferings. He gets it.

Jesus's Unconditional Love

Once we "get it" in terms of who Jesus is, even that is only a beginning. Frankly, it's just not easy to hang out with Jesus and be a proper Presbyterian. We find out surprising things about the real Jesus that aren't always comfortable. For instance, I noticed that Jesus is a lot more unconditional in his love than I thought he was.

I once thought that Jesus was conditional in his love and acceptance. What was I thinking? I was the one who set conditions.

Jesus said that if we're tired, we can go to him, and he will give us rest—that when our way is hard, his way would be easy (see Matthew 11:28–30). The condition is being tired.

Jesus said that he had come to love sinners (see Matthew 9:13). The condition was being a sinner.

Jesus said that he had come for the sick (see Mark 2:17). The condition was being sick.

Jesus hung out with prostitutes, drunks, and bad people. It quickly becomes clear that if I want to be his friend, I can't be a "proper" Christian.

I serve on two boards, and they both bother me. I've served on the boards of Christian magazines, Christian evangelistic ministries, and Christian sports ministries. I was sort of proud of being on those boards. They defined me as a Christian who is committed to God's work in the world.

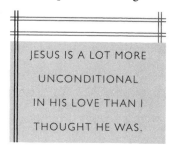

JESUS IS A LOT MORE UNCONDITIONAL IN HIS LOVE THAN I THOUGHT HE WAS.

Over the last few years, though, I resigned from those boards. I now serve on two boards. One is Harvest USA, started by my friend John Freeman as a ministry to gays and lesbians. Most of the staff and some of the board members at Harvest are homosexuals who are celibate or who have moved into a heterosexual life. When I was asked to serve on that board, I told God that it would hurt my reputation. "God," I said, "people are going to think I'm gay."

"So?" I think he said in response. "You may not be gay, but you're sinful, dirty, and screwed up. And if they call you gay, be glad, because when people 'utter all kinds of evil against you falsely on my account' (Matthew 5:11), you're to rejoice."

So I winced and signed up.

Then God, in his wisdom and graciousness, gave me another place to serve. I'm also on the board of Victoria's Friends. Victoria

Teague, my friend, is a former strip-club dancer and drug addict. Now, when she goes into strip clubs to minister, she weeps. She remembers the pain of that lifestyle and has incredible compassion for those who still experience that pain.

I told Jesus that I was sort of pleased that he had balanced out the homosexual and heterosexual sin groupings but that I still wasn't altogether happy with where he had sent me. What I had in mind, I told him, was a ministry where "normal" Christians reached out to "normal" people to make them more "normal." "Lord," I said, "what will people say? This could really hurt my reputation and my witness."

"It hurt mine," I think he said. Then he said, "You go, and I'll go with you."

JESUS AND RELIGION

So I went. You see, the only place it really would hurt my reputation was among religious people. I once thought we were called to be religious, but I was wrong. I was the one who took pride in religion. Jesus is far less positive about it than I thought he was.

Some of the harshest words Jesus ever spoke were spoken to and about religious people. He called them hypocrites, narrow-minded, whitewashed tombs, dishonest, and manipulative. He argued with them and told them that they didn't really know or understand the Scriptures. He offended them—he even seemed to go out of his way to offend them. He told stories about them, insulted them, and refused to be more religious to please them.

And he loved them.

In Matthew 5:20 Jesus said something that has always both-

ered me: "Unless your righteousness exceeds that of the scribes and Pharisees, you will never enter the kingdom of heaven."

Now, before you jump to any conclusions, you need to know that when Jesus said that, the most "righteous" people around were the scribes and Pharisees. You may not want to go to a movie or a football game with them—you may not like them at all—but that doesn't mean that they weren't righteous. These were the folks who came the closest to obeying the law of God—all of it. They were religious professionals who, if they lived today, would be leaders of the church.

If I have to be better than that, I don't stand a chance.

As I mentioned earlier, I'm the host of a syndicated radio talk show. At the time of this writing, a prominent religious leader has advocated the assassination of the president of another country. People who do talk shows *live* for this sort of comment. Everybody else thinks, "How could he?" But a talk show host says, "Cool." We have to find material somewhere.

Just before I started preparing my diatribe about this religious leader's assassination advocacy, someone handed me an article written by another religious leader who declared that this pro-assassination leader was "an embarrassment to the church and a danger to American politics." He went further to say the man was not much different from "Muslim extremists."

Well, I thought, *he may be right, and he probably said it better than I could have said it.* Then I thought, *But how insufferably arrogant and self-righteous he is!*

That's when a question popped into my mind (it may have been God, but I want to be careful here): *And you're not?!*

I thought about the righteousness of the Pharisees and scribes and about how Jesus said that I had to be more righteous than they were. Then I saw what Jesus was saying. He defined righteousness differently than religious people usually define it.

I might be one of the most religious people around, but don't confuse that with righteousness. I once thought that Jesus would be pleased with me because . . . well . . . because he was religious too. Now I'm not so sure. It kind of scares me when I consider the number of times I've used religion as a substitute for God, a method to tell others how good I am, or a badge of honor among the less religious.

Now all of that religiosity isn't looking so good.

A friend of mine says that anybody who makes his or her living at religion is probably going to lose one or the other. I don't totally agree with that, but it's close enough to the truth to cause me to wince. One must be careful about religion, because it can make you feel that you're close to God—that you're pure and that you're serving him—when, in fact, you aren't.

JESUS AND PARTISANSHIP

I once thought that Jesus took sides. But I was wrong. I was the one taking sides. I'm always taking sides. But when I hang out with Jesus, I find that he is far less partisan than I thought he was.

A friend of mine told me many years ago, "Steve, I don't know where you'll be in twenty years, but wherever you are, you'll be waving a flag for something!"

I don't care so much what you believe, but I hope you believe something strongly enough to fight and die for it. If you're a Democrat, don't shilly-shally about your political beliefs. If you're

a Republican, be a Republican. If you're a Christian, tell everybody you know and dare them to challenge you. If you're an atheist, be a real one. There's nothing worse than a "weenie" atheist except, maybe, a weenie Christian.

Then I find out that Jesus doesn't choose sides that way. For instance, his criticism of the Pharisees was so harsh that one cannot read it without wincing (see Matthew 23). And yet, on more than one occasion, he went to dinner parties with Pharisees. What's with that?

Jesus reached out to the oppressed and was on the side of the poor while, at the same time, being friends with the oppressors and the ones who helped keep the poor, poor.

He was clear about sexual morality, and in the Sermon on the Mount he went further than the Law did in his comments, saying lust was no better than actual adultery. His teaching on divorce is cut-and-dried—and goes beyond what Moses taught. So what in the world was Jesus doing spending time with adulterers and divorced people?

He lived in the middle of an occupied country, and yet he was often seen reaching out to and loving the occupiers.

It just doesn't make sense.

I'm quite political. On occasion I've been called opinionated. (Well, maybe more than occasionally.) I have strong theological, social, and moral convictions and have no hesitation about sharing those views with anyone who will listen. I draw a circle, and I put Republicans, Christians, Presbyterians, and good citizens in

> ONE MUST BE CAREFUL ABOUT RELIGION, BECAUSE IT CAN MAKE YOU FEEL THAT YOU'RE CLOSE TO GOD—WHEN, IN FACT, YOU AREN'T.

the circle and everybody else outside it.

So sometimes I want to say to Jesus, "Just take a side!"

But he doesn't have a side.

I recently spoke at a conference for Christian counselors, who have been criticized by other Christians for being too wishy-washy. At a dinner for the leaders of the conference, I brought up the criticism to see how they would respond. The president said, "While there are many who draw lines, we believe we've been called to build bridges."

Maybe there's something to both methods, and the key is knowing when to draw lines and when to build bridges.

Jesus drew lines, and they were clear, absolute, and hard. I knew that. But he also crossed every one of those lines and loved people on the other side.

The more I walk with him, the more I'm learning to see people through his eyes. That means I'm called to reach out to people who aren't the kind of people I want to know, people who are on the other side of the line. In other words, I like Republicans and Presbyterians; but the more I walk with Jesus, the more I understand that he probably wouldn't spend as much time with them as I do.

Jesus's Open Invitation

I once thought that Jesus's invitation was pretty exclusive. But I was the one who was into exclusivity. His invitation is far more open than I thought it was.

One wonderful image in the Bible is the marriage supper of the Lamb. Jesus referred to it at the last meal he shared with his disciples before his crucifixion. Revelation 19:6–9 gives a wonderful description of that marriage supper:

Then I heard what seemed to be the voice of a great multitude, like the roar of many waters and like the sound of mighty peals of thunder, crying out,

> "Hallelujah!
> For the Lord our God
>   the Almighty reigns.
> Let us rejoice and exult
>   and give him the glory,
> for the marriage of the Lamb has come,
>   and his Bride has made herself ready;
> it was granted her to clothe herself
>   with fine linen, bright and pure"—

for the fine linen is the righteous deeds of the saints.

And the angel said to me, "Write this: Blessed are those who are invited to the marriage supper of the Lamb."

I used to think that the marriage supper of the Lamb would be like a covered-dish supper at the local Protestant church: great food, good people, and the security of knowing that our fellowship is with those who belong to God.

C. M. Ward, the great Assemblies of God preacher and voice of the old *Revival Time* radio program, was one of my favorite preachers long before I started believing anything he said. Even as a teenager I was fascinated with his ability to effortlessly put together a long list of adjectives relating to God and the things of God. As I remember it, Ward often closed his broadcast by talking about the "long, long altar, where there is room enough for you."

I think the marriage supper of the Lamb will be like that. It will have a long, long table, and there's room enough for you.

That table will include those who were murderers, thieves, liars, adulterers, homosexuals, politicians, lawyers, tax collectors, prostitutes, drug addicts, and strippers.

I know what you're thinking: *Wait, wait. You don't mean to tell me that the marriage supper of the Lamb will include people like that?!*

Yes, the marriage supper of the Lamb will include people "like that"—people whose lives were once full of sin but who have been forgiven and redeemed. After all, it's going to include, I'm told, people like me.

It will include arrogant Christians whose self-righteousness will be hard to maintain in that kind of company. Some there might once have found it difficult to reconcile their theological views with the people they'll be sitting alongside. Some at that table may be the religious who would normally want to close their eyes and pretend that "those" folks aren't there. We'll undoubtedly find at that table preachers, elders, deacons, and leaders of the church who believed that the church was an institution. Sprinkled in will be some who have Sunday-school attendance pins that reach down to the floor.

The marriage supper of the Lamb will be for sinners like all of us.

It's a long, long table.

And there's room enough for you!

I used to think there wasn't.

I was wrong.

MANY ARE DECEIVED IN THE END,

WHO AT FIRST SEEMED TO BE LED BY THE HOLY SPIRIT.

THOMAS À KEMPIS

THE HOLY SPIRIT IS WORKING IN A LOT MORE PLACES THAN I THOUGHT HE WAS

O Lord, you have searched me and known me! You know when I sit down and when I rise up; you discern my thoughts from afar. You search out my path and my lying down and are acquainted with all my ways. . . . Where shall I go from your Spirit?

PSALM 139:1–7

THE HOLY SPIRIT is a lot busier than I thought he was. Right now, he might be in places you never expected, doing things you never anticipated, and acting in rather shocking ways.

I used to have a very limited view of the Holy Spirit. What was I thinking?

I once wrote a book about the Holy Spirit titled *Follow the Wind.*[1] In it I attempted to convey what the Bible says about the Holy Spirit, and I stand by what I wrote.

If you read it, you'll learn a lot about the Holy Spirit, the history of the doctrine of the Holy Spirit in the church, and the work of the Holy Spirit in the believer and in the world. The book deals with some of the controversies about the Holy Spirit in church history and with some of the modern controversies about the gift of tongues, the "baptism" of the Holy Spirit, and the work of the Holy Spirit in the sanctification of the Christian.

If you want to know the truth about the Holy Spirit, I highly recommend that book. After all, I'm not above trying to sell books

to earn a little extra money. (Actually, the ministry for which I work and which gets the profits from all my books, Key Life, needs the money.) So buy it—I think you'll like it.

However, if you want to know everything I've discovered about the Holy Spirit, you won't find it in that book.

One of the interesting things about the Holy Spirit is his job description. He never points to himself; instead, he always points to the first person (God the Father) and the second person (God the Son) of the Trinity. In John 15:26 Jesus said this about the Holy Spirit: "When the Helper comes, whom I will send to you from the Father, the Spirit of truth, who proceeds from the Father, he will bear witness about me."

In John 16:14–15 Jesus said, "He will glorify me, for he will take what is mine and declare it to you. All that the Father has is mine; therefore I said that he will take what is mine and declare it to you."

> THE HOLY SPIRIT NEVER POINTS TO HIMSELF; HE ALWAYS POINTS TO THE FIRST PERSON (GOD THE FATHER) AND THE SECOND PERSON (GOD THE SON) OF THE TRINITY.

So it's risky business to start talking about the Holy Spirit. We can miss him in a lot of places.

The late H. R. Rookmaaker, a professor at Free University of Amsterdam, would, I'm told, show two paintings to his classes. One of the paintings would be clearly religious and might portray Jesus on the cross. The other would not be religious, in the sense that it portrayed no religious subject. Then he would ask his students which of the paintings was Christian.

The students would, of course, point to the overtly religious painting. That's when Dr. Rookmaaker would explain that the

true Christian painting was not necessarily the one with the cross but rather whichever one reflected integrity, power, and beauty and that glorified God, from whom those things flow.[2]

Of course the Holy Spirit has a special place in the lives of believers. He guides, comforts, reveals truth, teaches, convicts, applies God's Word, gives spiritual gifts, and manifests the fruit of the Spirit (love, joy, peace, patience, kindness, goodness, faithfulness, gentleness, and self-control). The Holy Spirit interprets believers' prayers before the throne of God; lifts up, honors, and glorifies the Father and the Son; guides the church; and does a whole lot more.

You knew that.

The fact is, if you've been a Christian for very long, you've been taught about the Holy Spirit. Perhaps you even know more about the Holy Spirit than most Christians do. But, as Paul Harvey says, "You know the story . . . now let me tell you the rest of the story."

The Holy Spirit's work is not limited to Christians and the church.

"Secular" and "sacred" are categories that enable us to separate "us" from "them" or to divide our lives into "God stuff" and "not God stuff." However, those categories are not biblical categories. The Scriptures never put God in a box of the "sacred." Nothing is beyond his domain. He isn't just the ruler of a place; he's the ruler of *all* places. He isn't just the sustainer of religious stuff; he's the sustainer of *all* stuff. He isn't just the master of his own people; he's the master of *everyone*. Consider:

- "To the LORD your God belong heaven and the heaven of heavens, the earth with all that is in it." (Deuteronomy 10:14)

- "Blessed be the name of God forever and ever, to whom belong wisdom and might. He changes times and seasons; he removes kings and sets up kings; he gives wisdom to the wise and knowledge to those who have understanding." (Daniel 2:20–21)

- "O LORD God of hosts, who is mighty as you are, O LORD, with your faithfulness all around you? You rule the raging of the sea; when its waves rise, you still them. . . . The heavens are yours; the earth also is yours; the world and all that is in it, you have founded them. The north and the south, you have created them." (Psalm 89:8–12)

The Bible is a covenant book for God's covenant people. The Holy Spirit is, in a very particular and important way, the gift God gives to his people. Jesus said, "I will ask the Father, and he will give you another Helper, to be with you forever, even the Spirit of truth, whom the world cannot receive, because it neither sees him nor knows him. You know him, for he dwells with you and will be in you" (John 14:16–17).

But while the Bible is a covenant book for God's covenant people, it would be a disastrous mistake to think of God as only the God of the church or to think of God's chief concern as religion. If God is sovereign over all his creation, it stands to reason that he is acting everywhere he rules. And that, of course, is everywhere.

In the Old Testament, the word for God's Spirit is *Ruah*, and it means both breath and wind. The Holy Spirit, the Bible teaches, is God's power in action, or God's energy let loose. If that's true—and the Bible clearly states that it is—then the Holy Spirit is operating in a whole lot of places we might not expect.

The Activity of the Holy Spirit

Let me share with you five areas in which the Bible teaches that the Holy Spirit is active. This may seem rather pedantic and dull, but if you'll stay with me, we'll see some incredible implications of the Holy Spirit's involvement in those areas.

1. *The Holy Spirit Is Active in Creation*

The first place we encounter the Holy Spirit in the Bible is in the opening verses of the first chapter of Genesis, the first book of the Bible. Those verses say that God created everything, and they give us a glimpse of what it was like before God created: "The earth was without form and void, and darkness was over the face of the deep. And the Spirit of God was hovering over the face of the waters" (Genesis 1:2).

In creating the first human being in Genesis 2, the Spirit was active: "The LORD God formed the man of dust from the ground and breathed into his nostrils the breath [the word for *Spirit*] of life, and the man became a living creature" (Genesis 2:7). The psalmist said, "By the word of the LORD the heavens were made, and by the breath [there it is again] of his mouth all their host" (Psalm 33:6). The psalmist also stated, "When you send forth your Spirit, they are created, and you renew the face of the ground" (Psalm 104:30).

2. *The Holy Spirit Teaches and Affirms Truth*

Jesus called the Holy Spirit the "Spirit of truth" (John 14:17). Then he expanded on that by saying, "The Helper, the Holy Spirit, whom the Father will send in my name, he will teach you all things and bring to your remembrance all that I have said to you" (John 14:26).

Jesus also said about the Holy Spirit, "When the Spirit of truth comes, he will guide you into all the truth" (John 16:13).

The apostle Paul said that the Holy Spirit lives within believers and that he is a sort of truth detector. Paul wrote, "These things God has revealed to us through the Spirit. For the Spirit searches everything, even the depths of God. For who knows a person's thoughts except the spirit of that person, which is in him? So also no one comprehends the thoughts of God except the Spirit of God. Now we have received not the spirit of the world, but the Spirit who is from God, that we might understand the things freely given us by God" (1 Corinthians 2:10–12).

3. *The Holy Spirit Creates Righteousness*

In Isaiah 61 the year of the Lord's favor was proclaimed. This, by the way, is the passage Jesus read at the synagogue in Nazareth (Luke 4:16–22), adding, "Today this Scripture has been fulfilled in your hearing" (Luke 4:21). In Luke, quoting the Isaiah passage, Jesus said, "The Spirit of the Lord is upon me" (Luke 4:18). This simple yet provocative statement is followed by a list of what is proclaimed and accomplished by the Spirit of the Lord's anointing: "He has anointed me to proclaim good news to the poor. He has sent me to proclaim liberty to the captives and recovering of sight to the blind, to set at liberty those who are oppressed, to proclaim the year of the Lord's favor" (Luke 4:18–19). But further along in the Isaiah passage is this additional function of the Holy Spirit's anointing: "That they may be called oaks of righteousness, the planting of the LORD, that he may be glorified" (Isaiah 61:3).

The first chapter of Ezra opens with these words: "In the first year of Cyrus king of Persia, that the word of the LORD by the

mouth of Jeremiah might be fulfilled, the LORD stirred up the spirit of Cyrus king of Persia" (Ezra 1:1). In Isaiah 45:1, that same Cyrus is called God's "anointed" (anointed, I presume, by God's Spirit) who will fulfill God's purpose. Cyrus was the king of Persia and not a part of the covenant community of God, yet the Holy Spirit anointed Cyrus and used him to accomplish God's righteous plan.

Then, in Galatians, Paul talks about righteousness—"love, joy, peace, patience, kindness, goodness, faithfulness, gentleness, self-control"—as "fruit of the Spirit" (Galatians 5:22–23). While the fruit of the Spirit primarily is produced in the Christian in whom the Spirit dwells, one can safely say that wherever the Holy Spirit works in the world, we can see the same fruit.

4. The Holy Spirit Originates and Inspires Beauty so That God May Be Glorified

When God gave Moses instructions for creating the art and beauty of the Tent of Meeting (the tabernacle), he was not just concerned with function and form but also with beauty. The Holy Spirit would inspire God's anointed craftsmen to make beautiful the place where God would meet with his people. In Exodus 31:1–5 God told Moses, "See, I have called by name Bezalel the son of Uri, son of Hur, of the tribe of Judah, and I have filled him with the Spirit of God, with ability and intelligence, with knowledge and all craftsmanship, to devise artistic designs, to work in gold, silver, and bronze, in cutting stones for setting, and in carving wood, to work in every craft."

In the book of the prophet Haggai, God called to mind the glory of the temple that had been destroyed. God promised to re-

store the temple to its former beauty and glory. Through Haggai, he said, "Who is left among you who saw this house in its former glory? How do you see it now? Is it not as nothing in your eyes? Yet now be strong. . . . Be strong, all you people of the land, declares the LORD. Work, for I am with you, declares the LORD of hosts, according to the covenant that I made with you when you came out of Egypt. My Spirit remains in your midst. Fear not" (Haggai 2:3–5).

5. *The Holy Spirit Works in People*

Finally, the Holy Spirit works in people to give them an awareness of truth and to draw them to God.

In Jesus's rather long teaching about the Holy Spirit in John 16, he said, among other things, "When he comes, he will convict the world concerning sin and righteousness and judgment: concerning sin, because they do not believe in me; concerning righteousness, because I go to the Father, and you will see me no longer; concerning judgment, because the ruler of this world is judged" (John 16:8–11).

THE HOLY SPIRIT AND RELIGION

Got it? Creation, truth, goodness, beauty, and reality. If you've got that, we can "boldly go where no one has gone before"—or, at least, where very few Christians will go.

Henry P. Van Dusen, once president of Union Seminary in New York, wrote extensively about the Holy Spirit. He identified the modern-day Pentecostal movement (a movement that takes seriously the supernatural work of the Holy Spirit) as a "new reforma-

tion." He called it a kind of third force, standing alongside Roman Catholicism and historic Protestantism in its significance.

While I have some serious differences with Dr. Van Dusen about some of the things he said and wrote, his comment on the Holy Spirit's work in the world is so profound that I must tell you what he said. He wrote, "[Those of us who] cleave to the Scriptural conviction that God has not left Himself without witness, at any time or among any people, [will] find abundant confirmation of that belief in the awareness of His Spirit—however dim and however crude—in the consciousness of humanity virtually everywhere and always."[3]

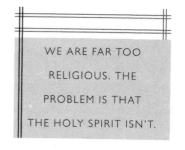

WE ARE FAR TOO RELIGIOUS. THE PROBLEM IS THAT THE HOLY SPIRIT ISN'T.

Now, let me get to my main point. One of the great dangers for Christians and for the world is that we are far, far too religious. We go to religious movies, we read religious books, we associate with religious people, we eat religious cookies, and we wear religious underwear that is far too tight. Our problem is that we spend too much time in church and far too little time in "the world." Jesus said that we are like leaven, and that's true. As someone has said, though, we have become a "lump of leaven," and lumps of leaven are no good to anybody.

Don't get me wrong. I'm religious too. The problem is that the Holy Spirit isn't.

We linger far longer than we should at church, thinking that's where God would have us stay. But it isn't. We should be there, but not for long. The church should be the "gasoline station," not the place where we park the car. When Jesus said

that we are to "go into all the world" (Mark 16:15), he didn't say that we should stay at the "gas station" holding hands and thanking the service manager for filling our tanks. He was saying that he planned to "leave the building"—and that we should go with him.

You're probably saying, "But of course. That's what Christians do. We share the gospel. We go on the mission field and reach out to the world with compassion and love." Yes, that's true, and that's a part of it. But being a Christian is far more than that, and what we're going to talk about shortly may shock you.

It has shocked me, and I like to spread the shock around.

RUNNING FROM THE WORLD

Let me deal with an issue that Christians have long used to run from the world. Paul wrote to the church at Corinth, "Do not be unequally yoked with unbelievers. For what partnership has righteousness with lawlessness? Or what fellowship has light with darkness? What accord has Christ with Belial? Or what portion does a believer share with an unbeliever? What agreement has the temple of God with idols?" (2 Corinthians 6:14–16).

It's important that we understand what Paul meant. Fortunately, we don't even have to ask; he told us. In fact, in 1 Corinthians 5:9–11 Paul referred to what he had written previously. (The time line of 1 and 2 Corinthians is a bit skewed in our present manuscripts. Many scholars think that some of 2 Corinthians actually came before 1 Corinthians.) Paul said this: "I wrote to you in my letter not to associate with sexually immoral people—not at all meaning the sexually immoral of this world, or the greedy and

swindlers, or idolaters, since then you would need to go out of the world. But now I am writing to you not to associate with anyone who bears the name of brother if he is guilty of sexual immorality or greed, or is an idolater, reviler, drunkard, or swindler—not even to eat with such a one." Then Paul goes on to say that his admonition had to do with Christians who betray the name of Christ—not with the world, where betrayal is rather difficult given the fact that these people don't even know Christ.

Various studies have shown that believers are as involved in and as affected by popular culture as anyone else. Christians, in about the same numbers as non-Christians, attend concerts, go to museums, and watch the same television programs as everybody else. I'm involved in and affirm the ministry of Christian media; but if numbers are any indication, Christian media have far less impact on professing Christians than mainstream media do. In fact, if just the Christians in America listened to and watched Christian media, the ratings would be phenomenal. They aren't.

In other words, Christians are just about like everyone else in terms of their involvement in and their support of "worldly" culture.

That's bad!

No, that's good. And I'm going to tell you why.

BACH, BUBBA, AND THE BLUES BROTHERS

Reggie Kidd, my friend and colleague at Reformed Theological Seminary, where I teach, wrote a profound and wonderful book about worship, *With One Voice: Discovering Christ's Song in Our*

Worship.[4] This book is, I believe, one of the most important popular books on worship ever written.

Reggie and I team-teach a Theology of Ministry course, and in his lectures Reggie often refers to various forms of music used in worship. In that course (and in his book), he describes those forms of worship as "Bach, Bubba, and the Blues Brothers."

He is, of course, teaching the many voices of worship.

The interesting thing about Reggie's lectures is that he often uses secular music, imagery, and art to illustrate what he's teaching. I asked Reggie (who has a PhD from Duke) how he knew what was good and what was bad in terms of culture. He said that if one's worldview is right (i.e., if one has a biblical worldview), then almost anything can be used to reflect and glorify God. He also said that if one's worldview is not stable, then everything else is dangerous.

> IT'S WHAT WE BRING TO WHERE WE GO, TO WHAT WE SEE, AND TO WHAT WE HEAR THAT DETERMINES WHAT IS APPROPRIATE AND RIGHT FOR US AS BELIEVERS.

Recently Reggie went to a U2 concert. He later kidded that it was so wonderful that he wouldn't have to go to church for the next two months.

That brings me to say something I believe to be biblical, surprising, and exciting: It isn't where we go, what we see, and what we hear that determines what is appropriate and right for a believer. It's what we bring to where we go, to what we see, and to what we hear that determines what is appropriate and right for us as believers.

I can hear you saying, "Steve, that can't be right!" Oh, yes,

it is. I didn't say it; God did: "To the pure, all things are pure" (Titus 1:15).

In writing about popular culture, William Romanowski, professor of communication arts and sciences at Calvin College, wrote something that's applicable to believers and our relationship with all kinds of cultural and "worldly" expressions:

> Limiting Christian criticism of the popular arts to confessional and moral content has fostered an understanding of popular art in terms of good/bad, right/wrong dichotomy. Consequently, many Christians have a difficult time evaluating popular art beyond the most superficial level. . . . We have not thought deeply enough about the nature of popular art and its role as a cultural communicator, which leaves us with very little to contribute to the discourse about popular art and culture. In varying ways, these approaches prohibit believers from distinguishing redemptive aspects of popular culture, determining appropriate Christian participation, and developing tools for constructive criticism.[5]

Leland Ryken addressed the same issue in his book on the arts. He wrote:

> Involvement in the arts allows Christians to respond to their surrounding culture. Christians are responsible to be a redemptive influence in their culture. That responsibility begins by understanding their culture, including its artistic expressions.[6]

The Russian novelist Fyodor Dostoyevsky wrote that "man has no right to turn back and to ignore what is going on in the

world—and there are supreme moral reasons for not allowing him to do so."

THE HOLY SPIRIT AND THE WORLD

I don't know about you, but church is comfortable for me. The people there talk the way I talk, believe what I believe, dislike what I dislike, and affirm all that I hold dear. When I venture into other places, even if it's God's Spirit who leads me there, I'm uncomfortable and afraid. We don't venture much outside the church because we're sure that the world is dirty, angry, wrong, and maybe even a bit too tempting.

When I was growing up, I was not the best student. Well, that may be an understatement. I was a horrible student—rebellious, bored, and distracted. I was trouble looking for a place to happen. It was rare (so rare that it happened only once) for me to have a teacher who was even worse at teaching than I was at learning. In third grade, however, one teacher singled me out as the object of her wrath.

I went to school in an era when the teacher was always right. If I complained to my mother about a teacher, my mother would discipline *me*. If I questioned a teacher, my mother always took the teacher's side. And if I ever came home with a note from a teacher about my bad conduct in class, that note might as well have been from Sinai, the "mountain of God." Teachers were without fault and well respected. If I ever had a problem with a teacher—no matter what the circumstances were—it was assumed to be my problem, certainly not the teacher's.

I didn't find out until I was an adult that there had been one

major exception. As I mentioned earlier, my third-grade teacher was abusive and angry, and it seemed she directed all her abuse and anger at me. I could do nothing right. I found it impossible to please her. I tried. I really tried to please her . . . but to no avail.

I suppose my mother noticed my black mood (mothers do notice such things). Perhaps she heard me crying. Maybe she just knew my heart and knew when it was broken and afraid. She asked me what was wrong, and at great personal risk to my own well-being, I told her about the teacher. She said, "Son, she's your teacher, and I don't expect to hear anything about her again."

It was settled. I would just have to deal with it.

Then something strange happened. The next week that teacher changed. It was like she'd taken a "nice" pill or something. Whereas before I had been the brunt of her anger, jokes, and abuse, I now seemed to be her favorite person in the world—and I hadn't even given her an apple. She praised my work in front of the class, told me how nice I looked, and even, on occasion, hugged me.

Frankly, that made me a bit uncomfortable. Even at that young age, I figured my teacher must be drunk.

She wasn't.

She had, however, received a visit from my mother. You don't know my mother, but if you did, you would know that this was not a woman you'd want to cross. The only person I knew who could be meaner and more dangerous than my teacher was my mother. If my mother had a "come to Jesus" meeting with you, all you wanted to do was repent and run. When my mother was angry, she could spit on the grass and it would wither. (My mother was the earthiest Christian I've ever known. She loved

Jesus, and she loved my brother and me without reservation or exception. The fact that it didn't always feel like love was a tribute to the kind of love with which she loved us. I know of no person, with the possible exception of my wife, who has had a greater and more positive influence on my life and my walk with God than my mother.)

Anyway, I was never privy to the conversation that took place between my mother and that teacher. Knowing my mother, I do know that whatever she said wasn't subtle. My mother was not a subtle woman. I suspect it was something like, "Do you like being a teacher? If you do, you will stop abusing my son. If you don't, I'll make sure you never teach again." Possibly my mother said, "You mess with my son again and I'll break your face!" All I knew was that the meanest teacher I'd ever had became the nicest.

Why am I telling you this? Because that's what the Holy Spirit has done in the world. The Holy Spirit has sent you into the world, and when you go, you'll find that he has gone before you. If you're willing to risk, you'll be surprised at how much creativity, truth, goodness, and beauty is out there. Not only that, but you'll also find that people—people out there—have a great yearning for God.

Is "out there" a dangerous place? Are you crazy? Of course it is. Christians get killed "out there." Great darkness, greed, and lust can be found "out there." You'll find selfishness and hatred of God and of anything or anyone associated with God . . . like us, for instance. Perversion is out there, and egos so big that there's no room for truth, goodness, or beauty.

But in the midst of that mud, there are diamonds.

Now for the Shock

Now for the shocking part: If you're a Christian, Jesus did not remove you from the world. Nor, believe it or not, does he keep you from enjoying it.

Contrary to a lot of Christian drivel, just because you like something doesn't mean it's sin. And if you don't like something, that doesn't necessarily mean it's good for you. In fact, it could be that the opposite is true. The Holy Spirit is doing great things in the world, yet we are in great danger of missing it—and him. We're also in danger of walking away from the world's culture at the very point at which, if we speak with authenticity and humility, our message just might be heard.

> EVERYWHERE YOU GO, YOU'LL FIND THE HOLY SPIRIT CREATING BEAUTY, REVEALING TRUTH, MANIFESTING GOODNESS, AND STIRRING A HUNGER FOR THE REALITY OF GOD.

Don Richardson, in his book *Eternity in Their Hearts*, makes the point that wherever missionaries go they find that God has been there first, going before them.[7] It's time we made the same discovery about wherever we may go in the world.

The Holy Spirit works in churches. But never forget that he's also working in bars and theaters, in ballparks and stadiums, in museums and concert halls, in politics and government, in novels and journals. In short, our Lord the Holy Spirit has gone wherever believers can go. Everywhere you go, you'll find the Holy Spirit creating beauty, revealing truth, manifesting goodness, and stirring a hunger for the reality of God.

Christians are human beings who rejoice in God's creation and who, with other human beings, enjoy the fruits of culture. We *are* human beings, but we are also more than that. We're human beings in whom the Holy Spirit (who is working in the world) resides. The Holy Spirit, by his very presence in our lives, gives us (even if we don't know it) a "baloney detector." While there is much evil in our culture, there's much good too. We've been given the gift of knowing the difference.

Our gift to the world is to show up and engage. Too often we've run *from* the world when we ought to run *toward* it. Our gift to the world is not one of anger, judgment, or condemnation. Our gift to the world is to find where the Holy Spirit is creating beauty, speaking truth, and manifesting goodness—and when we find it, to identify it, enjoy it, affirm it, and get involved in it.

Paul said, "Finally, brothers, whatever is true, whatever is honorable, whatever is just, whatever is pure, whatever is lovely, whatever is commendable, if there is any excellence, if there is anything worthy of praise, think about these things" (Philippians 4:8).

Good heavens! I always thought he was talking about religion.

I was wrong.

I'm going to a movie.

So there.

FOUL SHAME AND SCORN BE ON YE ALL
WHO TURN THE GOOD TO EVIL,
AND STEAL THE BIBLE FROM THE LORD
AND GIVE IT TO THE DEVIL.

JOHN GREENLEAF WHITTIER

The Bible Reveals a Lot More Than I Thought It Did

In that day the deaf shall hear the words of a book, and out of their
gloom and darkness the eyes of the blind shall see.
The meek shall obtain fresh joy in the LORD, and the poor among
mankind shall exult in the Holy One of Israel.

ISAIAH 29:18–19

IN HIS BOOK *Journey into Light*, the late Émile Cailliet wrote about his first encounter with the Bible. His philosophical naturalism had prevented him from considering God or theology. However, Cailliet knew there had to be something more than what he had experienced. He had tried to compose a book that expressed who he was by writing down quotes he had read from a variety of sources that had resonated with him. As he read through the book he had compiled, he recognized the futility of his efforts and was quite depressed.

Earlier his wife had visited a French Huguenot chapel, and the pastor had given her a Bible. When she saw her husband so despondent, she hesitantly (knowing his views on religion) offered the Bible. Cailliet had never seen a Bible before, but he wrote:

> I literally grabbed the book and rushed to my study with it. I opened it and chanced upon the beatitudes! I read, and read, and read—now aloud with an indescribable warmth surging

within. . . . I could not find words to express my awe and wonder. And suddenly the realization dawned upon me: This was the book that would understand me—I needed it so much, yet, unaware, I had attempted to write my own—in vain. I continued to read deeply into the night, mostly from the Gospels. And lo and behold, as I looked through them, the One of whom they spoke, the One who spoke and acted in them, became alive to me. . . . While it seemed absurd to speak of a book understanding a man, this could be said of the Bible because its pages were animated by the presence of the living God and the power of his mighty acts. To this God I prayed that night, and the God who answered was the same God of whom it was spoken in the Book.[1]

Cailliet then described how, as he read the Gospels, the One about whom they spoke became real to him. In other words, he discovered the Bible and then became a Christian by reading the Bible. It often happens that way.

That's not what happened to me.

It might surprise you to know that I became a Christian long before I believed in or took the Bible very seriously. I thought I was an intellectual, and I thought intellectuals were immune to the silly religiosity of the Bible. I didn't believe in things like seas that parted, virgin births, or resurrections.

French mathematician and religious philosopher Blaise Pascal said he would never have found God if God had not already found him. I guess that was true for me, even if I didn't know it. I had a spiritual hunger, and that hunger presupposed the existence of food to satisfy it. I had a sense of guilt, and that guilt presupposed

the existence of someone who could forgive me. I wanted meaning in my life, and that desire presupposed that something beyond me was the source of meaning. Even intellectuals eventually will die, and most are not altogether happy about the prospect. I wanted to have some kind of hope that my life would not come to an abrupt end in a graveyard.

Then Jesus came.

I didn't know much about Jesus except what I had learned in Sunday school as a child, but I suppose that was enough. When I really got to know Jesus, the spiritual hunger I had felt was somewhat bearable; I felt forgiven; I found a modicum of meaning. And while I didn't want to ask too many questions about it, I thought there might be something on the other side of the grave.

Jesus did that for me, but the Bible was something else altogether. The theological education I received at a very liberal graduate school at a major university didn't help me appreciate the Bible much. In fact, my professors almost took away the minimal relationship I had with Jesus along with any possibility of my having a Cailliet-like experience with Scripture.

It's a long story, and I won't bore you with the details, but because of some wonderful people who really were intellectuals—people who had read all the books I'd read, knew all the words I knew, *and* believed in the Bible—I came to the position that I now hold and have held for most of my adult life: the Bible is the absolute Word of God. I believe and teach the verbal plenary inspiration of Scripture (*verbal* referring to the words and *plenary* meaning all of it—thus, every word of the Bible is true), and I believe the Bible to be revealed propositional truth and to be accurate in everything it affirms.

Because the journey from where I was (a liberal this side of crazy) to where I ended up (believing in the full authority of the Bible) was such a rigorous and difficult one, when I got there I spent a considerable portion of my time simply holding, as it were, the land I had acquired.

Today I'm quite good at defending the eternal verity of the Bible and biblical truth. If you should visit my study, you would note that a large section of my library is devoted to the defense of the inspiration and authority of the canon of Scripture.

But I haven't been to that section of my library much lately. And I want to tell you why.

You may be thinking that it's because I've changed my views. Not even close. In fact, my views on biblical authority are, if anything, stronger and more firmly settled in my mind and heart than ever. Those views are the anchor of how I define myself. One doesn't give up what one has worked so hard to attain.

WE CAN BE SO ENAMORED WITH THE BIBLE'S TRUTH THAT WE FORGET THAT THE TRUTH IS TO BE LIVED AND USED, NOT JUST ACQUIRED AND MEMORIZED.

In attaining the doctrinal position I now hold, my problem was that I had lost something extremely important. The liberals tried to take away the Bible's import with the unbelief they fostered. They needn't have bothered. My high view of Scripture and my unrelenting defense of its truth had done the same thing to me that the liberals had done so many years before: it robbed me of the power, the reality, and the joy of the Bible. You see, I had made the Bible too religious. I had put a candle on each side of it and placed it on an

altar in my heart and dared anybody to mess with it.

A friend of mine says that much of the evangelism and witnessing done by Christians is a pyramid scheme. The purpose is to acquire the product (i.e., salvation), sell it to others, and then train those others to sell it . . . so those others will, in turn, acquire it and train others to sell it. The problem, my friend says, is that nobody ever uses the product. We just sell it.

That's a good point.

It can be true with the Bible too. We can spend so much time defending and "selling" the Bible to others that we don't use the product very much. And we can spend so much time articulating and defending our doctrinal position from the Bible that we forget why it was even important in the first place. Just as it's easy to eat so many doughnuts that we forget how good they taste, we can be so enamored with the Bible's truth that we forget that the truth is to be lived and used, not just acquired and memorized.

I want to share with you some things about the Bible that are more important than what I just told you . . . and maybe some things that will be more important than what you already knew.

Let's start with the bad news, and then it will get better.

The Bible Isn't a Magic Pill

The Bible is not a magic book to put under our pillow at night to make all our bad dreams go away. The Bible was never meant to be worshiped or to be used as a magic cure-all to fix everything that's wrong.

I'm sure you've heard advice like this: Are you depressed? Read the Bible. Are you falling into temptation? Memorize Scripture. Are you scared? Read the Bible through in a year. Do you struggle

with obedience? You're simply not studying the Word enough. Do you have doubts? Just keep reading until your doubts go away. Are you trying to be a better mother, father, husband, or wife but failing miserably? The solution is the Bible, and your problem is that you've gone everywhere else but there for help.

In other words, fill your mind with the Bible (i.e., take the magic pill), and there won't be room for any of the bad stuff.

What? That's crazy. First, it's not true. Second, it grossly underestimates the human capacity for multitasking.

I know more of the Bible and have memorized more of it than, I think it's fair to say, the majority of people have. That's not pride (well, maybe a little); it's simply a statement of fact. It's part of what I do for a living. I've been a Bible teacher for most of my adult life. I can hardly think a thought without thinking of a biblical text. If the Bible were the magic book we've been taught it is, I would be far more spiritual and obedient and far less frightened and angry than the majority of people, but I'm not. I may even be worse.

People who believe the way I do about the Bible often use this slogan: "God said it, I believe it, and that settles it for me." It sounds nice, but that doesn't settle it for me anymore. I've been asking an important question: so what? Just believing it because God said it used to settle it for me, but as of late it doesn't even come close. There are, however, some things (even if they don't settle it) that make it better.

THE BIBLE ISN'T JUST ABOUT RELIGION

I feel better, for instance, when I remember that the Bible is actually far less religious than I thought it was.

It might surprise you to learn that the Bible's original lan-

guage had to be "cleaned up" in our modern translations because . . . well . . . because it would offend the sensitive tastes of "nice Christians." We take a book of the Bible about sex and make it a book about the church. We sanitize the imagery in the Bible and "fix" the "inappropriate" parts. (I would go into detail here, but I simply cannot . . . because of my very point!) We often simply ignore the numerous warts of Bible characters. We take the common Greek of the New Testament (Koinê), formalize it, bring it into the church, and make it hallowed as if it had been dropped out of the sky in a golden wrapper.

I have a minister friend whose young pastoral associate usually read the designated scriptures during the church worship services. The problem was, the associate hardly ever read the passage ahead of time, in preparation. My friend decided to break him of that habit, so one week he assigned a reading that included some rather earthy verses not usually read in public worship services. (Oh yes, there are a number of those.)

The young associate stood before the congregation and started reading. When he realized what he was reading, he started blushing, stumbling over the words, and pausing in places where a pause wasn't necessary. He got through it, but he never read a text "cold" again.

If you haven't blushed, been shocked and embarrassed, and said to yourself, *I don't believe I would have said that*, then you've probably read more nursery rhymes than Bible texts.

At certain times in the church's history, some believed the Bible was so sacred that it should not even be read by "common" people. The thought was that if people read the Bible without the proper interpretation, it would be dangerous. How ironic, when

you consider that for the most part, the Bible was written by common people—common people under the inspiration of God's Spirit.

Eventually some godly servants of Christ (some of whom lost their lives for their trouble) worked to translate the Bible into the language of common people so everyone could read it for himself or herself. Martin Luther's translation of the Scriptures into German changed the religious and cultural landscape. Luther spent a considerable portion of time in nearby towns and markets listening to how people spoke because he wanted to make sure they would be able to understand his translation. He said that when he finished his translation, the gospel would be understood by a farm boy behind a plow as well as by the scholars and the priests at a university.

My point is this: we must avoid the pitfalls and danger of taking the Bible back to where it was before these Reformers succeeded in translating the Bible into the common languages. Of course we wouldn't translate it back into Greek, Hebrew, Aramaic, or Latin. The danger is that we'll translate the Bible into the language of "holy," and nobody will want to have anything to do with it if they don't speak "holy."

THE BIBLE IS ABOUT REAL PEOPLE

I also feel better when I remember that the Bible has a far more realistic view of humans and of the world itself than I once believed.

Many people think the Bible is a book written to tell us about the lives and teachings of radically spiritual and super believers who had it all together because of their extreme spirituality. But nothing could be further from the truth. The Bible was written

(under the inspiration of the Holy Spirit, of course) by people who were as scared, depressed, sinful, doubting, flawed, and human as we are. Some of them wanted nothing more than to run from their calling. Some even questioned whether God had truly called them to write.

The people of the Bible—those who wrote, those who spoke, and those whose stories unfold on its pages—are not superheroes who will inspire you to be a superhero yourself. They are people like you and me who discovered a merciful, kind, and sovereign God—one who cared enough about their humanity to come as a baby in a dirty stable.

If you ever want to feel better about yourself, read what the Bible has to say about certain members of the family of God. You might find yourself saying, "Well, I may be bad, but I'm not that bad!" (And when you really understand, you'll repent for saying it.) The fact is that sometimes these "Bible heroes" were a bunch of reprobates and scoundrels. If you want to hear from people who have it together and will tell you how you can get it together too, the Bible is not your book. If you want to find out how to be more religious and nicer, good luck trying to force the Bible into that mold. It's not a manual for the religious or the nice.

> THE PEOPLE OF THE BIBLE ARE PEOPLE LIKE YOU AND ME WHO DISCOVERED A MERCIFUL, KIND, AND SOVEREIGN GOD.

Alcoholics Anonymous asserts that only a drunk can help a drunk. That may be true. The reason the Bible seems of so little help to many Christians is because we simply don't feel we can identify with the people in the Bible. We're "drunks," and we need

a word from "drunks," not from people who will be shocked at our drunkenness. With our institutional and religious sermons, our books and our seminaries, we've made the Bible religious, and frankly, it's killing us. (And, God help me, I've been as much to blame as anybody I know.)

The Bible makes a difference in our lives not because we memorize it, teach it, and defend it. It makes a difference in our lives because the God who loved, guided, forgave, and cared for the people in the Bible when they didn't deserve it will also love, guide, forgive, and care for you and for me when it's painfully obvious that we don't deserve it either.

Now get out your Bible and read it, keeping in mind what I just told you.

THE BIBLE IS FREEING

I also feel better when I remember that the Bible is far more freeing than I thought it was.

Do you get tired of people who try to "fix" you all the time? I do, and there are a whole lot of them. You should see the thousands of letters and e-mail messages I get from people who are sure that with just a few words—written in the "love of Jesus," of course—they can straighten out my bad doctrine, make me nicer, and maybe even get me to a place where I won't cause so much damage to the church.

Just last week one of our receptionists buzzed me and said, "Steve, I hate to do this to you, but I can't find anybody else to take a call. A man on the phone is very angry. He wants to talk to you, and he's not going away until he does. Would you please talk to him? I've just about had it with him."

Being the kind and benevolent boss that I am, I picked up the phone and said in my best kind and benevolent voice, "Hi, this is Steve. Can I help you?"

"Mr. Brown," the man shouted from the phone, "there are millions of people in hell because of you."

"Cool," I said. "I didn't know I had that much power."

Evidently the man didn't share my sense of humor, because he went on to tell me that my teaching was blasphemous and doing great damage to Christians. I listened for a while and then said, "I guess this means you aren't going to send a contribution to our ministry."

He hung up.

Do you know what I felt when he hung up? I felt—and this means I'm just as neurotic as the man who called—condemned and guilty. I felt that way because I'm conditioned to feel that way. Most Christians are. We choose not to read the Bible because we already feel guilty and condemned, and we just don't need any more rules and regulations when we can't even keep the ones we know.

The Bible does have rules and regulations (they're called laws and commandments), but you'll be surprised to find out that God didn't make the rules to save us, to make us better, or even to grant us the permission to be self-righteous. (A friend of mine says self-righteous people are merely those who know the rules and can "fake it" better than those who don't.)

God gave us the rules and regulations of the Bible so we would know our need, understand our helplessness, and accept our inability to live up to them. Then—and this is why we were created—we would run to the only helper, forgiver, and redeemer around—God.

However, instead of focusing on his love, forgiveness, and kindness, we obsess on our failure to live up to all those rules and regulations. That inappropriate obsession keeps us from opening the Bible, because we already know we're sick, and we just can't stand to feel any sicker than we are.

But take heart: Jesus's angriest words were not spoken to the people who didn't live by the rules; they were spoken to those who *did*. When I remember that, I go to the Bible not with fear but with great joy—the joy of a child reading a letter from his beloved father. When a person is obsessed about his sin, he goes to a bar. When he's obsessed about God's love, he goes to the Bible.

The Puritans understood that point. (Their stern image is a myth created by people who don't know and have never read the Puritans' writings.) Consider this Puritan prayer:

No day of my life has passed
that has not proved me guilty in thy sight.
Prayers have been uttered from a prayerless heart;
Praise has been often praiseless sound;
My best services are filthy rags.

All things in me call for my rejection,
All things in thee plead my acceptance.
I appeal from the throne of perfect justice
to thy throne of boundless grace.
Grant me to hear thy voice assuring me:
that by thy stripes I am healed,
that thou wast bruised for my iniquities,
that thou hast been made sin for me,
that I might be righteous in thee,

that my grievous sins, my manifold sins, are all forgiven,
buried in the ocean of thy concealing blood.
I am guilty, but pardoned,
lost, but saved,
wandering, but found,
sinning, but cleansed.[2]

Studying the Bible didn't make the Puritans mean; it made them free.

THE BIBLE IS MORE THAN JUST A THEOLOGY BOOK

I want to share with you one more thing about the Bible. Even though just believing the Bible doesn't "settle it" for me, I do feel better when I remember that the Bible is less a theology book than I thought it was.

Donald Grey Barnhouse used to say that all of life illustrates Bible doctrine. I agree with that but would also add that all of the Bible illustrates doctrine too. In other words, the Bible isn't primarily a book about doctrine and theology.

Does the Bible teach propositional truth? Of course it does. But that's only one part of its function. Mostly the Bible is a big story encompassing many lesser stories that draw us to a God who has always revealed himself in stories. A colleague at Reformed Seminary, Richard Pratt, has written a wonderful book titled *He Gave Us Stories*.[3] God has given us stories, and when we forget that, we miss one of his great gifts to us.

Systematic biblical theology is an important discipline. Systematic theologians are scholars who take the Bible in all of its varied expressions and forms and create a system that enables us

to organize, teach, and apply the "whole counsel of God" (Acts 20:27). John Calvin said of the Bible that the Old Testament interprets the New Testament, the Epistles interpret the Gospels, and the whole interprets its different parts. That's a hermeneutical principle (i.e., a principle of interpretation) that stands at the very heart of systematic biblical theology.

Truth isn't merely what works for me. It isn't whatever I say it is or whatever I decide I like. Truth is truth because God said it. We have a tendency to major on minors, to go off on tangents, to create cults, and to turn weird. Systematic theology is a helpful tool in preventing such error.

Let me ask you a question: why do we have to create a systematic theology? We have to do it because God hasn't done it. The Bible is a book that teaches us to write poetry, to tell stories, and to dance in the presence of a merciful God.

So go ahead—get the truth from the Bible. But don't forget how to dance.

A friend of mine says that belief in the Bible isn't the standard for measuring its effectiveness any more than belief in a gun is the standard for measuring its effectiveness. If someone breaks into your home and you have a .45 pistol aimed at him, even if he says he doesn't believe in guns, you wouldn't respond, "Oh, then I guess I can't use this gun. I'll have to let you rob me."

No, you'd simply pull the trigger. (Or, if you're more benevolent, you might say, "I'm getting ready to shoot the place where you're standing. If you're still standing there when I shoot, you should prepare to meet your Maker.")

The Bible doesn't need to be defended any more than God needs to be defended. I've come to see that neither God nor the

Bible needs my puny efforts to help them stand the test of truth. The Bible and God were around a long time before I got here, and they'll both do fine long after I'm gone.

I've spent too much time admiring the "gun" and defending its effectiveness.

I've decided to pull the trigger.

THERE ARE MORE THINGS IN HEAVEN AND EARTH,
HORATIO, THAN ARE DREAMT OF IN YOUR PHILOSOPHY.

SHAKESPEARE

THE BATTLE IS A LOT MORE SUPERNATURAL THAN I THOUGHT IT WAS

We do not wrestle against flesh and blood, but against the rulers, against the authorities, against the cosmic powers over this present darkness, against the spiritual forces of evil in the heavenly places.

EPHESIANS 6:12

THE PSYCHIATRIST John White, in his book *The Fight*, wrote about Christian conversion. He said that Christian conversion is like conversion to any worldview. The psychological manifestations of conversion are well known and have long been recognized and described.

Then he wrote:

What makes Christian conversion different is that supernatural events also occur. The feeling states in non-Christian conversion are temporary. They are equally temporary in Christian conversion.

But the supernatural, and often unfelt, events are permanent. They mark you in the sight of demons and angels as a human who is different. They bring your body into touch with eternity and with the Eternal God.[1]

I read those words years ago, when I was a young man. But I dismissed them. It wasn't so much that I disagreed with what Dr.

White had written, but being far from my personal experience, as I refused even to acknowledge the supernatural, it was hard to identify with his view.

I just read those words again, and like the young man who recalled his teenage years and was surprised at how much his father had learned since then, I was surprised at how profound and cogent Dr. White's words seem to me now.

The Bible is replete with evidence of the supernatural. You'll find it all in there: devils, angels, miracles, signs, wonders, magic, exorcisms, healings, prophecies, resurrections, visions, cosmic manifestations . . . and even a virgin birth. If naturalism (as opposed to supernaturalism) is your worldview, though, you'll simply dismiss all of that.

You might be surprised at how many Christians dismiss it too. I don't think very many would admit it, but they do. I know, because I was one of them.

My mentor, Fred Smith, told me once that Christians, if given the choice between spiritual power and political power, will almost always choose political power. I agree with that and would even expand on it. Given the choice between the supernatural power described in the Bible and the power of money, fame, and status, for most Christians it's a no-brainer. Money, fame, and status win every time.

We're sort of like the man in the old story who was in a flood. He scrambled onto the rooftop as the water rose. As it threatened to reach the top of his house, he cried out to God to save him. Shortly after that, a man came by in a boat and offered to take him to safety, but he said, "No, thank you anyway. I'm waiting for God to save me." Then a crudely crafted raft floated by, and he almost

jumped on it. But he kept waiting for God to save him. Finally, a helicopter descended and threw him a rescue line, but he waved off the helicopter. He would rather wait for God.

The man drowned.

When he stood before God's throne, the man complained, "I trusted you, and you failed me."

"I didn't fail you," God replied. "I sent a boat, a raft, and a helicopter to save you, but you turned them all down."

That's a mildly funny story because it shows what we believe to be the narrow-mindedness of relying on the supernatural when we have the natural right at hand. And who knows? Those natural occurrences could even be God. Maybe not, but one never knows. Not only that. The story shows how really dumb it is to hold out for God's supernatural intervention when it becomes obvious that God isn't going to supernaturally intervene.

I used to think that story was funny too. Now I'm not so sure. What if the man had turned down all of the other forms of help, had trusted in God, and God really had intervened, say with a golden stepladder from heaven, an angel who performed a miracle, or perhaps a supernatural parting of the waters so the man could have climbed down from his roof and simply walked away? What if he had trusted God and there had been a definable, clear, and certain moment when God came and rescued him?

Frankly, throughout most of the "floods" in my life, I've jumped on too many boats and bailed out too quickly. That's true for most of us. But then, as the years go by, you eventually encounter something you can't fix or escape, and you begin to realize that unless God does something, all the boats in the world won't make any difference. *There just aren't that many boats, and I can't*

swim as well as I thought I could. If God doesn't intervene, I'm going to drown.

Author Anne Lamott has been a guest on my talk show a couple of times. I don't agree with her about much of anything except Jesus, but that's enough. She's the real deal, and she has experienced God in a variety of wonderful events in her life. Her book *Traveling Mercies* is the record of God's actions in her life in some specific, merciful, and often supernatural ways.[2]

I once heard Lamott say that she only believed in three kinds of prayer:

First, "God, help me, and help me right now!"

Second: "Wow!"

Third: "Thank you, God."

Those are the prayers, I believe, that arise when we need—and then see—God's supernatural intervention in our lives.

IDENTIFYING THE SUPERNATURAL

And that brings me to an important principle, which is our starting point: We fail to recognize a lot of the supernatural that happens in our lives.

When we misidentify supernatural things as natural, our faith is not reinforced, and we tend to see less of the supernatural. When the supernatural is correctly identified in our lives, our faith grows—and so does the supernatural reality in our lives.

I often preach at a large church in Orlando (Northland, A Church Distributed) that features seven services (which are then multiplied, using satellite technology, in several additional locations throughout the city so that many people in many locations all worship together). When I preach the same sermon seven times

between Saturday and Monday evening, a number of things happen. If the sermon is reasonably good in the first service, it gets a lot better, and by Monday night I sound like Charles Spurgeon. (Sometimes it goes so well, I want to take notes on myself!) On the other hand, if the first sermon on Saturday night is bad, I know I'm going to have a very bad weekend.

> WHEN THE SUPERNATURAL IS CORRECTLY IDENTIFIED IN OUR LIVES, OUR FAITH GROWS —AND SO DOES THE SUPERNATURAL REALITY IN OUR LIVES.

As you might imagine, preaching the same sermon that many times can produce a great deal of boredom. If you think listening to one sermon can be boring, you ought to try preaching the same one seven times. So in order to get some relief, I usually change things a bit for each service. These aren't big changes, but just enough to keep me from falling asleep during my own sermon.

Recently, when I preached at Northland, a friend of mine brought an acquaintance, whom he'd practically had to drag to the worship service. His friend was not a believer, mainly because of the hypocrisy he had encountered in the churches where he'd been involved.

My friend hadn't told me this person was coming, but for some reason, in the one service his friend attended, I started talking about the church. I said, "Whenever someone complains about the church, I want to say, 'You don't know anything. I could tell you stories that would curl your toes!' The church is a place where very human and sinful people get together. If you want to be committed to Christ and to the church, you have to be committed to hypocrisy, to bad communication, to anger,

and to division. And, if you aren't willing to commit to that, don't be a part of the church."

While that comment wasn't totally irrelevant to the sermon topic, it was the only service in which I said anything even remotely like that. I had no idea why I said it or why I said it in that particular service. That is, I didn't know until my friend told me what happened as a result of those words.

His friend had been deeply touched by those words and was very close to becoming a Christian because of what I'd said. My friend thanked me. When I told him that the service his friend had attended was the only one in which I'd made that point, my friend said, "Wow. And they say there's no God."

In other words, my friend saw, experienced, and identified a supernatural work of God in that service. He could have said, "Man, what a coincidence!" He might have asked, "Wonder how that happened?" Or he could have just shrugged his shoulders and said, "Go figure."

I recall a time when that would have been my reaction. But as I've grown older, I've come to realize that the battle is so fierce and I'm so weak and sinful that what I do or don't do makes little difference. It really is God. And so, with Anne Lamott, I'm saying far more often than I used to: "Wow!"

In the parable of the talents in Matthew 25, Jesus tells a story of a master who gave one servant five talents (a talent was a measure of money), another servant two talents, and a third servant a single talent. You may remember that the first two invested the money and got a good return for their master. The third man, however, hid his one talent in the ground and then returned it to his master exactly as he had received it. The displeased master took

away the one talent from the servant who had buried it and gave it to the servant who had used his original five talents and increased them to ten.

The interesting thing about that parable is the commentary on it. Jesus said, "To everyone who has will more be given, and he will have an abundance. But from the one who has not, even what he has will be taken away" (Matthew 25:29).

Many legitimate interpretations of that parable have been given; but for our purposes here, I believe the parable also applies to the principle I mentioned above. When we don't see God's supernatural hand in our lives, we'll come to see even less of his supernatural hand in our lives. When we do see it, identify it, and thank him for it, then his supernatural work increases, and we'll come to depend on it. It's like the old sermon illustration in which a young boy asks his grandfather where he sees God. His grandfather answers, "Son, I hardly ever find a place where I don't see God."

As I mentioned before, when my students express their strong (and often wrong) views on a matter of Christian importance, I often point out, "You haven't lived long enough, sinned big enough, or failed nearly enough to even have an opinion on that." (I don't say that in a critical or mean-spirited way. It's just a fact, and somebody needs to say it.)

Well, I'm not a spiritual giant or anything, but I've lived long enough and sinned big enough to see God's supernatural works in places I never expected to see them. Not only that, the years and the sin are not irrelevant to the very subject of this chapter. We'll get to that shortly.

I have some good news and some bad news: The good news is

that there is a God who will operate in amazing and supernatural ways in your life. The bad news is that you usually have to be on the rooftop without a boat, as it were, before God's supernatural work is clearly perceived.

What does it mean to be on that rooftop? And, after all these years, what have I discovered?

OUR WEAKNESS

I've discovered that I'm not nearly as gifted, as strong, or as skilled as I thought I was. I've grown less sure of what I can do and the difference I can make—and far more dependent on what God does. I don't particularly like it, but it has become necessary.

It's like the line says in "Mercy Came Running," originally recorded by Phillips, Craig, and Dean: "When I could not reach mercy, mercy came running to me." The helplessness expressed in that song is the experience of any Christian who has lived long enough and sinned big enough to know much of anything. When you haven't, the natural is sufficient. When you have, the natural is not enough. Not nearly enough.

As a young man, I was sure there was no problem I couldn't solve and no mountain I couldn't climb. My youthful self-confidence could be summed up by paraphrasing the old military slogan: the difficult I'll do now; the impossible will just take a bit longer.

In the Bible God says, "My grace is sufficient for you, for my power is made perfect in weakness" (2 Corinthians 12:9). But we don't really believe that, do we? Or, if we do, it's a theory we'd rather not test—a sort of safety net we resort to only if we get into trouble.

But something happens after you walk with Christ for a long while. As the years go by, you begin to realize that if God's grace isn't sufficient and his supernatural power doesn't work in weakness, then you don't have a chance. In other words, we don't believe the teaching of 2 Corinthians 12:9 until we have to. Then, even if we don't like it, we realize that we just don't have a choice.

I love the story of the pastor who, in his twenties, prayed, "Lord, give me the grace to win this city to Christ."

In his forties, he prayed, "Please, Lord, grant me the grace to win my church for Christ."

In his sixties, he prayed, "Lord, don't let me lose too many."

I've stood beside more deathbeds, listened to more confessions, and confronted more loss and pain in myself and in others than I ever thought possible. On those occasions I knew that I was inadequate to say or do anything that would make any real difference. I've listened to people who desperately wanted answers, and I had none. I've prayed for the sick and felt that my prayer wasn't reaching any higher than the ceiling. I've watched people I loved weep over open graves, felt intimidated by people I feared, been betrayed by people I trusted, and grieved when people I'd taught about God turned away from him.

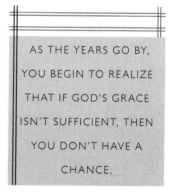

AS THE YEARS GO BY, YOU BEGIN TO REALIZE THAT IF GOD'S GRACE ISN'T SUFFICIENT, THEN YOU DON'T HAVE A CHANCE.

And over and over again, I've experienced a power far beyond me . . . teaching, healing, changing, comforting, strengthening, caring, loving, and empowering. The more I've seen it, the more

I've depended on it. And the older I've gotten, the more I've realized that I can depend on little else.

There's a reason for that even beyond my own weakness, and I'll tell you what it is.

OUR STRONG ENEMY

I've also discovered that the enemy is a lot more gifted, strong, and skilled than I thought he was.

Back in the days when I was an "intellectual," I couldn't bring myself, in sermons and speeches, to refer to the devil. I always referred to him as "the metaphorical personification of evil," and even then, I wasn't convinced of the reality or power of evil.

I remember one cold, dark, and rainy night on Cape Cod. A young man sat across from me in my small study—a study barely large enough to accommodate the desk and the two chairs in which we sat. He was angry. He had abused his family. He had physically attacked his employer. He had made fun of the church, of Christ, and of me. He talked about Satan in the most positive terms and God in the most negative.

Then, to my shock, he started cursing. I mean real cursing—foul, harsh, and offensive. He ended his long string of expletives with a statement that ended our conversation. "If there is a God," he said in a deep and guttural voice, "I curse him!"

I remember the hair standing up on the back of my neck and the sense of fear I felt. I had the impulse to call the police. I also remember what I thought then: "My, my, this young man is paranoid schizophrenic; he clearly needs some therapy and medication."

A few years later I visited the Philippines and a small mountain church that was packed with people. In fact, people stood all along

the back and sides of that church, and the crowd spilled out into the streets. Every open window had people crowded around it.

I asked the pastor why so many had come. He told me that it was because he and the elders of the church had cast a demon out of a woman in their village after the local witch doctor had failed. He said, "Steve, this is what happens when God's power is manifest." We prayed and thanked God for his faithfulness and his supernatural power.

Between those two incidents, something had happened to me. It's called experience. Between those two events, I'd seen Satan walking down the streets of a city slum, watched him do his work with a needle dripping heroin, and seen his destructive power in the bottle clutched by a drunk sleeping it off on a bench on Boston Common. I read his handwriting on a suicide note and saw him smiling as the crowds lined up to watch an "adult" film. I saw his work in a crushed automobile, in a starving nation's desperate hunger, and in a soldier's death. Between those two incidents, I'd seen Satan in the sneer of the racist and in the lies of a politician whose only concern was power. I encountered Satan in the evils of poverty and oppression and in the death of a man who wept as he died of AIDS.

In short, between those two incidents, I grew up and realized that evil is personal, scary, and powerful. Peter wrote, "Be sober-minded; be watchful. Your adversary the devil prowls around like a roaring lion, seeking someone to devour. Resist him" (1 Peter 5:8–9).

The Bible has a lot to say about Satan. He's called a liar, the accuser, the dragon, the serpent, and the ruler of the world. Jesus prayed for Peter because "Satan demanded to have" him (Luke

22:31), and he said that religious leaders were of their "father the devil" (John 8:44). He talked about the sower whose good seeds are taken away by Satan (see Mark 4:15). Throughout the Bible the presence of the good, the pure, and the loving are juxtaposed with the presence of evil. The Bible teaches that there is a kingdom of light and a kingdom of darkness (see Colossians 1:12–14).

Here's the good news: the Bible also teaches that the battle has already been won. The Bible informs us (in Colossians 2:15 and Revelation 20:10) that the believer is playing in a ball game that's already over. It teaches that the Spirit of God in us is far greater than the spirit of Satan in the world (see 1 John 4:4) and that all we have to do is stand.

As someone has said, the dragon has been slain, but his tail still swishes. I've learned to identify the swishing of that tail. And when I see that happening, I've learned to run to the God who intervenes in a battle I'm too weak to fight—and that he has already won.

OUR CHOICE

One other thing must be said: I've also discovered that I have a choice in my life and work. I can do it my way (the natural way), or I can do it God's way (the supernatural way). You have this choice too.

Have you heard about the pastor who played golf? After a terrible drive, an eagle picked up the man's golf ball and dropped it onto the green. Then a rabbit pushed it across the green, and finally, a beaver kicked it into the hole. "Please Lord," the pastor said, "I'd rather do it myself!"

That's the way most of us (myself included) deal with our lives.

Maybe God would intervene to help us, but then we'd owe him, and we're not into owing God. He might send us as missionaries to some third-world country with no cable television. He might even make us become preachers. So we just keep on keeping on, doing it our way, until we're so tired and have made such a mess of it that we don't have any choice but to try it his way.

When you've lived long enough and have sinned big enough, your heart turns to God more often. It's because you discovered that, if he doesn't open the door, you'll be stuck outside in the cold.

As of late, I find myself saying more often, "Help me, God—right now."

"Wow!"

"Thank you, God."

SIN IS STRONG AND FLEET OF FOOT,

OUTRUNNING EVERYTHING.

HOMER

PEOPLE ARE A LOT WORSE THAN I THOUGHT THEY WERE

I know that nothing good dwells in me. . . . For I do not do the good I want, but the evil I do not want is what I keep on doing.

ROMANS 7:18–19

DON'T YOU JUST hate cynical people? I do too.

It was horrifying to me to discover that I had become one. I called it "Christian realism," but that isn't what it was. It was plain, old-fashioned cynicism. I often quoted Jesus's words that we needed to be "wise as serpents and innocent as doves" (Matthew 10:16), but one day I realized that my serpent side had won out. I had discovered that people really are a lot worse than I thought they were. And with that discovery, something terrible happened.

I became a cynic.

Paul wrote to the Philippians, "Whatever is true, whatever is honorable, whatever is just, whatever is pure, whatever is lovely, whatever is commendable, if there is any excellence, if there is anything worthy of praise, think about these things" (Philippians 4:8). Cynicism robs you of seeing anything as true, honorable, just, pure, lovely, commendable, excellent, and worthy of praise. Cynicism is a hard and dark place to live.

93

Now I'm what you might call a recovering cynic. I still have to fight cynicism, but I'm better. I'm not better because people are, at heart, good and pure; they aren't. I'm not better because *I* am, at heart, good and pure; I'm not. I'm better because of Jesus.

Later I want to tell you what happened to make me better, but we have miles and miles to go before we get there. I could have titled this chapter "I'm a Lot Worse Than I Thought I Was," and it would have been accurate. In fact, that particular discovery was more important than my discovery about people in general, and it's one of the reasons I'm better about my cynicism. But I'm getting way ahead of myself.

THE ONE REALITY OF CYNICISM

Before we dig deeper into this, let me share with you an important truth. Cynicism and Christian realism are similar in that they both see reality. Cynicism, however, looks at only one reality.

In John 2 we're told that when Jesus was in Jerusalem, many people were impressed and believed in his name when they saw the miracles he did. Then John says that Jesus "did not entrust himself to them, because he knew all people and needed no one to bear witness about man, for he himself knew what was in man" (John 2:24–25). Jesus was a realist.

We see this realism again in Mark 3:5, when Jesus was angry at the shallowness and lack of compassion in the religious people, yet he was also "grieved at their hardness of heart."

Jesus understood that people are a lot worse than most people think they are. In fact, he understood this far better than the most

hardened cynic. At the same time, though, he grieved. Perhaps one way to define Christian realism is to say that it perceives the dark side . . . and weeps. But Christian realism also goes beyond weeping; it never loses hope.

The problem with most Christians is that we have a naive belief in the goodness of people. We really believe that we're all reasonably good folks who have some stuff in us that's a bit skewed, so can't we all just get along?

Einstein is reported to have said that he wouldn't give a nickel for simplicity on this side of complexity, but that he would give his life for the simplicity on the other side of complexity. Christian realism is like that. Hope on this side of knowing the reality about the dark side of human nature isn't worth a nickel, but the hope we find on the other side of that knowledge is worth everything.

> PERHAPS ONE WAY TO DEFINE CHRISTIAN REALISM IS TO SAY THAT IT PERCEIVES THE DARK SIDE . . . AND WEEPS, BUT IT NEVER LOSES HOPE.

Our problem, I fear, is that most Christians have never faced the hard and scary side of sin—both others' sin and their own. Do you remember Jim Jones's Peoples Temple? It was a cult that started out doing good works, helping the poor, and reaching out to the disenfranchised, but it ended with the mass suicide of more than 900 people in the jungle of Jonestown, Guyana.

Deborah Layton was a member of that cult—and a survivor. In her book *Seductive Poison*, she looks back over her experience and, for the sake of her questioning daughter, tries to understand

how something that started out so good could end up being so horribly evil. She wrote:

> On my own, with no one to answer to, I have kept my shame locked in a small compartment just beneath the surface. But my daughter's innocent probing has emboldened me to face the horror again, after twenty years.
>
> "Why didn't you just leave when Jim got mean?"
>
> I'm not sure. What took me so long to comprehend and finally heed the danger signs? Was it my naiveté? Perhaps it was my childlike belief in my own papa's goodness that kept me from grasping the truth . . .
>
> I'm propelled by my daughter's innocence to turn inward to my cavern of painful, frightening memories. But facing them requires that I first learn how to cope with the shame.
>
> How could we do such awful things?[1]

We all—even if the sin in our own lives is less obvious and less horrific than in that tragedy—must ask those same questions. If we don't ask them, we end up living in a fantasy world of denial.

Nothing is more dangerous than an unrealistic view of human nature. It will cause you to leave your car and your home unlocked, invest in the latest "Christian" money-making scheme, or send generous gifts to those who tell you they're trying to stand for God and save Christian values from the hordes of unbelievers bent on destroying all that's good and pure.

When we live in denial of the dark side of human nature, we get hurt needlessly, often get conned, and should never play poker. It's the difference between believing that democracy is a wonderful form of government because people are basically

good and should participate in their government, and believing in democracy because people are basically bad and no one person should be entrusted with too much power. It's the difference between being genuinely surprised by evil and being genuinely surprised by good.

But coming to the discovery that people are a lot worse than I thought they were was a process.

MY THEOLOGY

It started with my theology.

The world is not a pretty place. Once I accepted that the Bible is true, I had to deal with what the Bible said about the world and about human nature. And, frankly, it's not a pretty picture.

We may like to think that people are basically good, but the Bible says that "the heart is deceitful above all things, and desperately sick; who can understand it?" (Jeremiah 17:9).

In Romans 3:10–18 Paul quoted a string of Old Testament passages that should cause us to wince:

"None is righteous, no, not one;
>   no one understands;
>   no one seeks for God.
All have turned aside; together they have become worthless;
>   no one does good,
>   not even one."
"Their throat is an open grave;
>   they use their tongues to deceive."
"The venom of asps is under their lips."
>   "Their mouth is full of curses and bitterness."

"Their feet are swift to shed blood;

in their paths are ruin and misery,

and the way of peace they have not known."

"There is no fear of God before their eyes."

It isn't just us; it's where we live. Although Christians have sometimes ignored biblical environmentalism, the Bible makes clear that we should act as stewards of creation and protectors of life. However, biblical environmentalism is a long way from the silly and superficial view of the environmentalist who calls earth "our mother" and worships at the altar of nature. Biblical environmentalism looks at the world the way it really is: a world in which the strongest survive and eat the weakest; a world in which earthquakes, hurricanes, and floods bring destruction and death; and a world in which very little is safe or controllable. Genesis 3:16–17 talks about the curse of the ground and the horror of pain. Paul wrote about creation being "subjected to futility," being in "bondage to decay," and "groaning together in the pains of childbirth" (Romans 8:20–22).

> THE BIBLE SAYS THAT GOD IS IN HIS HEAVEN; BUT ALL IS NOT RIGHT WITH THE WORLD, OR WITH US.

The late Christian comedian Jerry Clower used to tell a story about a wealthy farmer who, when asked, refused to donate to the local volunteer fire department. The farmer objected that, should there be a fire, his own people at the large farm would do a lot better than a bunch of volunteers.

Shortly after that, his barn caught fire. Despite the efforts of his own people, the barn continued to burn. So the farmer called

the local volunteer fire department. They came in their old fire truck with its worn-out engine. With water spraying everywhere, they drove right into the burning barn and put out the fire.

The wealthy farmer was so impressed that he gave the firefighters a check for $10,000. One of the firefighters turned to the other and said, "Wow, $10,000. The first thing we're going to do is get those brakes fixed!"

It may appear, because of the thin veneer of civilization that keeps the dark side of human nature somewhat in check, that people are basically good. It can seem almost as if we even have the weather under control, because specialists can tell us what the weather will be—and after all, we have strong levies to keep out the water. It can appear that, as Robert Browning wrote, "God's in his heaven and all's right with the world." The Bible says that God is in his heaven; but all is not right with the world, or with us. Not even close.

A lot can be said about goodness in people (and we'll get to that in the next chapter), but only a shallow, unthoughtful person fails to note that our brakes, as it were, need to be fixed.

MY EXPERIENCE

The discovery that people are a lot worse than I thought they were was a process that started with my theology, but it didn't stop there.

It was also confirmed by my experience.

I didn't start out being cynical. It almost happened without my noticing it. I began with high hopes for people, for me, and for the church. I started out accepting the tenets of American optimism: that every problem had a solution, every human being

wanted to be better, and every situation was redeemable.

Have you heard about the little boy who was digging in a pile of manure? Someone asked him what he was doing. The boy said, "With this much manure, there has to be a pony in there somewhere." I thought the pony was in there too. I kept digging and digging . . . only to give up in the end. You can only keep digging for so long before you at least start to suspect that the pony has long since left the scene.

Cynicism goes with the territory of being a pastor. Your heart breaks, your hopes shatter, and your mind is overwhelmed by the dark secrets of people you love. When that happens often enough, you either become a sweet, nice, and insipid clown saying things nobody believes and everybody expects, or you move into a mode of cynicism about almost everything. It's not easy to live in denial and be a pastor—at least not a sane one.

My late brother was a district attorney, and a good one. (Our father used to say that between his two sons—one was a lawyer and one was a preacher—there wasn't any problem he faced that one of them couldn't fix.) My brother once told me that in spite of the dark side of human nature he saw and the confessions he'd heard as a district attorney, he believed it wasn't even close to what I faced every day.

Someone has said that anyone who likes the law and sausage should never watch either one of them being made. I would add that anyone who likes the church should never watch how church is done. Paul wrote to his young friend Timothy that a leader of the church should never be a new Christian. I used to think that all Paul was saying was that he wanted discipline, knowledge, and maturity in the church leaders. I suppose that was a part of it.

Paul pointed out the danger of a new convert becoming "puffed up with conceit" and falling "into the condemnation of the devil" (1 Timothy 3:6).

But I'm older now, and I think I better understand why Paul didn't want new Christians leading the church. More than the fear of conceit and a need for godliness drove this injunction. I believe Paul was aware that, after just one board or congregational meeting, a new Christian might be driven to become a Buddhist.

One problem seminary faculty members encounter is that students frequently go into the church unaware of its dark side. As a result, they often are hurt badly, and their ministry suffers. After discussing that particular problem at a faculty meeting a while back, we agreed that someone had to warn students and teach them how to survive the harsh reality of the church. Given that practical theology is my area of teaching, they commissioned me to do something about it.

So now, in my classes, I spend a number of lecture hours talking about how human sin is manifested in the church and how to identify and understand the dark side. I cover subjects like how to develop a "Christian mean streak," how to win the political battles without losing your salvation, how to identify "pockets of power," how not to be a weenie, how to deal with your discouragement and broken heart, and how to collect "political chips" in the poker game of church politics.

The students hate it.

In fact, often they're so irritated that they make angry comments to me. (Not an easy thing to do when a professor has the power of the grade.) They say that I'm teaching them to be manipulative and underhanded, that I'm giving them an undue

negative view of the institution they will serve and the people they are supposed to love, and that I'm turning them into cynics. (Just so you know, I generally assign to one student the job of raising his or her hand when I'm so negative about the church that the students begin to think about leaving the seminary and the church altogether. When that hand goes up, I tell them about the high and holy calling of ministry, the great privilege it is to serve God's people, and stories about the people of God, their love, their faithfulness, and their kindness.)

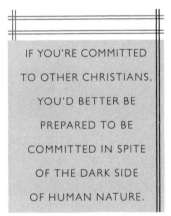

IF YOU'RE COMMITTED TO OTHER CHRISTIANS, YOU'D BETTER BE PREPARED TO BE COMMITTED IN SPITE OF THE DARK SIDE OF HUMAN NATURE.

When the students complain, I say to them, "I know . . . but you'll learn this, and I'll test you on it. One of these days, believe it or not, you will rise up and call me blessed."

And they do. I can't tell you how many times a former student has called or written to say, "Steve, do you remember how negative I was about those lectures on church politics? I repent. That stuff was better than Greek."

When you have a pastor who thinks people are wonderful, the occurrence of sin is minimal, and Christians are entirely sanctified, you've met a pastor who has never gone through a building program, offended the wealthy, stepped on the toes of an elder, preached from a text he wished wasn't in the Bible, or taken an unpopular stand. Either that, or you're dealing with a person who has lost his mind.

A pastor friend of mine founded a church and served as its pastor for more than twenty-five years. The church became a major

witness to the city, and what God did there was nothing less than phenomenal. My friend finally decided to retire, and I, thinking he might need the comfort of a brother, visited him in his study.

"Next Sunday is your last Sunday, right?"

"Yes, it is, and it's going to be hard. I'm going to look out at those people, and it's going to be a struggle to keep from falling apart."

"You want some advice?"

"This would be a good time."

"Next Sunday, when you're preaching your last sermon and are about to lose it, think of someone who really ticks you off . . . someone in the church who has made your life miserable. Of course, you'll have to repent when the service is over, but it'll get you through it."

"Steve," he said, "I can't do that. I love these people. I'm their pastor. I can't think of a single person like that."

"OK," I responded as I headed for the door. "Then you're on your own. I'll be praying for you."

"Steve, wait!" he called after me, laughing. "I just thought of three."

If you're committed to other Christians, you'd better be prepared to be committed in spite of the dark side of human nature. I can't tell you the number of times people have told me that they wanted a career change because they were tired of working "in the world." They want to work in a place where their coworkers are Christians and where people love one another. "I'm tired of the struggle, the politics, and the difficulty of maintaining my witness in the secular workplace," they say. "Can you help me find a job in a Christian ministry?"

I respond in a loving and pastoral way: "Are you a fruitcake?

No place you can go is free of sin. If you like Christian organizations and the church, it's better not to work there."

If you're not a believer and have somehow picked up this book, you'll notice that I've spent a lot of time talking about us, the believers. I do so because this book will be read mostly by people who have at least a minimal commitment to Christ. Don't think for one minute, however, that I couldn't have addressed human evil among nonbelievers—and had enough material for ten books.

MY SHAME

People are a lot worse than I thought they were. I got that from the Bible (my theology) and from my experience. Christian realism has its anchor in both theology and experience, but it also has its personal application. When I discovered that people were a lot worse than I thought they were, I also found out that I was a lot worse than I thought I was.

It was verified by my shame.

I've told you some of the bad things about being a pastor. Now let me tell you one of the good things: I know that I'm not alone in this. Most people think that they are the only ones who are lonely, afraid, angry, doubting, and sinful. When you talk to as many people as I do, have as much contact with students as I do, and get as many letters as I do, you begin to get the feeling that we're all very human.

That's particularly true when it comes to sin.

I remember when "Sam" (not his real name) came into my office, confessing that he had stolen money from the city in which he was the city purchasing agent. It wasn't a lot of money, but if

you steal ten dollars, it's no less stealing than if you'd pocketed ten thousand dollars.

Sam had lowered the price of a confiscated car that was being sold by the city. The car was priced at $600, and he marked it down to $450 so he could buy it for his daughter. No one would have ever known had it not been for a major audit of city records and the fact that Sam was thrown in with some really big-time embezzlers who had taken money from the city for years. Again, the amount wasn't what was important. My friend was guilty, and he told me so.

The next day Sam's name was in the local paper, and three or four months later, he went to trial and was convicted. He was an officer in our church, and because we had so many new Christians, I asked if we could use his story to teach them how Christians should deal with sin. (The matter is never one of *whether* Christians sin; that's a given. The only question is how we will deal with it.) "Steve," Sam said, "that would be a privilege. I would like what I've done to be of use to the Kingdom."

It's a long story, and I don't have room here to go into details. The end of the story, though, is so good that I have to share it with you. Sam resigned from the board of deacons, and during the entire process of his trial, when he was without a job and facing the horror of his shame, the entire church stood with him emotionally, financially, and spiritually.

I'll never forget the scene after Sam was (along with others) found guilty. The others held press conferences at which they proclaimed their innocence. But in the courthouse rotunda, a whole bunch of Christians surrounded Sam, placed their hands on his head, and prayed that God would be glorified through the sad

episode. Many tears were shed, amid great joy that God was in charge. The day Sam was restored to the board of deacons, the entire congregation applauded.

So did the angels.

The reason I'm telling you this story is to tell you what happened the day before Sam confessed his sin to me. I was in Los Angeles and had left my car parked in the lot at my local airport. When I returned from that trip, I retrieved my car and headed to the booth where one pays the (exorbitant, I'd say) parking fees. Then, to my surprise and joy, I realized that the woman in the booth had charged me ten dollars less than I owed. I thanked her and started to drive away.

PEOPLE—MYSELF INCLUDED—REALLY ARE A LOT WORSE THAN I THOUGHT THEY WERE.

Just then I thought it would be a smart thing for me to go back and pay the right amount. I'm not altogether that pure, but being a fairly well-known preacher in our town, I was afraid she would realize what happened and know that I had cheated.

So, with great reluctance, I backed up and told the woman that I owed her some more money. She was surprised, looked again at the ticket, and then thanked me. She told me that if I had not come back, the money I failed to pay would have been taken out of her paycheck.

As Sam told me about his stealing from the city, I thought about my "almost" stealing from the city. I realized then that it could have gone either way for me—or for him.

That's a "safe" sin and one I feel comfortable telling you about. Others, though, haven't been so safe. Time and time again, people

would confess their sins to me and I would think, *That could have been me.* Or, on several occasions, *I've been there and done that . . . I just haven't been caught—yet.*

To be honest, there is no sin of which I'm not capable or haven't committed. Not only that, but there are a lot of sins I would have committed if I'd had the time or was sure I wouldn't get caught.

Gradually I had become a cynic about other people; but more importantly, I became a cynic about me.

MY FAITH

People—myself included—really are a lot worse than I thought they were. I learned that from my theology, my experience, and my shame. But I started moving from cynicism to Christian realism because of what happened to my cynicism.

My cynicism was redeemed by my faith.

I don't want to get ahead of myself here, but I just can't leave this chapter (or you!) in the mud. When you realize that people are a lot worse than you thought they were, and when you realize that you're not above the rest of the human race, you'll have a choice to make. You can deny the reality, you can become bitter, you can run, or you can just accept the dark side as a part of what it means to be human. On the other hand, you can discover the joy, the power, and the freedom of being loved even when you don't deserve it.

Jesus really is a friend of sinners. In fact, he didn't come for the healthy but for the sick. The angel who appeared before the birth of Jesus told Joseph, "She [Mary] will bear a son, and you shall call his name Jesus [meaning 'the Lord is salvation'], for he will save his people from their sins" (Matthew 1:21).

Author Brennan Manning wrote:

The fierce mercy of Jesus is at work protecting moral failures from the fierce shaming and moral debasement of religious bureaucrats who have severed spirituality from religion, the heart from the head, and grace from nature. Real sinners deserving real punishment are gratuitously pardoned; they need only accept tenderness already present. Forgiveness has been granted; they need only the wisdom to accept it and repent. There are the ragamuffins, the poor in spirit whom Jesus declared blessed. They know how to accept a gift. "Come all you who are wiped out, confused, bewildered, lost, beat-up, scarred, scared, threatened, and depressed, and I'll enlighten your mind with wisdom and fill your heart with the tenderness that I have received from my Father." This is unconditional pardon. The sinner need only live confidently in the wisdom of tenderness.[2]

The church is not a place for people who are "together," obedient, and spiritual. If you really think it is, then you were conned. The church is actually a place for people who are needy, afraid, confused, and quite sinful. But even more important than that, the church is a place for people who have been loved . . . and have no idea why. Each congregation is, as it were, a local chapter of "Sinners Anonymous."

I have a friend, Ray Cortese, who is the pastor of one of the most dynamic and effective churches in America. It's in the small community of Lecanto, Florida, and people from all over the state attend. This man's ministry is a powerful witness to the truth of the gospel.

Ray said that when he first came to Lecanto, he thought the

community was a "sewer" where there was little concern for God, for truth, or for God's law. Ray knew he'd been sent as a prophet, so he preached powerful, prophetic sermons condemning evil and pointing to God.

Do you know what happened? Nothing. Jesus left the building.

Allow me to relay Ray's testimony and the reason he believes so many have come to his church. Ray has said, "I thought there was a sewer, and there was. It was not in the community; it was in my own heart." It was this knowledge that revolutionized his ministry, his relationships with others, and his sermons. Once he knew the truth about himself and let God love him and forgive him, Ray became a powerful voice for those who needed God but didn't think they were good enough.

The people in the church Ray serves are getting better, but they're getting better because they know that getting better isn't the point. The point is that God's power is made perfect in weakness, God's grace shines clearest through sinners, and God's message can only be heard from people who are beggars telling other beggars where they found Bread.

As I mentioned before, Alcoholics Anonymous teaches that only a drunk can help a drunk. They're right. That's why drunks get help from AA. Only people who truly understand that they're a lot worse than they thought they were can help people who are learning the same thing about themselves. Only sinners can help sinners.

People—you and I—really are a lot worse than we think we are. But as the late Jack Miller, founder of World Harvest Mission, said, "God's grace is a lot bigger than we think it is."

That's Christian realism.

THERE MAY BE SAID TO BE TWO CLASSES OF
PEOPLE IN THE WORLD: THOSE WHO
CONSTANTLY DIVIDE THE PEOPLE IN THE WORLD
INTO TWO CLASSES AND THOSE WHO DON'T.

ROBERT BENCHLEY

People Are a Lot Better Than I Thought They Were

Hold fast what is good.

1 THESSALONIANS 5:21

I HAVE TROUBLE loving three people (well, there are more, but that's a different story). Let me tell you about them.

The first is a television evangelist (and you would know his name). I disagree with almost everything he teaches. In fact, he drives me nuts. I was in a supermarket parking lot recently when a little boy ran up to this man's big car. I thought the evangelist was going to drive off, but he didn't. He stopped his car, got out, knelt down, and listened to what the child had to say. In fact, when I left that parking lot some time later, he was still talking to that little boy. He was nicer than I'd expected him to be.

Don't you hate it when that happens?

The second person I have trouble loving is one of the most cynical and pagan people I know. When I want to get angry (I think better when I'm angry), I think of some sarcastic comment he made: some slur against a brother or sister in Christ or some kind of caustic and flip remark about the church.

One of the great tragedies of my life was when my younger

brother died. He was my best friend, and I miss him more than I can tell you. Shortly after that event, I ran into this man, and do you know what he said to me? He called me aside and said, "Steve, I'm so sorry about your brother's death. As you know, I don't pray much and am not even sure that God exists, but I've been praying to God for you, and I've asked him, if he exists, to comfort you." He was more compassionate than I'd expected.

Don't you hate it when that happens?

The third person is a woman who had been quite critical of me to one of my friends. I called this woman, confronting her with her alleged comments and wanting to straighten her out. Needless to say, I was angry. When she picked up the phone, I said, "Betty [not her real name], let me tell you what someone told me you said; if you did say it, we need to talk."

To my shock, "Betty" started crying. She said that I didn't need to repeat what my friend had said. "I said it," she confessed through the tears, "and I'm so sorry. I said it because of my own insecurity, and it was a terrible thing to say about you. Please forgive me, and I'll make a call and confess my lie to your friend as soon as we get off the phone." Then Betty told me about the pain she'd been dealing with and how her life had been so devastated by it. She was more vulnerable and honest than I'd thought she would be.

Don't you hate it when that happens?

Do you know why we hate to lose our enemies, the ones we've demonized? It's because we need our enemies to feel better about ourselves. We're right and they're wrong; we're good and they're bad; we're in and they're out; we know the truth and they don't.

We hate to lose our enemies because they define who we are.

And therein lies a great problem for Christians. The more we define ourselves in terms of "us and them," the greater the gap in relationships, and the more marginalized we become. Then we wonder why we're so lonely.

You've heard the old story of the uptight and condemning group of Christians who went to heaven. Saint Peter was showing some new arrivals around heaven, and they walked by a house. Peter told everyone to remain quiet and not to say a word. After they passed the house, someone asked Peter why they had to be quiet. He said, referring to the uptight and condemning Christian group, "The people in that house think they're the only ones here. It would greatly disturb their happiness and tranquility if they knew about you."

> THE MORE WE DEFINE OURSELVES IN TERMS OF "US AND THEM," THE GREATER THE GAP IN RELATIONSHIPS, AND THE MORE MARGINALIZED WE BECOME.

In the last chapter we talked about Christian realism. This chapter is the flip side of Christian realism: the recognition of the image of God in people, even in our enemies. People really are a lot worse than I thought they were, but they're also a lot better and more valuable than I thought too.

In the first chapter of the Bible, we find the story of the creation of Adam and Eve. That chapter has astounding implications for how we should view others: "God said, 'Let us make man in our image, after our likeness. And let them have dominion over the fish of the sea and over the birds of the heavens and over the livestock and over all the earth and over every creeping thing that creeps on the earth.' So God created man in his own

image, in the image of God he created him; male and female he created them" (Genesis 1:26–27).

My colleague and friend Richard Pratt, in his book *Designed for Dignity*, refers to the doctrine of Adam's fall and its tragic results. (The Fall is when sin entered our world and spread like a disease, to wit the Puritan rhyme, "In Adam's fall / We sinned all.") Richard wrote about the image of God in which all human beings are created:

> How do fallen people remain the image of God? In what ways are they still God's likeness? First, people possess many basic characteristics granted to Adam and Eve in the beginning. We exhibit rational and linguistic capacities; we have moral and religious natures; we are immortal souls. Sin severely mars these aspects of our character, but it does not obliterate them. . . .
>
> Whatever else we may say about fallen humanity, we must remember that we remain the image of God. We have rebelled against our Maker, but we are still people. All of us are special creations designed with marvelous abilities and blessed with unique responsibilities in this world.[1]

A well-known song says that "people who need people are the luckiest people in the world." That may be true, but let me tell you something else that's true: people who need people and build walls to keep people out are the loneliest people in the world. For years I constructed those walls, but as of late I climbed up on a ladder and looked over the walls, sometimes even climbing down on the other side. And my life has changed as a result of that discovery.

People Are Just Like Me

I discovered that other people are just like me.

When I said that people are a lot better than I thought they were, I probably should have added that they are *sometimes* better than I thought they were. Sometimes they're worse. I'm that way too.

I remember the time, years ago, when I went with an evangelistic team into one of Boston's worst areas. It was one of those neighborhoods where white people were not supposed to go. But a number of us—both black and white—were going, and I felt I would be safe.

(I know, I know. That sounds racist, and it is. I repent.)

As a part of that evangelistic effort, we put up a screen in one of the parks and invited people to watch a film about Jesus. I don't remember the results, but what I do remember is a cacophony of feelings and perceptions. I felt fear and anxiety; if I had to die, I was glad I would die serving Jesus. By far the most salient memory I have, though, is of watching the African Americans in that community playing with their children. One father was carrying his daughter on his shoulders, and both were laughing. His daughter was the same age as my daughter, and I remember thinking, *He's just like me.*

As the film ran, I stood on a street corner adjacent to the park. I noticed a car parked there, and sitting in the car was what appeared to be a very angry black man. I thought of slavery and racism and how he probably had every right to be angry. Coward that I am, though, I started moving away from the car.

That was when this man rolled down his window and said, "Come here!"

I went. This white boy may not be the smartest you ever met, but I'm not dumb either.

"You with these people?" he asked.

"Yeah . . . ," I said hesitantly.

"Get in," he said in a gruff voice. "I want to talk to you." He reached over to the other side of the car, opened the door, and waited.

I got in, my whole life flashing before my eyes. I began thinking about my will and who would get all my stuff.

Do you know what happened? He saw my fear and started laughing. "Let me ask you a question," he said. "Do you really believe this stuff?" I allowed that I did, and he said, "Good—my life is a mess, and I want to know God. Can you help me?" Then, to my shock, he started crying.

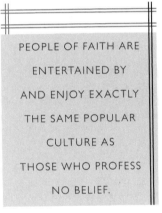

PEOPLE OF FAITH ARE ENTERTAINED BY AND ENJOY EXACTLY THE SAME POPULAR CULTURE AS THOSE WHO PROFESS NO BELIEF.

We talked for over an hour, and during that time we both shared our doubts and fears, our pain and our joys. If you'd been there, you would have seen two guys crying, holding hands, and praying together. I remember thinking about that incident after I got home. It dawned on me, with surprise, that my new friend was just like me.

That's not the only time I've discovered a common humanity in other people. I see it in my neighbors—the ones who would describe themselves as Christians and, more importantly, those who wouldn't. When we go through a hurricane (and we have gone through several together), I don't ask the guy who comes with the chainsaw whether he's a Christian. He's just a neighbor who wants

to help. As we all work together, I don't gravitate toward those who are my brothers and sisters in Christ. I gravitate toward those who, like me, have a mess on their hands.

As you already know, I'm a Republican. Bill Clinton is not my favorite person in the world. I didn't vote for him and didn't agree with his policies. I remember when his mother died, though, and I saw footage of the funeral. As President Clinton brushed the tears from his eyes, I was reminded of the time my mother died and of the loss and pain I'd felt. I thought, *He feels what I felt. He's mourning the way I mourned. He misses his mother just like I do. He's just like me.* (You have no idea what it took for me to admit that.)

The other day I talked to my friend Terry Mattingly, religion columnist for the Scripps Howard News Service. He had just finished his book on popular culture, *Pop Goes Religion: Faith in Popular Culture.* He told me that every study he's seen shows that people of faith are entertained by and enjoy exactly the same popular culture as those who profess no belief.

Let me recommend a surprising book about the discovery of faith and integrity in the filmmaking capital of the world. The title is *Behind the Screen: Hollywood Insiders on Faith, Film, and Culture.* Spencer Lewerenz and Barbara Nicolosi, the editors, write in the introduction:

Here's the situation as many see it (and if you don't think this way, you probably know plenty of people who do):

Most movies and TV shows are immoral, obscene, perverted, or some combination of the three (except *7th Heaven*).

Hollywood has it out for Christians in much the same way Tom had it out for Jerry or Foghorn Leghorn had it out for the dog.

The entertainment and news media are controlled by the "cultural elite," a cadre of ex-Ivy League dandies who, when not swiping manger scenes from suburban lawns, spend their time in idle cocktail chatter sneering at "conventional morality" and Costco. . . .

Blaming Hollywood has to be considered a failed tactic that needs to be abandoned.[2]

The point of that book is correct. It's easy to demonize other people as long as we can keep them at arm's length. For years I'd done that with Christians whose theology was different from mine and with unbelievers whose worldview was in opposition to mine.

So at last I looked over the walls I'd built . . . and found lonely people like me who needed a friend. I've found people who are sad, people who are funny, people who are afraid, people who are worried about paying their mortgage and about cancer. They laugh the way I laugh, at the same things I find humorous. They feel guilty the way I feel guilty and are just as insecure as I am. They bleed the way I bleed, they worry about their families the way I worry about my family, and they have moments of great courage, profound love, and graciousness—and other moments of incredible selfishness, arrogance, and self-righteousness.

In short, they are like me.

PEOPLE ARE BETTER THAN ME

But there's more: people are often better than me.

You've heard the comment, "So and so isn't a Christian, but he or she is a good person," right? While there are some theological niceties—in fact, true ones about sin and the Fall—that need

to be spoken to that particular idea, the statement (at least on a human level) is true.

I want to address this subject in more detail later, but here let me say that the definition of *Christian* is not "a good person." Being "good" is not the biblical faith; it's the American folk religion.

I used to think there were two kinds of people in the world: good people and bad people. The good people were Christians, and they were in the church. The bad people were not Christians. They were not in the church. In fact, they mowed their lawns, watched television, drank beer, and went to football games on Sundays—all while the good people worshiped.

I was right about the number. There are two kinds of people. I was just wrong about who they are. There are people who are needy, sinful, and worried—and know it. And there are people who are needy, sinful, and worried—but don't know it. As I understand the Bible, the church should be made up of the people who know it.

Let me make a surprising and truthful statement with which I believe you'll agree, at least if you stop and think about it. Some of the meanest, most condemning, angriest, and hardest people I know are people who call themselves Christians. Not only that. Some of the kindest, most compassionate, and most loving people I know don't claim to have made any kind of faith commitment. In fact, you'll find both kinds of people inside and outside of faith communities.

So what's the difference? The difference is that the Christians have run to Jesus, and he's accepted and loved them. That's it. Are they getting better? Well, at least in that they know what "getting better" is. Sometimes they are better. Sometimes they're not

better. And sometimes we don't know that they're better, simply because they were so bad in the first place that they had a long way to go before anybody could tell the difference. Some who ran to Jesus are better than unbelievers, and some are worse. Some are so beaten up that all they can do is be still and allow God to love them. And then there are others who've been loved long enough that they can now love others.

The difference is Jesus.

What about letting our light shine before others so they'll see our goodness and glorify God (see Matthew 5:16)? We should, of course, but goodness as defined by Jesus is quite different from what we might suppose. Usually those who are good don't know it, and others don't know it either because "Goodness" is a thing that takes place inside a person and has more to do with an attitude of love and graciousness than it does with obeying the rules. Sometimes the meanest, least godly people obey the rules. And sometimes the people of whom Jesus seems most fond have the hardest time getting it right. In the Bible, the people who obeyed the rules better than anybody else were, I would remind you, the very ones who ticked Jesus off the most.

PEOPLE NEED OTHER PEOPLE

I was quite surprised to look over my walls and find that people on the other side were often better than me. But I found out even more.

I discovered that other people need other people the way I need other people.

I smoke a pipe. (It's one of the few vices I have left. Don't

write me letters or try to persuade me to stop. People more spiritual than you have already tried . . . and failed.)

Contrary to what most Christians think, there are some good things about smoking a pipe. For instance, it always gives me something to look forward to when I'm in a boring faculty meeting or listening to a boring speech. In Florida, the smoke keeps away the mosquitoes. There's more: my smoking shocks other Christians who know I love Christ but can't make the fact of my smoking fit into that image. That's probably good for them.

One other benefit of smoking a pipe is that it has made me part of a small and ever-decreasing fellowship of smokers. Everywhere I turn smokers are quitting or . . . OK . . . dying. So, as our numbers decrease, we naturally are drawn to one another outside buildings, behind barns, and in small rooms designated for those who are ugly and their mother dresses them funny (i.e., smoking areas).

You'll probably never know this if I don't tell you, but when smokers get together, they laugh a lot. They like one another and relax in each other's company. Some of my Christian friends smoke and are members of the church where I often preach. Those guys have

> I DISCOVERED THAT OTHER PEOPLE NEED OTHER PEOPLE THE WAY I NEED OTHER PEOPLE.

formed a Bible study they call "Holy Smokes." They are among the most honest, authentic, and fun people I've ever met.

The fellowship of smokers is one of people who are drawn together by their sin and not by their goodness. They don't pretend to be better than they are by using mints to hide the smoky smell

on their breath. They don't blush when they're together and someone sees them smoke. They hardly ever appear to be holier than thou. They're just people who need people and who gravitate to one another because of their sin.

As I peer over my walls of isolation, I find that people who are needy are drawn to one another. They take off their masks and reach out to others. The need for each other is the reason television shows about friends, companionship, and community are popular. Those programs speak to the yearning we all have to be in relationships that are more than just superficial.

So I looked over my walls to see people who are like me, people who are better than me, and people who need me as much as I need them.

WHY DO I STAY BEHIND THE WALL?

Now to a question that must be addressed before we move on: if everything I just told you is true, then why do I stay behind the wall? Or, to meddle a bit, why do you stay behind a wall? I don't know your reasons, but I know why I do it.

I stay behind the wall because I'm afraid people will learn who I am but won't accept me.

I don't want to be known.

We all wear masks.

I just finished interviewing Peter Schweizer on our talk show. He is a wonderful writer and a research fellow at the Hoover Institute. His new book is *Do As I Say (Not As I Do): Profiles in Liberal Hypocrisy.* Peter is fun to talk to, and he takes great delight in punching holes in the self-righteous balloons of both liberals and conservatives.

I opened that interview by introducing him and saying, "Peter, before we get into your book, there is something I need to say first. I'm the biggest hypocrite I know."

"Of course you are," Peter responded, laughing, "We all are. The difference is that you know it, admit it, and just announced it to your audience. The people in my book don't think they are and deny it everyplace they go."

Without making a political comment, let me say that his insight into human hypocrisy is profound. The masks we wear are many, and we wear them for a variety of reasons. Bottom line, though, is that we're afraid that if people find out what we're really like, they will reject us, criticize us, or make fun of us.

The truth is that they might love us. But let's talk about that in a minute.

Do you know what's great about being a Christian? It gives me the freedom to stop pretending. I'm climbing up the ladder and looking over the walls and even associating with those on the other side of the walls because I don't have anything to protect anymore. According to the Bible, the church is the only organization in the world where the only qualification for membership is to be unqualified. By my very membership in the church, I have proclaimed to the world that I'm a sinner, I'm needy, and I can't fix me.

If I already know that and people find out that it's true, it doesn't matter. It is a great freedom.

I also stay behind the wall because sometimes I think God wants me to stay behind the wall.

I don't want to displease God.

A misguided kind of Christianity suggests that believers

must not look at or touch anything that isn't intentionally Christian. Just as the religious people in Jesus's day were shocked that he was a friend of prostitutes, winebibbers, and sinners, so perhaps religious people today ought to be shocked that I'm friends with the same kinds of people.

> THE PEOPLE WHO SHOUT THE LOUDEST ARE OFTEN THOSE WHO ARE LEAST SURE ABOUT WHAT THEY'RE SAYING.

For about a year, when I was a teenager, I got involved in a Christian group that believed it was a dangerous sin to go to movies or to associate with people who did. I've always had a heart and a hunger for God, and when I was younger and less cynical than I am now, I listened to and believed just about anybody who spoke with authority about God. The people in that group spoke with sureness and conviction about God and what he expected of me. So, I bought it. And it almost killed me.

After that year I decided I was going to hell. I just couldn't live by the rules anymore. And I decided that if I was going to hell, I was going to have some fun doing it.

I went to a movie.

No no no. It wasn't a skin flick or a violent film. It was a Jerry Lewis and Dean Martin movie. (Now I've seen more obscene things in church than in that movie.)

During the film, though, I remembered what I'd been taught—that Jesus would return when I least expected it, and, "Do you want him to find you in sin when he returns?" I had a horrible time. I kept looking around, thinking that Jesus was coming and I was going to be in serious trouble. I knew that tell-

ing him I was there to witness wouldn't wash. And he'd never believe I'd wandered into the theater by mistake.

Then I sensed that Jesus came and sat beside me . . . and that he was laughing at me . . . and at the movie.

Since then I've learned to be very, very careful about listening to people who tell me where I shouldn't go, what I shouldn't do, what books I shouldn't read, and to what music I shouldn't listen. Instead of paying too much attention to those voices, I've decided to check out what the Bible really says. As a result, I'm a lot freer than I thought I was—and a whole lot freer than they said I was.

I am glad for this discovery, because otherwise I might never have even dared look over the wall.

Still, sometimes I stay behind the wall because I'm not completely secure in the truth I believe.

Have you ever noticed that the people who shout the loudest are often those who are least sure about what they're saying? It's like a poker game. The winners laugh and make jokes while the losers say, "Shut up. Deal and bet." When you have a winning hand, you don't have to be uptight or angry. You just enjoy the game.

Some time ago I started, and for a number of years moderated, a group called Skeptics Forum. The ministry consisted of a weekly meeting of atheists, agnostics, and all sorts of nonbelievers. Only one Christian was allowed to attend the meetings, and that was me. The purpose of the forum was to provide honest answers to honest questions from nonbelievers.

Do you know my initial feelings when I began the Skeptics Forum? I was scared spitless. I had nightmares in which these learned nonbelievers destroyed my faith. I was sure they would

have me for lunch. I thought I would probably make a fool of myself, bring shame on Christ, and destroy his kingdom with my shallow and insufficient answers.

What really happened was just the opposite: many of the people who joined the forum eventually became Christians, and the others stopped laughing.

The point is this: the genuine can be tested. Truth is truth, and a good place to see if the truth will stand up under questioning is among people who don't believe it. You may be surprised at how well the truth holds up. Once I discovered that, it was easier to climb over the wall.

Finally, I stay behind the wall because I'm afraid of love.

Love brings with it obligation, and frankly, I'm already more obligated than I can handle.

In honest and authentic relationships, you climb over the wall. You start talking. You discover that these aren't half-bad people. The truth is, you kind of enjoy being with them. You begin to realize that they like you and you like them.

That's when you notice their tears—and you find that you care.

It can be uncomfortable to love. It's messy, and it puts you in a position of obligation. But not to love is dangerous. Oh, you may not get hurt or disappointed. And it feels safe on this side of the wall, even if it is boring. The problem, however, is that once you start building walls, it's hard to stop. One day you'll wake up to discover you're closed in by those walls you built. You'll have just four walls and only a little room. You'll find that without intending to, you've become hard, angry, and very lonely.

Jesus saw the tears of those on the other side of the wall. He knew what his love for them would cost—and he chose to love anyway.

Then he told us to do what he had done, and he promised that if we did, he would always go with us.

OF ALL MARVELOUS THINGS, PERHAPS THERE IS NOTHING
THAT ANGELS BEHOLD WITH SUCH
SUPREME ASTONISHMENT AS A PROUD MAN.

Charles Caleb Colton

Self-Righteousness Is a Lot More Dangerous Than I Thought It Was

Do nothing from rivalry or conceit, but in humility count others more significant than yourselves.
PHILIPPIANS 2:3

I just bought a new Honda Accord.

I guess I started thinking about it when the producer of our radio program, Erik Guzman, bought an old car and converted it to run on cooking oil. He was quite pleased and, I might say, a bit self-righteous. He could go to McDonald's for a burger and fries and fill up his fuel tank at the same time. The problem was that his car smelled like French fries. Whenever I followed him in traffic, I got hungry. His car also put out a lot of pollution. While it may be better to smell French fries than gasoline fumes, the smoke from either is unpleasant.

Still, the more I thought about it, the more I thought I should do something for myself and for the world.

So I bought the Honda Accord. It isn't just an Accord. It's a hybrid Accord.

The combination gasoline and electric engine is a little more expensive, but I didn't mind. I was willing to pay more because I care. I care about the environment, and I care about

the quality of life. I'm concerned that people who don't care are buying gas-guzzlers with engines that pollute the atmosphere and kill the trees.

I don't want to sound overly harsh, but too many people don't care. They drive their big cars, and they're killing all of us. Every time I see someone in an SUV, I want to shout, "You cretin! Don't you care about the earth? Don't you care about our air? Don't you care about our children?"

I've even thought about printing cards to place under the windshield wipers of such cars: "Please save our children. Get a hybrid!"

There, I've said it, and it felt really good.

Of course, I get a tax write-off for buying the hybrid, I save money on gasoline, and the hybrid isn't tested enough to be sure that the batteries won't explode and ruin an entire forest. Doesn't matter that I could have bought a cheaper car and given what I saved to missions or that a lot of people can't afford a car at all.

> WHEN WE START THINKING ABOUT IT, WE BEGIN TO REALIZE THAT SELF-RIGHTEOUSNESS IS PERHAPS THE MOST DANGEROUS OF ALL HUMAN SINS.

I feel good about myself and my environmentally friendly decision. That's what's important. Perhaps I was even able to make you feel guilty. It hardly gets any better than that, right?

In Luke 18 Jesus tells a story about self-righteousness. The story has two characters: a religious man and a horrible sinner—a dishonest tax collector. Jesus said that the religious man came to the temple to

pray, looked down at the sinner, and then prayed, "God, I thank you that I am not like other men, extortioners, unjust, adulterers, or even like this tax collector. I fast twice a week; I give tithes of all that I get" (Luke 18:11–12).

The tax collector's prayer was considerably shorter. Jesus said that he wouldn't even look up when he prayed, "God, be merciful to me, a sinner" (Luke 18:13).

Jesus explained that the tax collector found favor in God's eyes (i.e., was justified); the religious man didn't. Then Jesus made an astounding statement. He said, "Everyone who exalts himself will be humbled, but the one who humbles himself will be exalted" (Luke 18:14).

Let's talk about self-righteousness. I only recently found out that I was an expert. You may not know it, but you probably are too. I'm not trying to put down or demean anyone. I'm simply stating a conclusion that's hard to avoid when we think about it. And when we start thinking about it, we begin to realize that self-righteousness is perhaps the most dangerous of all human sins.

In its religious form, self-righteousness is a conviction that one is better than others, morally, spiritually, or theologically. Yet the word has come to connote something more than that: it is the spurious view that one is not like other people. Self-righteous people always think they speak as outsiders. The religious man opened his prayer with an interesting statement: "God, I thank you that I am not like other men" (Luke 18:11).

I didn't always think of self-righteousness as altogether that dangerous. But it is. Let me tell you why, and why it doesn't seem so.

SELF-RIGHTEOUSNESS IS SUBTLE

First, self-righteousness doesn't seem dangerous because it's quite subtle.

I never thought I was self-righteous. In fact, the more self-righteous I became, the less self-righteous I thought I was. Being a religious professional, especially if you have any success at it, can be dangerous in this respect. I know. The churches I served all grew, the books I wrote sold, and the invitations to speak were so numerous that I couldn't even accept a small portion of them. And then there was radio and television. I was, of course, doing it all for God. When others criticized me, I was kind but rather cool. After all, I knew I was God's servant doing God's work, and doing it with a degree of excellence that gave me the sense that I was OK and others weren't.

Paul wrote, "Let anyone who thinks that he stands take heed lest he fall" (1 Corinthians 10:12). I never underlined that verse because I never thought I had to underline it. That's the very nature of self-righteousness: it's a disease that can hardly ever be diagnosed by the person who has it.

I'd like to tell you that I'm cured, but I'm not even close. I am, however, beginning to realize that when I die, I'm not going to even leave a hole—that God doesn't *need* me, and that my sin is so great that I need to be very careful in talking about anyone else's. It took a near nervous breakdown, acute embarrassment, and some honest brothers who forced me to look at myself for me to become the spiritual giant now writing this book. (And if you believe that last part, you need help as much as I need to repent for writing it.)

Let me tell you about my friend Rusty Anderson. Rusty died in an automobile accident a few years ago, and I miss him more than I can express. He and I had been friends for twenty-five years, and in that time we had come to trust each other with our secrets. Rusty loved me and I loved him, and in the context of that love, we spoke truth to each other.

I was once offered a position as president of a prominent educational institution. A number of people I respected told me they were sure I was the man God had called to that place.

Before I tell the rest of this story, there's something you need to know. I ran away from kindergarten, and school was a struggle for the next twenty years. Frankly, it seems to me insane that I'm teaching in a graduate school of theology with people who have their doctorates from places like Oxford, Harvard, Cambridge, and Duke, when I'm not even a nurse.

I remember my brother Ron on his first day of school. Our mother asked him how he liked it, and Ron said that it was OK, but he wasn't going back. When she told him that he didn't have a choice, he cried. I was older than he was and found that funny— but I understood.

Back to the story.

Some well-known and discerning people decided that I should be the president of this academic institution. At first I thought they had lost their minds, but then I started thinking perhaps they were more discerning than I'd first believed. Perhaps I knew more than I thought I knew. Perhaps I had become such an example of integrity, morality, and purity that I was the right person for the job. Perhaps my humility had blinded me to my own insight, my own depth, and all the knowledge I'd acquired over the years. I

moved from surprise to consideration and was quickly moving up to a coronation when Rusty called.

I don't even know how he found out where I was or that I'd been offered the position. Maybe God told him. I was in a hotel room in another city, getting ready to speak at a conference when he called. Rusty didn't even say hello or ask me how the conference was going. "Who do you think you are?" he almost shouted over the phone. "Are you nuts? You can't do this. You will fail at it, embarrass yourself and your family, and destroy the place."

Shortly after Rusty's somewhat less-than-kind call, I phoned the people on the committee and told them to find somebody else.

Self-righteousness is so subtle that sometimes someone who loves you has to step in and tell you the truth.

Are you an obedient Christian, a respected leader, an esteemed expert—and know it? That can be the most dangerous thing in your life right now. If you've failed, been dishonored, or are in sin—and know it—right now, that might just be the best thing you have going for you.

SELF-RIGHTEOUSNESS IS INCREMENTAL

Self-righteousness is also dangerous because it's incremental. It never starts out as self-righteousness; it starts out as something fine and good.

My friends and colleagues Charlie and Ruth Jones (of the ministry Peculiar People) are among the finest and most gifted dramatists I've ever seen. They are a part of the Key Life team when we do Born Free seminars (a seminar on radical grace, infectious joy, and surprising faithfulness) and The Great American

Medicine Show (a fun evening during which grace and freedom are demonstrated, and people don't bring Bibles).

One of their dramatic sketches touches on the story Jesus told in Luke 18 to which I referred above. Their sketch, however, has a twist to it that is profound. The religious man prays his prayer, and the tax collector asks for mercy; then, immediately after that justifying prayer, the forgiven sinner stands up and shouts, "Thank God, I'm a Christian and I'm free!"

Then, during the remainder of the sketch, the new Christian encounters a variety of people who—while mildly pleased with his new status as a believer—try to teach and disciple him. One tells him that it's fine that he's saved but that he isn't really saved until he speaks in tongues. Another recommends the study of Reformed theology. One woman shows him how he should get up in the morning and have devotions. And it goes on and on until that new Christian is burdened down with all it "means" to be a Christian.

> IF YOU'VE FAILED, BEEN DISHONORED, OR ARE IN SIN—AND KNOW IT—RIGHT NOW, THAT MIGHT JUST BE THE BEST THING YOU HAVE GOING FOR YOU.

In the final scene the new Christian enters a church to pray and opens with these words: "Lord, I thank you that I'm not like other men. I get up at four in the morning to have devotions, I speak in tongues, I read theology, I . . ." And the sketch ends.

That is precisely the way it happens. I know. I've lived there a long time. The sin of self-righteousness is always built on the foundation of the good and the pure. The man in Jesus's story really had done all the things he said he had done. He tithed, and

he fasted twice a week. He was an honest and just man. He did not commit adultery. And yet he was not justified in God's sight. If that doesn't scare you, self-righteousness has blinded you.

It does me sometimes.

SELF-RIGHTEOUSNESS IS ADDICTIVE

I am simply amazed at what I will do to appear to be better than others. I suspect it may be one of the reasons I do what I do for a living. When you're a pastor, a seminary professor, or a Bible teacher, people think of you as spiritually a cut above others. I, of course, deny any such assertion. Then people tell me they're impressed with my humility. That makes me feel good, and then I want to fake being even more humble. It's a vicious cycle.

Why do you think the religious man in Jesus's story stood so tall while the tax collector only looked at the ground? It was because the religious man not only *felt* he was more righteous than others, but he also wanted everyone to see him and to *know* he was more righteous than others. The tax collector didn't want anybody to notice his level of righteousness.

The nature of self-righteousness is that it is never a private sin. Most people know (even if they don't admit it to themselves) what they're really like. Jesus warned about practicing one's righteousness in public (Matthew 6:2–6):

> When you give to the needy, sound no trumpet before you, as the hypocrites do in the synagogues and in the streets, that they may be praised by others. Truly, I say to you, they have received their reward. But when you give to the needy, do not let your left hand know what your right hand is doing, so that

your giving may be in secret. And your Father who sees in secret will reward you.

And when you pray, you must not be like the hypocrites. For they love to stand and pray in the synagogues and at the street corners, that they may be seen by others. Truly, I say to you, they have received their reward. But when you pray, go into your room and shut the door and pray to your Father who is in secret. And your Father who sees in secret will reward you.

This morning I went by our local doughnut shop. As I'm writing this, I'm having coffee and a doughnut. Well, I probably should tell the truth. I've had more than one doughnut.

I ate six. OK?

I honestly didn't mean to eat that many doughnuts. I bought the half dozen so I could share them, but nobody came into my study. (It is a fairly safe bet that no one else in the office gets here this early, so maybe there was a volitional element in my eating all of the doughnuts.) I thought I'd have just another one. Before I knew it, the box was empty. I couldn't believe I'd eaten them all.

Do you know why I ate all of the doughnuts? I ate them because I like doughnuts, and the more I eat them, the more I like them. In fact, after I finish this paragraph, I may go back to the doughnut shop and get some more so I can share them with others when they come in later this morning. I might even have one or two more myself.

Jesus talked about the reward for people who give to the needy so others will notice or who pray so others will see. Reward is the stuff of which addictions are made. The more one is rewarded, the more one will do that which brought the reward.

It's called positive reinforcement. Once you get a lot of praise for your beauty, your spirituality, your academic ability, or your righteousness, that praise can become habit forming—and then, in your addiction, you will do almost anything to get more.

People will sell their souls in order to receive praise. I've been there—and still visit on occasion.

SELF-RIGHTEOUSNESS IS INDISCRIMINATE

If you're not religious, you may be intrigued by what I've said about religious folks. Perhaps you're saying to yourself, *Yeah! They're a bunch of hypocrites, and I always knew it.*

Do you know what you just did? You just manifested a self-righteousness that is equal to and perhaps greater than the religious self-righteousness about which I've written.

Once we see how pervasive self-righteousness is, we begin to see it everywhere—in ourselves and almost everywhere else. I challenge you to start observing the world where you live from the perspective of what we've considered in this chapter. You'll be amazed. Instead of seeing politics in terms of left and right, religion in terms of God haters and God lovers, environmentalism in terms of those who love and those who hate the environment, look for the self-righteousness. Instead of seeing issues, look for the ego.

A friend of mine is a consultant to major industry. I asked him how he knew what to do and how to find problems. He said, "I always look for the ego."

Don't define everything in terms of wicked capitalists and naive socialists, those who are at war with Christmas and those who are trying to preserve our best traditions, or those who be-

lieve the Bible and those who don't. Not even in terms of those who stand for God, motherhood, and justice and those who don't. Look for the ego.

In whatever issue being addressed, you'll usually find that the self-righteous quotient is far higher than the concern quotient. You will find criticism of Christian fundamentalists by people whose secular fundamentalism dwarfs the fundamentalism of the people being criticized. Political correctness and the attendant feelings of self-righteousness have their equivalent in religious communities with religious correctness. If you look at victims (the ones who talk the most about justice), you'll find self-righteousness. On the other side, if you look at the people who wield power, they do it with the self-righteous notion that they know better, understand more, and are more informed than others.

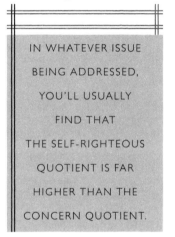

IN WHATEVER ISSUE BEING ADDRESSED, YOU'LL USUALLY FIND THAT THE SELF-RIGHTEOUS QUOTIENT IS FAR HIGHER THAN THE CONCERN QUOTIENT.

And if you look hard enough, you'll find self-righteousness in what I just wrote.

Arrogance, condescension, disdain, contemptuousness, aloofness, and pomposity are everywhere. You'll find it in the good guys, in the bad guys, and in those you think are good guys and bad guys. It's in the religious and the nonreligious. You can find it on both sides of every political and social issue. You'll find it in Washington, in Hollywood, and in your own town.

And if you look hard enough, you'll find it in what I just wrote.

Self-righteousness is so subtle, so incremental, and so addictive

that most folks don't see it in others or in themselves. Once you get it, though, you simply can't get away from it.

My wife, Anna, just read what I wrote above. She said, "That's true except for our dogs, Annie and Thor." She's right. It's in everybody but Thor and Annie. Well, everybody but Thor. Annie is a bit self-righteous with Thor.

Before we look at some ways to fix self-righteousness, let me say one more thing.

SELF-RIGHTEOUSNESS IS DESTRUCTIVE

Self-righteousness makes genuine love almost impossible. My friend Fred Smith says it's impossible to love anybody who has sinned unless you're aware that you are capable of the same sin. Self-righteousness, then—believing ourselves better than others—makes it almost impossible to love, and thus destroys relationships.

One of the most effective prison ministries I know of is Riverside House in Miami. My friend Cleve Bell is an incredible force for good inside the prison system. Prisoners love him because he loves them.

I've often accompanied Cleve and watched him minister to prisoners. Cleve is a great communicator, but that isn't why he's great with prisoners. He's an exciting musician, but that isn't the reason for his effectiveness. He runs an administratively tight ship at Riverside House and at the halfway house it operates, but that's not why Cleve has success with prisoners.

Cleve is good at what he does because he found Christ when he was in prison. Cleve was convicted of first-degree murder, so when he talks to prisoners, he's pretty sure they haven't done any-

thing he's not capable of doing—or has done. Prisoners listen because Cleve loves them, and he can love them because he knows the truth about himself.

Do you ever wonder why Christians are ineffective in evangelistic efforts? It's because most people who aren't believers think of us as angry, condemning, uptight, and judgmental. (I know, I know; they are too, but that isn't the issue. We're talking about us.) Do you know why they think that? Because it is—God help us—a lot truer than most of us would like to admit. And the reason we are that way is because of self-righteousness.

In Calvin Miller's wonderful book *The Singer*, he has woven in statements (outside the movement of the story) that are like little bursts of light. Let me share one of them with you:

Institutions have a poor safety record. The guillotines of orthodoxy keep a clean blade that is always honed for heresy. And somewhere near the place where witches die an unseen sign is posted whose invisible letters clearly read:

WE ARE PROUD TO REPORT 0 WORKING DAYS
LOST TO INJURY OR ACCIDENT.

—THE MANAGEMENT

Let us pray.[1]

We destroy people with our guillotines of self-righteousness.

Perhaps more important than what self-righteousness does to relationships and to the church is what self-righteousness does to our personal relationship with God. The first thing a sane person feels when standing before a holy, righteous, and sovereign God

should be extreme humility. If we don't feel that way, we've been worshiping an idol.

In fact, if you're a Christian and can take communion, can worship and be involved in ministry without wondering why in the world God would forgive, love, and save you, you simply haven't understood the gospel.

It must be hard to be a king, to have won many battles and have people singing your praises, without becoming self-righteous. Ask David. Don't ask him when he's doing fine and wielding power; ask him after his fall—his acts of adultery and murder. This is a hard lesson, but an important one, and maybe even worth the pain: "The sacrifices of God are a broken spirit; a broken and contrite heart, O God, you will not despise" (Psalm 51:17).

I sometimes tell my students a story about a young, arrogant preacher who climbed into the pulpit with his "peacock feathers flying in the breeze." The sermon was a colossal failure, and the young man was devastated. As he walked down from the pulpit, tears of shame filled his eyes. An old saint standing at the foot of the stairs said, not unkindly, "Son, if you had entered the pulpit the way you left it, you might have left the pulpit the way you entered it."

That principle holds true when we enter the throne room of a holy God too.

WHAT'S THE SOLUTION?

I have no idea.

I suppose we could have no convictions, never be obedient, and fail at everything we do. That, however, violates everything

I know about what God would have us be. He wants us to have strong convictions, to be obedient, and to reach for excellence.

I used to counsel single people who wanted to be married that they should place that desire on the altar and give it up to the Lord. When they had sacrificed the desire, perhaps God would give the gift of marriage to them.

My friend Genevieve Caldwell, whose book *First Person, Singular* dealt with the topic of singleness, heard about the advice I was giving. She said, "Steve, I love you, but I just heard what you've been telling single people. That's the dumbest thing I've ever heard. You're telling them that they should relinquish their God-given desire to be married, and when they get to the point where they don't want it anymore, God will give it to them. That's crazy!"

It was crazy—about as crazy as rejecting the gifts God has given you, setting aside the convictions that have come from him, and deliberately failing at the tasks to which he has called you, and then hoping God will give them back to you when you don't want them any longer.

I guess we could pretend we don't have those convictions and those gifts. But that's even crazier than trying to get rid of them. There's already enough pretending, and besides, if you've read this far, you probably can see that we'd only become self-righteous about what we pretend: "Hey, everybody, look at me. You know I'm beautiful, gifted, and bright, but I'm pretending I'm not, and you should praise me for that."

So, what to do? I don't know. I wish I did. I wish I could give you a formula or a ten-step program to deal with self-righteousness. But there is no system. I wish I could teach you a prayer that would

fix it. No prayer like that exists, that I know of. I wish I could tell you how to be really, really humble. But I don't know how.

Wait.

Maybe that *is* the solution. Maybe the solution isn't in anything we *do* but rather in what we *know*. Could it be that the solution isn't in making ourselves less self-righteous but rather in recognizing that we *are* self-righteous?

In fact, the secret to getting better might be to simply recognize how difficult it is to get better, take our self-righteous shortcomings to Jesus, and tell everybody we know that we've been to him—and why we went there.

Oh, and by the way . . . God said I could keep the hybrid if I quit talking about it.

WICKED MEN OBEY FROM FEAR;

GOOD MEN, FROM LOVE.

A<small>RISTOTLE</small>

OBEDIENCE IS A LOT MORE DIFFICULT THAN I THOUGHT IT WAS

Truly, I say to you, the tax collectors and the prostitutes
go into the kingdom of God before you.
MATTHEW 21:31

IS IT RELATIVELY easy for you to be obedient to God and his commandments? If it is, then you can skip this chapter. In fact, go right on to the next one.

I'll wait while you do.

Okay, now that it's just us sinners, can we talk?

When I was younger, I bought into the philosophy that the world was getting better and better, in every way, every day—and that most people were too. And even if they weren't, Christians certainly were. It was called sanctification (i.e., the process whereby a believer, by God's grace and the work of the Holy Spirit, gets better and better), and it was promised by God. Paul said that what God begins in my life, he'll be sure to complete (see Philippians 1:6).

I still believe that. It's just a lot harder than I thought it would be.

That's bad. Well, sort of, but it isn't as bad as you might think. I know I'm supposed to get better, and I know that God would

have me be his obedient and holy child. I also know that I'm not even close.

If you know much about my ministry and what we teach at Key Life, you know that our purpose is to get you and those you love Home with radical freedom, infectious joy, and surprising faithfulness to Christ. The operative words there are *radical, infectious,* and *surprising.* I often teach that your sin can be the best thing in your life—*if you're aware of it*; and your obedience can be the greatest danger in your life—*if you're too aware of it.* Having read the material in the previous chapter, you know that's true because of the horrible danger of self-righteousness.

Now I want to take that teaching a bit further. I want to do something that may surprise you and will almost certainly offend you. Stay with me, though, because what I'm going to say now is the essence of the gospel and, frankly, a lot more helpful than religion. I want to say a good word about sin.

What? A good word about sin?

Yes, but I'm not the first one to do that. Martin Luther once wrote a letter to George Spalatin, a Christian brother who had worked with Luther during the Reformation. Spalatin had a difficult time dealing with overwhelming feelings of guilt over some spurious advice he'd once given. When Luther learned of Spalatin's condition, he wrote to him the following:

> My faithful request and admonition is that you join our company and associate with us, who are real, great, and hard-boiled sinners. You must by no means make Christ to seem paltry and trifling to us, as though He could be our Helper only when we want to be rid from imaginary, nominal, and

childish sins. No, no! That would not be good for us. He must rather be a Savior and Redeemer from real, great, grievous, and damnable transgressions and iniquities, yea, from the very greatest and most shocking sins; to be brief, from all sins added together in a grand total. . . .

Dr. Staupitz comforted me on a certain occasion when I was a patient in the same hospital and suffering the same affliction as you, by addressing me thus: Aha! you want to be a painted sinner and, accordingly, expect to have in Christ a painted Savior. You will have to get used to the belief that Christ is a real Savior and you a real sinner. For God is neither jesting nor dealing in imaginary affairs, but He was greatly and most assuredly in earnest when He sent His own Son into the world and sacrificed Him for our sakes.[1]

I like to sin. If I didn't like to sin, I wouldn't sin. In fact, one of the most difficult things I do as a Christian leader is try to persuade people not to do what they obviously would like to do. When the bank robber was asked why he robbed banks, he said, "Because that's where the money is." Duh. Sin is attractive, and we sin because we like it.

Other than that (and that only sounds positive), though, there are some positive things one could say about sin.

KNOWING GOD

If it weren't for sin, I would never have known God.

When Luther made his oft-quoted comment to the effect that one who sins ought to "sin boldly," he was not saying that sin is a good thing but rather that Jesus was a bold Savior. If your sin is

small, the savior who saves you will be rather small. In fact, your small savior will not be Jesus but a substitute. After all, you won't need the real thing.

However, the intensity of a problem can be measured by the intensity of the solution. In other words, the bigger the problem, the bigger its solution must be. If our sins had been little and our needs small, God could have sent a book. But he sent his Son. That ought to give us some idea of how big the problem is. As I pointed out before, when Jesus's disciples were asked why he spent so much time with sinners, Jesus explained that he was a physician and had come for the "sick" people—not for those who were well (see Matthew 9:10–13).

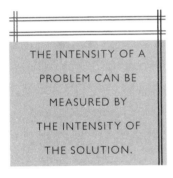

THE INTENSITY OF A PROBLEM CAN BE MEASURED BY THE INTENSITY OF THE SOLUTION.

Let me tell you about my lawyer friend John Longino. He moved to the mountains of north Georgia to escape the fast track he'd been on in Miami. John had been on the fast track because he's good at what he does. For a number of years, John was the corporate attorney for some major companies and was much in demand as a trial lawyer. He finally made enough money to move to the mountains, and that's where he is now.

John is smart, gifted, articulate, and mean . . . really mean. Don't get me wrong—he loves Jesus. In fact, in the national park near his home, John often takes doughnuts and coffee to the campers on Sunday mornings and leads a worship service for them. If you first saw John doing that, you'd be surprised to see him in court. There John doesn't seem at all the same nice, mild-mannered, spiritual person who would conduct a worship service

in the woods. When John is in court, he's one of the most effective advocates I've ever seen.

At Key Life we've owned a certain 800 number (1-800-KEY LIFE) for several years. It's a long story, and I'll spare you the details, but while two other companies (which we had once hired to collect order information from calls to that number) were in litigation, one of them stole our number. That's right, they just took it, turned it off, and closed it down.

I tried to talk to AT&T about getting the number back, but they said (firmly but nicely) that we had lost it, and their policy was not to make a number available again for six months. Even then, we would simply be one among others who wanted that number. That meant that Key Life was in serious trouble: we get thousands of calls each month through that number.

So I called John, and he went to work.

John eventually found out the name and private phone number of the corporate attorney at AT&T. "I'm getting ready to bring the mother of all lawsuits against you guys," John told the attorney. "And not only that; I'm going to make a ton of money doing it. However, I work for these crazy Christians in Florida, and they say I have to talk to you before I sue."

That afternoon AT&T gave us back the number.

I could tell you a bunch of stories about John and about his kindness to me. One time, as we sat on his front porch in the mountains, John said, "Brown, I love for you to get into trouble." I asked him why, and he said, "I love you, and the only time I see you is when you're in trouble."

Jesus says sort of the same thing to me. Did you ever think that grace (i.e., God's unmerited favor) is attracted to sin? That's what

the apostle Paul said: "The law came in to increase the trespass, but where sin increased, grace abounded all the more" (Romans 5:20). In other words, if it weren't for my sin, I never would have known Jesus. And while I hate my sin, seeing it makes me thankful for my closest friend and my King, Jesus Christ. If not for my sin, I never would have known him.

LOVING OTHERS

If it weren't for sin, I never would have loved you, and you never would have loved me.

Well, you probably don't know me, and I probably don't know you; but if we knew each other, the only way we could love each other would be because of our sin.

Do you remember when Jesus washed his disciples' feet (John 13)? During his last supper with them, to their astonishment, Jesus took a towel and did what only servants were called to do: he washed the guests' dirty feet. As he did, he talked about being made clean. Then, when he had finished, Jesus said something important:

> Do you understand what I have done to you? You call me Teacher and Lord, and you are right, for so I am. If I then, your Lord and Teacher, have washed your feet, you also ought to wash one another's feet. For I have given you an example, that you also should do just as I have done to you. Truly, truly, I say to you, a servant is not greater than his master, nor is a messenger greater than the one who sent him. (John 13:12–16)

The dean of our seminary chapel, Reggie Kidd, decided to devote one of the weekly services to a foot-washing ceremony. When he told me about it, I said something spiritual, like, "I'll

participate in that kind of service when a hot place freezes over! Hope you guys have a really good service. I won't be there."

I'm driven by guilt, though. As the day approached, I decided I ought to go. I carefully washed my feet that morning and put on clean socks, and I went. Do you know what happened? It was one of the most emotionally moving and profound worship services I've ever attended. You have no idea what faculty washing each other's feet and faculty washing students' feet does to a professor. You have no idea what students washing each other's feet or students washing faculty members' feet does to a student. At the end of the service, we all came down to the front of that big chapel and held hands while we sang:

> Amazing Grace! how sweet the sound,
> That saved a wretch like me!
> I once was lost, but now am found,
> Was blind, but now I see.

Why did Jesus wash his disciples' feet? They were dirty (a metaphor for sin). Why did Jesus tell us to wash one another's feet? They are dirty. In the context of our human contact, who washes dirty feet? People with dirty feet wash the dirty feet of others. Therein is the profound truth about sin: Love in response to goodness, perfection, and obedience isn't love; it's a reward. Only those who don't deserve it can be loved, and only those who have been loved can love.

Discovering Joy

If it weren't for sin, I never would have discovered joy.

Earlier I referred to a Luther quote on sinning boldly. Now

let me give you the entire quote. Luther wrote to his friend and colleague Philipp Melanchthon, "God does not save people who are only fictitious sinners. Be a sinner and sin boldly but believe and rejoice in Christ even more boldly for he is victorious over sin, death, and the world."[2]

> IF NOT FOR MY SIN, I NEVER WOULD HAVE COME TO KNOW JESUS . . . OR LOVE OTHERS . . . OR EXPERIENCE THE JOY AND RELEASE OF ACCEPTANCE.

I asked a friend how he was this morning, and he responded, "I'm doing so good that I think God has overlooked me. I think if he had not overlooked me, I would have been dead from the lightning bolt he would have thrown at me." My friend then told me that he never wanted to be like Job, about whom God said to Satan, "Have you seen my servant Job?"—and then some very bad things happened. "Steve, I want to be obedient and stuff, but not that obedient. I prefer God to overlook me."

Then my friend said, "But he hasn't overlooked me, has he? He has even numbered the hairs on my head, and he continues to bless me, to be fond of me, and to forgive me. Go figure."

He's got it, and "it" is the source of true joy. I don't care what you say about me, how much you dislike me, or whether you want to be with me, because I have a Friend who is quite fond of me. Of course, that fondness is the result of the Cross; nevertheless, it's genuine and a source of great joy.

Jesus said that the kingdom of heaven is like "treasure hidden in a field, which a man found and covered up. Then in his *joy* he goes and sells all that he has and buys that field" (Matthew 13:44, emphasis added). If it weren't for my sin, I never would

have known the joy, the release, and the pleasure of knowing that I'm accepted and acceptable—no matter what I've done, no matter where I've been.

Do you remember where Jesus found you? I remember where he found me. I was living in an apartment near Boston where, from my front porch, I could see the bay on my left and the ocean on my right. I remember the money I made and the beautiful wife God had given me. I remember the baby (our first) we were expecting. I also remember standing on that porch and crying like a baby. I was miserable, empty, lonely, and sinful. And my life had little meaning.

Then Jesus came. Just thinking about where I was when he found me is a source of great joy. If not for my sin, I never would have come to know him . . . or love others . . . or experience the joy and release of acceptance.

Hating Sin

I don't want to go too far down this road without also saying that, not only am I thankful for my sin, but I also hate my sin. My friend Tony Campolo is a regular on our talk show. We call him our "go-to liberal"—and he is that, at least politically. Tony is also one of the most compassionate and unconditionally loving people I've ever met. Tony, as you may know, was a friend of Bill Clinton's (who probably wouldn't be my best friend), and he has reached out to the gay community with love and without compromising the truth of what the Bible says (which is something I'm not sure I could do).

Last week Tony was on our show as we discussed televangelist Jim Bakker. Shortly after Bakker had been exposed for some sinful

behavior, Tony had preached a sermon titled "I Am Jim Bakker." Tony's wife, Peggy, told me then that she wished Tony hadn't done that, because "everybody now thinks he's messing around."

On our show I mentioned what Peggy had said, and Tony responded with something I've thought about ever since: "Steve, do you know how people say that one should love the sinner and hate the sin? That's not what my Bible says. My Bible says that we should love the sinner and hate our own sin."

I agree with Tony. I gave you an "argument for sin." But that's not all: I hate my sin. I really do. I'm not a good person, and I've given you sufficient evidence of that in this book. However, you probably don't know many people who want to please God more than I want to please him. When I thought my sin would make God angry, I was rebellious and angry with him. But when I found out how much he loves me, I was drawn to that love. In the light of his love, I see things about myself that embarrass me, that offend me, and that cause me to cringe. I'm not good, but I want to be.

OBEDIENCE AND HOW TO GET THERE

And that brings me to the main question: If obedience is so hard, how can we be obedient? How can we get better?

In the previous chapter, on self-righteousness, I ended with a suggestion for becoming less self-righteous—for how to get better. That truth is a powerful weapon against all of our sin and disobedience: the secret to getting better might be to simply recognize how difficult it is to get better, to go to Jesus with it, and to tell everybody we know that we've been to him and why we went there.

One of the most radical passages in the entire Bible is found in Luke 7. In that chapter Luke tells about a dinner party Jesus

attended. It took place at the house of Simon, a Pharisee—a very religious and good person. I suppose the people at the dinner were all religious and good people like Simon. The dinner party was interrupted by a commotion—a prostitute had "crashed" the party because she wanted to see Jesus. Jesus treated her with kindness: he did not condemn her but rather forgave her sins and then held her up as an example of love.

For those of us who want to get better but are finding out how difficult that really is, this story is instructive. If you haven't yet discovered how difficult obedience is, then you haven't tried very hard to be obedient. I've walked with Jesus for a long time now, and sometimes (not all the time, or even most of the time, but sometimes) I find myself following closely in his footsteps. When I do, though, it isn't for the reasons you may think.

Let's consider some things Luke's story reveals about the prostitute's going to Jesus, about Jesus's response, and about what these things mean for us.

The prostitute in the story knew she was a sinner and ran to Jesus. Yet when we know we're sinners, too often the last place we want to go is to him.

Luke says "a woman who had lived a sinful life brought an alabaster flask of ointment, and standing behind him at his feet, weeping, she began to wet his feet with her tears and wiped them with the hair of her head and kissed his feet and anointed them with the ointment" (Luke 7:37–38). This woman risked embarrassment, ridicule, and condemnation because she saw something about Jesus that most of us forget: he welcomes sinners.

A lot of people have given us a terrible misrepresentation of God. Parents use him to scare children into obedience ("I may not

see you, but God sees you!"). We use his anger at and hatred of sin to gain power and to manipulate others. We speak of God as a "consuming fire"—and that's true—but we forget to tell the rest of the story. We self-righteously talk about hell with an attitude of, "You'll get yours, and I'm glad!"

But don't forget that the Word (which was God) "became flesh and dwelt among us . . . full of grace and truth" (John 1:14). If you forget that, trying to be obedient will kill you.

At the risk of repeating myself over and over again, remember that even if you never get any better, God won't love you any less than he does right now. And even if you get a lot better, God won't love you any more than he does right now. But if you don't understand that, you'll never get better, because only those who know that God will love them even if they don't get better will ever get any better.

The prostitute didn't go to Jesus to get better; she went to Jesus to be loved by the one man who would love her unconditionally—without wanting anything from her in return.

The prostitute not only knew that she was a sinner and ran to Jesus, but she didn't care who noticed. And we care way too much.

One of the interesting things about this incident is that Jesus seems almost to have wanted to embarrass the prostitute. A kinder man, we suppose, would have excused himself and gone outside to talk with the woman. A more compassionate man, we suppose, would have talked to her in private and would have helped her. That's not what Jesus did. He pointed her out. In fact, Jesus turned to his host, Simon, and asked, "Do you see this woman?" (Luke 7:44).

What's with that?

I think Jesus pointed out the prostitute because he knew she

wouldn't mind being pointed out. One of the most surprising things about the whole episode is the fact that she would crash a Pharisee's dinner party at all. I don't know about you, but if I were a prostitute, the last party I would want to attend would be one at the house of the chairman of the board of deacons.

If you were sleeping with your girlfriend, no longer liked her, and wanted to sleep with someone else, to whom would you go for advice, Dr. Laura (Schlessinger)? You'd have to be crazy. I don't know if you've ever heard her popular talk show, but I can't listen when someone like that calls her. I want to say to the caller, "Are you out of your mind? She's going to kill you." As you may know, Dr. Laura af-

ONLY THOSE WHO KNOW THAT GOD WILL LOVE THEM EVEN IF THEY DON'T GET BETTER WILL EVER GET ANY BETTER.

firms traditional and biblical values, clearly calls for responsibility, does not abide idiots easily, and will call it like it is—as in, "You're a self-absorbed cretin who's thinking of nobody but yourself!"

For most of us, this prostitute's going to Jesus would seem like a promiscuous and arrogant teenager going to Dr. Laura. But that's not the case. The prostitute wasn't arrogant. She was a moral failure, her life was a mess, and Jesus was all that mattered.

In Don Miller's wonderful book *Blue Like Jazz*, he tells of some Christian students on a secular campus who set up a confessional booth at a college fair. No, they weren't taking confessions . . . they were giving them. When a student came into the booth, wondering what in the world was going on, he or she was asked to

sit down in the confessional chair. Then the Christians confessed their sins to the person in the chair![3]

That's so astounding and so good that I can hardly stand it. It may also point to a major secret to obedience: being authentic about our own sin. When we care too much about what other people think, we start pretending we're something they might like. And when we pretend too much, we end up discovering that it's almost impossible to become what we fake.

In chapter eight we talked about the tax collector in Jesus's story who wouldn't even look up and could only pray, "God, be merciful to me, a sinner!" (Luke 18:13). We saw that the repentant tax collector was justified in God's eyes. Now let me tell you something else that happened. By way of commentary on his story, Jesus said, "Everyone who exalts himself will be humbled, but the one who humbles himself will be exalted" (Luke 18:14).

What does that mean? It means that authenticity and honesty (as in confession without caring who knows) is a source of great help in our efforts to be obedient. James wrote, "Confess your sins to one another and pray for one another, that you may be healed" (James 5:16). The great and important supernatural principle is this: honesty about who we are makes us better than we are. After all, the Holy Spirit's power, like a stream, only runs downhill.

So, if you've discovered that obedience is more difficult than you thought it would be, go tell someone. Tell him or her who you really are, what you've really done, and how often you've been disobedient. You'll be embarrassed. But you'll be better too.

Jesus didn't tell the prostitute in the story to get better. Yet we think that's all he does.

If you're really religious, then you're not going to like what Jesus said next: "'Her sins, which are many, are forgiven—for she loved much. But he who is forgiven little, loves little.' And he said to her, 'Your sins are forgiven.' Then those who were at table with him began to say among themselves, 'Who is this, who even forgives sins?' And he said to the woman, 'Your faith has saved you; go in peace'" (Luke 7:47–50).

Go in peace?! What about discipleship, joining a good synagogue, and studying the Scriptures? What about obedience?

Listen: Jesus didn't tell the prostitute to be better, because he didn't have to tell her to be better. Her sin was not the issue; her love for Jesus was the only issue. Jesus knew she would walk the walk, or at least walk it better than she had before.

Christians are too often obsessed with sin. You know it's true. An outsider would think that it's all we care about—being pure and holy. If an unbeliever is asked about what we do, he or she will probably say something like, "Those Christians are miserable and won't be happy until everyone else is miserable too." And they may have a point. I remember a man telling me, after I had talked to him about Christ, "No thanks! I'm already guilty enough—I don't need any more guilt."

The truth is, almost everything of any importance is found while looking for something else. You can't chase peace, love, or happiness. Those things result from pursuing, or in relation to, something else. The same is true with obedience. I've decided to accept the fact that obedience is harder than I thought

it was, and because it is, it's going to be slow in coming. I don't like it, but it's true. So if I can't get better quickly, then what am I to do?

I'm going to Jesus. I'm going to him because he doesn't care how I come. My purity, my goodness, and my obedience aren't the issues. My guilt, I believe, has only one purpose, and that isn't to make me better; it's to send me to him, the only one who loves me, forgives me, and will accept me no matter where I've been, what I've done, or where I'm going.

One other thing about this story—it's a side road, but it's important nonetheless:

I believe Simon became a follower of Jesus because of the prostitute.

Simon had a question, but he never asked it: "When the Pharisee who had invited him saw this, he *said to himself,* 'If this man were a prophet, he would have known who and what sort of woman this is who is touching him, for she is a sinner'" (Luke 7:39, emphasis added). Then notice the next words: "And *Jesus answering said to him . . .*" (Luke 7:40, emphasis added).

Do you see it? Simon never asked his question aloud, and yet Jesus answered it. How do you think we know Simon asked that question if he never voiced it? Where did we get that detail of the story if no one ever heard Simon's question?

From only one person: Simon. I submit that the only possible reason Simon would have talked about it would be as a part of his testimony about Jesus. I can see him, months after that incident, telling his friends—perhaps during a worship service in the early church or in some kind of public forum—"Hey, let me tell you about Jesus. One time when he was at my house for dinner, he read my mind. Is Jesus great or what?"

Obedience really is more difficult than I thought it was. But God's grace is a lot bigger than I thought it was too. Again, the secret to getting better is simply to recognize how difficult it is to get better, go to Jesus with it, and tell everybody we know that we've been to him and why we went there.

When we do that, not only do we get better . . . everybody else does too.

LOVE IS INDESTRUCTIBLE;

ITS HOLY FLAME FOREVER BURNETH;

FROM HEAVEN IT CAME,

TO HEAVEN RETURNETH.

ROBERT SOUTHEY

LOVE IS A LOT STRONGER THAN I THOUGHT IT WAS

Above all, keep loving one another earnestly,
since love covers a multitude of sins.

I PETER 4:8

A NUMBER OF years ago I spoke at a conference in a rather large convention center. I was the preacher/teacher for the plenary sessions in the auditorium, and running concurrently in another part of the center was a conference for young people whose parents were attending the larger conference. The teacher for the youth conference was a prominent professor. He was (and is) a brilliant scholar, a profound thinker, and a much-respected Christian leader . . . but, frankly, in spite of all his gifts, he had no business leading a conference for teenagers.

When I first learned that this man would lead the youth conference, I wondered who had invited him and what they were smoking when they did. I thought, *Those teenagers are going to eat him alive!* I didn't believe there was any way he'd make it through the week.

I often tell youth pastors and parents of teenagers that, if they die while doing either, they get a free pass to heaven. In fact, they won't even be asked about Jesus when they get to heaven. The

angels will just say, "You poor dear, you come right on in." It's a joke, of course, but people laugh because they know that teenagers are a tough audience. The teens at this conference were not the "nice" ones who operate the rides at Disney World or who usher on Youth Sunday in your church. These were teenagers with black fingernails, purple hair, rings in funny places, and clothes that have been designed to keep adults away.

Anyone who speaks at a teen conference had better be charismatic and exciting. And I don't want to be unkind, but this man was anything but charismatic and exciting. In a contest of which was most exciting, listening to this man speak or watching paint dry, watching paint dry would win every time.

Anyway, on the final day of the conference, everybody—teenagers and adults—came together to talk about the event, to praise God for what he had done, and to pray together. Some nice things were said about me during that final session, but what was said about this dull and boring professor was "over the top." A steady parade of teenagers got up and talked about how God had touched their lives, about what their conference leader had taught them, and about what was going to be different when they returned home. Many of them wept as they told how this man had deeply affected them.

The next year both this professor and I were invited back to speak at that same conference. I determined to find out his secret for working with teenagers. So toward the end of the conference, when I was on a break, I sat at the back of the youth auditorium, watched, and listened. The man was as dull as I thought he would be—pedantic, boring, and long-winded. I had just about decided

that there was no accounting for taste and got up to leave when something happened that I'll never forget.

This professor began to cry. In the middle of his presentation, he got emotional and lost it. And when it happened, he turned his back on his audience. (That's *not* a good communication technique.) With his back to the teenagers, the professor took out his handkerchief and wiped the tears from his eyes. I noticed that while this professor wept, there wasn't a single smart comment, no derision, no snickers. It was as quiet as a tomb—the kind of quietness that suggests awe.

When the professor pulled himself together, he turned back to face the teenagers, and this is what he said:

"I'm so very sorry. I hate it when I do that.

"I've been spending a lot of time with you young people. I've been listening. You've been kind enough to tell me your secrets, to confess your sins, and to describe the hard places in your lives. It's a great privilege and honor that you would trust me with that. As I promised, I've been praying for you and thinking about you a lot.

"And, no, I'm not going to tell anybody what you told me . . . as long as you're nice to me."

Everybody laughed.

The man continued: "But just then, while I was teaching, I couldn't think about what I was teaching; I started thinking about you. I hate for this conference to come to an end, not because I like conferences, but because of you. You've gotten under my skin and into my heart, and I will continue to think about you and pray for you long after this conference is over. I want you to know that I love you, and deeply.

"But I don't love you nearly as much as God loves you. Try to remember that."

That was it! That was his secret. Love trumped power, charismatic speaking, authority, and skill. Love trumped everything else.

It always does, you know.

I didn't know for sure what it was that I was witnessing then. That conference happened a lot of years ago, but even then I knew I'd seen something authentic and powerful, maybe even supernatural. I saw tears I didn't expect and power I couldn't explain.

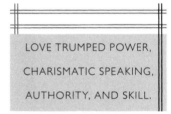

LOVE TRUMPED POWER, CHARISMATIC SPEAKING, AUTHORITY, AND SKILL.

I had seen a profound love—both human and supernatural. I might have been able to name it then, but I didn't understand it. I understand it better now . . . because I've been loved longer. A degree of wisdom comes with long and enduring love. Love sees things the mind can miss.

One of the great love stories of history is that of Martin Luther and Katharina Von Bora. As a monk, Luther had pledged not to marry. The more he studied, the more Luther realized that marriage was a gift from God . . . but only for others. Certainly not for himself.

When Luther finally did decide to marry, it was not for love. He wrote to a friend, "The rumor of my marriage is correct. I cannot deny my father the hope of progeny, and I had to confirm my teaching at a time when many are so timid."[1] Luther married to confirm his teaching, to irritate his adversaries, and to give his parents grandchildren. Those aren't the most romantic reasons for

marriage, and it's surprising that Katharina (or any other woman, for that matter) would have him, with a mindset like that.

But Katharina loved Luther, and in time Luther found the wonder of love in the arms of his "beloved Katie." He wrote, "I would not exchange my Katie for Paris or all of France, for Venice or all of Italy, for God has given her to me and has given me to her. . . . There is no sweeter union."[2]

It took me a long time to discover that love is a lot stronger than I thought it was. I was so busy practicing my religion, getting my theology right, teaching the truth, and working for God that I almost missed love.

I INCORRECTLY DEFINED LOVE

I almost missed love because I didn't understand what it was.

I suspect you've heard the often-quoted words of C. S. Lewis on the various forms of love.[3] Lewis wrote about four Greek words for love, each meaning something slightly different (*storge*—affection, *philia*—friendship, *eros*—romantic love, and *agape*—charity). Lewis explained that agape love is from God. Without it, the other kinds of love become distorted.

In 1 Corinthians 13 Paul wrote that agape love is patient, kind, and without envy or boastfulness. It isn't arrogant or rude, and it doesn't insist on its own way. Love isn't irritable or resentful, and it rejoices in truth. Love, Paul went on to say, bears, believes, hopes, and endures all things . . . and it lasts forever.

I find Lewis's comments on love helpful, and I'm moved by Paul's great chapter on love. I've often taught on the "concept" of love, defining it in terms of what I had learned. The problem with

propositional truth about love, though, is that it's not love. It's like the difference between reading a book on lions and meeting one, or between looking at an advertisement for Florida oranges and eating one.

The song says we're "looking for love in all the wrong places." I suppose there's some truth to that, but it would be more correct to say that we fail to see love in those "wrong places." Love is everywhere, but we can easily miss it. You have to have experienced the real thing before you can see it in the "wrong places." As with the professor I described at that conference, love was there—but I missed it.

I once saw love in a prostitute's weeping for another prostitute who had been abused by a client. I watched love as a gay man nursed his partner, who was dying of AIDS. A friend of mine told me about love when he went to bars because that's where his friends were, and he felt more comfortable there than in church. You can find love in a cult where doctrines are wrong and at a party where drunks are cursing. You can find love in a racist as he watches his child being born. You can find love in a Muslim mosque where a father weeps for his son, who just blew himself up thinking he was doing it for God. I've seen love in a liberal church that was feeding the poor and in a fundamentalist church that forgave and restored a sinful preacher.

Sometimes love is masked by harshness, lust, and booze; but if you know where to look, you can find it. Love hangs out in brothels, churches, bars, and missions. Love is in the homes of the rich and of the poor, in the smoke-filled back rooms of the powerful, as well as the smoke-filled back rooms of the unpowerful. Love is sometimes emotional and sometimes unemotional. Love is sometimes harsh and sometimes gentle. Love can be a mighty river or

a gentle stream; but mostly, love hangs out in the "wrong" places . . . or else it isn't love.

What matters isn't *where* you go to find love; it's what you're looking for. It's not really the wrong place that causes you to miss love but the wrong definition. It's not what's in your head but what's in your heart.

If you can't define it with the experience of your heart, you can miss love. I know.

Love Is Subtle

I almost missed love because love is quite subtle.

Hosea is one of the great love books in the Bible. It's the story of how Hosea—a religious professional—is called to marry a prostitute by the name of Gomer. Needless to say, that's not the best career move for a preacher. (Just try introducing that new wife to the deacons or the Ladies Aid Society at your church.) But Hosea was an obedient servant of God and did what God called him to do. He married Gomer. Three children were born into that marriage.

Then she left.

I guess Gomer remembered the "good times," the parties, and the gifts. For whatever reason, she left her husband and went back to her old life. Hosea was devastated. I can only imagine he was in the process of healing when God came to him a second time. God told Hosea to go back into the red-light district of the city to find his wife, who, having hit some hard times, had sold herself into slavery. God instructed Hosea to bring Gomer back home and to love her. And Hosea was obedient to God.

As I mentioned in chapter four, Donald Barnhouse, great

Philadelphia preacher of another generation, used to say that all of life illustrates Bible doctrine. He wasn't the first preacher to understand that. Hosea understood it as well and used his experience to illustrate an incredible truth about a God who loves those who are unlovely. God loved the "prostitute" (his unfaithful people) with a love that would never let go—even though, like Gomer, they certainly didn't deserve it. Consider Hosea's wonderful description, a powerful image of subtle love: "When Israel was a child, I loved him, and out of Egypt I called my son. The more they were called, the more they went away; they kept sacrificing to the Baals and burning offerings to idols. Yet it was I who taught Ephraim to walk; I took them up by their arms, but they did not know that I healed them" (Hosea 11:1–3).

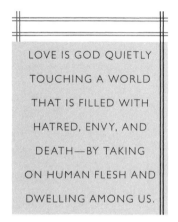

LOVE IS GOD QUIETLY TOUCHING A WORLD THAT IS FILLED WITH HATRED, ENVY, AND DEATH—BY TAKING ON HUMAN FLESH AND DWELLING AMONG US.

They didn't know?

That's the nature of love. When love comes with power and authority—with flags waving and swords swinging—it isn't love. Love never chases, it woos. Love never demands, it requests. Love never shouts, it whispers. That's why love is so easy to miss.

I have a problem with the Christmas holiday. And, no, it isn't because of the commercialism, the "pagans'" war against it, or Christ's being taken out of it. I have no quarrel with merchants making a living and being able to pay their employees. I don't mind unbelievers enjoying Christmas. I don't expect them to put Christ in Christmas. I love the gigantic and impressive Christmas spectaculars and the performances of Handel's *Messiah*. When the

"Hallelujah Chorus" is sung, I stand because I can't help it. I love the Christmas sermons and the decorated churches.

What really worries me is that the love that came down at Christmas was much quieter and more subtle than all that. I think Christmas bothers me because it's too loud, too clear, and too manipulative. Love is far more subtle than that.

"God so loved the world," the Bible says, "that he gave his only Son" (John 3:16). Love revealed itself in a stable and completed itself on crossbeams between two thieves. Love came to a small town and to a people who were conquered and weak. Love is easy to miss because love is not a thing; it's a person. Love is God quietly touching a world that is filled with hatred, envy, and death—by taking on human flesh and dwelling among us.

Jesus said, "Greater love has no one than this, that someone lays down his life for his friends. You are my friends. . . . No longer do I call you servants, for the servant does not know what his master is doing; but I have called you friends" (John 15:13–15).

We all live in the "wrong places." After all, it's the only place we can live. And love is there, but it's not until you've been loved by God that you see it.

But I'm getting ahead of myself.

I DIDN'T THINK I NEEDED LOVE

I also almost missed love because I didn't think I needed it.

Paul said that a person who's doing fine should be careful, because it's easy to fall (see 1 Corinthians 10:12). I did fine for only so long before the wheels came off my wagon.

The world in which we live is extremely dangerous. (More to come on that in the next chapter.) It's unforgiving, uncaring, and

harsh. We encounter so much pain, death, and sin in the world that sometimes I can hardly stand it. The world is far more dangerous than I thought it was when I was young.

Forgive me if I sound glib. I'm not trying to provide answers to the problem of pain and evil. I've already told you that I don't have the answers. But I do know one of them. The world in which we live is the only kind of world where, when it gets dark enough, you can see the light. It's the kind of world that will cause you to look for something better. The prayer that falls from the lips of those who have felt pain, been brushed by death, and struggled with sin is both honest and powerful: "God, the ocean is so very big. My boat is so very small. Have mercy on me."

When my father was dying, his physician said to him, "Mr. Brown, you have about three months to live. We're going to pray, and then I'm going to tell you something more important than what I just told you." They prayed, and then my father's doctor told him about Jesus and Jesus's love.

I almost missed the experience of love because I was doing fine, thank you very much. It was only when I was no longer doing fine—when my sin had almost overwhelmed me and when I grew sick of the lies and the pretense, realizing just how truly helpless I was—that I found love. Or, perhaps, love found me. When it did, I realized I had always known there ought to be a God like that somewhere.

I Thought I Had to Earn Love

I almost missed love because, once I knew I needed it, I thought I had to earn it.

Love, if it's earned, is not love; it's reward. Love, in order to be love, must be directed toward one who is unlovely. The Bible says,

"While we were still weak, at the right time Christ died for the ungodly. For one will scarcely die for a righteous person—though perhaps for a good person one would dare even to die—but God shows his love for us in that while we were still sinners, Christ died for us" (Romans 5:6–8).

Everything we know about the world suggests that if we work hard enough, we'll be rewarded. In school we did our homework, studied for tests, and were attentive . . . and got good grades. At work, if we perform well, we get bonuses, compliments, and promotions. As children, if we were nice, we got praised; and when we weren't nice, we got punished.

I know, I know. It doesn't always work that way, and things aren't always fair. But we all know that it ought to work that way, and more often than not it does. The golfer knows that, while practice may not make perfect, it does make him better. The hardworking teacher, doctor, or lawyer knows the rewards of that hard work.

It stands to reason, then, that God's rewards are given to those who work hard at being obedient, religious, and pure. Right?

No! That lie is from the pit of hell and smells like smoke. Therein is the reason so many miss God's love. As I mentioned before, the church is the one organization in the world where the only qualification for membership is not being qualified. The less qualified you are, the more qualified you become.

Now, that's crazy. And it would make us more comfortable if God got it right. In fact, the church—God have mercy on us— has been working hard at trying to remedy God's error. Jesus came for the sick . . . but if you get well, he'll like you a whole lot more. Jesus came for the sinners . . . but if you want to be blessed by

God's love, repent of your sin and get rid of it. Jesus came for the outcasts, the rebels, and the lost . . . but we, in our effort to fix God's mistake, turn them away.

In teaching my seminary students how to preach, I start by exposing a number of religious myths for what they are—myths. The biggest myth is that they shouldn't preach sermons they aren't living. In other words, they have to walk the talk. A preacher *should* be a model of love and grace, no question about it. A leader in the church *should* be following Christ. But if a preacher only preaches what he lives, then his sermons will be very short—and he'll only preach once or twice a year.

Even more importantly, that preacher will give credence to the lie that God had more than one perfect preacher. And he'll fail to communicate the most important and difficult truth of the Christian faith. As preacher Paul put it, "The saying is trustworthy and deserving of full acceptance, that Christ Jesus came into the world to save sinners, of whom I am the foremost" (1 Timothy 1:15).

My friend Jack Miller taught that the most repentant person in the congregation ought to be the preacher. In fact, without repentance, there is no power in what is taught. That point is profound, because anything less suggests that if one is good enough, one can be loved by God.

I believed that lie for a long time. I still struggle with it. But when I believe that lie, I miss the incredible and unconditional love of God.

LOVE IS STRONG

One other thing must be said: Love sometimes appears weak because it's so subtle that it whispers, and because people keep trying

to earn it and therefore never experience it. But love is not weak; love is a lot stronger than you think it is.

Paul wrote that three things will last forever: "Faith, hope, and love abide, these three; but the greatest of these is love" (1 Corinthians 13:13).

Love is incredibly strong because once you experience it, you can never "un-experience" it. You cannot stop love, and you cannot keep it from re-creating itself in you.

John the apostle wrote, "We have come to know and to believe the love that God has for us. God is love, and whoever abides in love abides in God, and God abides in him. By this is love perfected with us, so that we may have confidence for the day of judgment" (1 John 4:16–17).

LOVE IS INCREDIBLY STRONG BECAUSE ONCE YOU EXPERIENCE IT, YOU CAN NEVER "UN-EXPERIENCE" IT.

Paul wrote that when God starts something in the life of the believer, he will bring it to completion (see Philippians 1:6). What that means is this: what God begins, he always completes; so just the fact of its beginning is the absolute promise of its completion. That, of course, includes love. Paul also said that the love of Christ controlled him (see 2 Corinthians 5:14).

When John wrote about the incarnation of God in Christ, he said, "In him was life, and the life was the light of men. The light shines in the darkness, and the darkness has not overcome it" (John 1:4–5). "No one has ever seen God; the only God, who is at the Father's side, he has made him known" (John 1:18). And John is the one who told us that "God is love" (1 John 4:16).

At the coming of Christ, love was let loose in the world . . .

and nobody can stop it. God—the awesome and sovereign creator and sustainer of all that is—is love. God is not loving; he *is* love. God does not act in a loving way; he *is* love. God is not sometimes loving and sometimes not; he *is* love. The darkness has no reality of its own; it is only defined in terms of the absence of light. The Light has come, and everything that is dark will be destroyed in its wake.

Someone has said that as long as there are exams, there will be prayer in public schools. That's true, but let me tell you something else that's true: as long as there are sinful people who want to be forgiven, marginalized people who want to be accepted, frightened people who want hope, anxious people who want peace, and dying people who want life, there will be love—God's love, available to those in need.

I once heard a preacher say to a group of people, who were not altogether happy about his being there, that he loved them.

"Yeah, what do you want from us?" a man called out from the back row.

"I don't want anything from you. I have everything I need. I just want you to know that I'm going to be your friend even if you don't want me to be your friend, and I'm going to love you even if you don't want me to love you."

The people were quiet. What do you say in the face of that kind of love?

That's the message God has given to those who will receive it.

God has also called those who know him to that same message—to live and to give in love. Only those who have been loved can love, and their love is measured by the degree of the love with which they

have been loved. And here's what we know about God's love for us: "I am sure that neither death nor life, nor angels nor rulers, nor things present nor things to come, nor powers, nor height nor depth, nor anything else in all creation, will be able to separate us from the love of God in Christ Jesus our Lord" (Romans 8:38–39).

You can't stop love.

THE UNREST OF THIS WEARY WORLD IS

ITS UNVOICED CRY AFTER GOD.

THEODORE T. MUNGER

The World Is a Lot More Dangerous Than I Thought It Was

I am sending you out as sheep in the midst of wolves,
so be wise as serpents and innocent as doves.

Matthew 10:16

Monday morning is often depressing for me. But it's not depressing because I have to go to work.

It's depressing because I have to pray.

At Key Life we keep a list of people who have written, called, or e-mailed us, asking us to pray for their needs . . . and that list is updated every Monday. A number of staff and volunteers pray, and I'm one of them.

The list is quite long (often a couple hundred items), and it simply gives the first name of the person who requested prayer and a short statement about the need. Let me share with you some of the items on this morning's list:

- . . . just discovered lung cancer; doctor doesn't give much hope
- . . . husband whose wife left him and their three small children
- . . . sexually abused

... husband has been unfaithful and says he doesn't love her

... her baby just died, and she can't go on

... trying to deal with drug and alcohol addiction

... soldier in Iraq asks prayers for his wife and three children back home

... mother is dying

... just been diagnosed with MS

... pastor whose ministry has been destroyed by his sin

... single mother who lost her job

... was raped and is trying to deal with the pain and shame

... son has not spoken to him in more than four years (trying reconciliation)

... husband is in hospital and dying ... no place to turn

... son died in Afghanistan

... arrested, and the charges are false

... lost his home in the hurricane

... living in fear and can't sleep

... that her son will allow her to see her grandchildren

... dealing with divorce

... homeless couple with small child

... wife committed suicide

It goes on and on. By the time I finish praying, I'm depressed.

Did you read about the Romanian prisoner, Pavel M, who

filed a paper to sue God for crimes against his person? He claimed that his baptism was a pact he made with God in which God pledged to protect him. God had not followed through with his side of the bargain, so Pavel brought suit.

We, of course, would not file suit against God. That's silly. Whom are you going to get for a lawyer, and how will you get God to show up for the trial? But I can understand Pavel. I might try a lawsuit too if I knew God wouldn't strike me dead.

I have a book in my library that promises those who read it a way to have a "victorious and abundant life." That makes me wince, and it also makes me wonder where in the world the author has been living. I hope he reads this chapter. The fact is, a "victorious Christian life" is sometimes no more than keeping your nose above water. The fact is, the "abundant Christian life" is sometimes no more than getting by without messing it up so badly that it can't be fixed.

> A "VICTORIOUS CHRISTIAN LIFE" IS SOMETIMES NO MORE THAN KEEPING YOUR NOSE ABOVE WATER.

Sometimes we forget that we aren't Home yet. When we forget that fact, our expectations far exceed what God has promised. I'm afraid that honest unbelievers wonder about us: they think we may have lost our minds. It's quite clear to anybody who cares to observe that Christians are sometimes in great pain, have doubts, wonder about meaning, and suffer about the same as everybody else.

What thinking Christian has not wondered with the psalmist why God treats so well those who aren't even God's friends? "For the wicked boasts of the desires of his soul, and the one greedy for gain curses and renounces the Lord. In the pride of his face the

wicked does not seek him; all his thoughts are, 'There is no God.' His ways prosper at all times" (Psalm 10:3–5). And what thinking Christian doesn't affirm Saint Teresa and her humorous but profound comment, "Lord, you would have more friends if you treated the ones you had a little better"?

Today, the day I write this chapter, I interviewed Dr. David Downing, author of *Into the Wardrobe: C. S. Lewis and the Narnia Chronicles*, on our talk show. He also has written several other books about Lewis, including an award-winning biography, *The Most Reluctant Convert*.

When I asked Downing why he was so enamored with C. S. Lewis, he explained that had been raised in a kind but very strict home, and when he got to college, he began to have doubts about his faith. Someone gave him Lewis's book *The Problem of Pain*, and Downing was astounded by the honesty with which Lewis opened that book. Lewis articulated the reality of what Downing was experiencing. The book began with a strong statement of the conviction Lewis once held: if there was a spirit behind the universe, it was an evil spirit.

It's easy to buy into a kind of dream-world faith in which God is explained, questions are answered, and pain is denied. But it's dangerous, because no one can explain God, some questions simply don't have answers, and a life without pain is impossible.

Consider Lewis's words, spoken in a time of war:

[War] makes death real to us: and that would have been regarded as one of its blessings by most of the great Christians of the past. They thought it good for us to be always aware of our mortality. I am inclined to think they were right. All the

animal life in us, all schemes of happiness that centered in this world, were always doomed to a final frustration. In ordinary times only a wise [person] can realize it. Now the stupidest of us knows. We see unmistakably the sort of universe in which we have all along been living, and must come to terms with it. If we had foolish un-Christian hopes about human culture, they are now shattered. If we thought we were building up a heaven on earth, if we looked for something that would turn the present world from a place of pilgrimage into a permanent city satisfying the soul . . . we are disillusioned, and not a moment too soon. But if we thought that for some souls, and at some times, the life of learning, humbly offered to God, was, in its own small way, one of the appointed approaches to the Divine reality and the Divine beauty which we hope to enjoy hereafter, we can think so still.[1]

A number of years ago I wrote a book titled *When Your Rope Breaks*. That book has been translated into several languages, and I still hear from people who say they were helped by it. I'm glad. The book was written for those who are going through hard times, and I stand by everything I wrote. Theologically and biblically, it was accurate and correct. In fact, it wasn't half bad.

The only problem is that the author was too young to even know that the truth he wrote was true. Now I know that what I wrote so many years ago is still true. There are, however, a number of additions that I would make to that book if I had the opportunity.

I have a friend who was in a car accident nearly forty years ago. As she pulled out of a parking space, another vehicle plowed into

the side of her car. Even after all these years, my friend says she sometimes braces herself when she pulls out of a parking space.

If you're into looking away from hard places of truth, you might want to skip over what follows. This is not going to be pretty. If you stay with me, I promise it will get better. Before we see the light, however, it's important to recognize the dark.

Over the years, since I wrote the book on broken ropes, I've noticed that I brace myself far more often than I did back then. Bracing oneself is the curse of experience.

THE WORLD IS ATTRACTIVE

I have to brace myself, because the world is far more attractive than I thought it was.

That truth may seem strange given what I wrote above. It seems a little strange to me too. I'm sort of like the man who wrote to the magazine subscription department: "When I subscribed a year ago, you stated that if I was not satisfied at the end of the year, I could have my money back. Well, I would like to have it back. On second thought, to save you the trouble, you may apply it to my next year's subscription."

Why would I be attracted to a dangerous world in which there is so much pain?

1. *I'm Attracted to the World because It's a Good Place to Sin*

The apostle John said that "what we will be has not yet appeared; but we know that when he appears we shall be like him" (1 John 3:2). That thrills me! That means the time is coming when I'm going to be like Jesus. I won't struggle with sin anymore; I won't

have to deal with my addictions; I won't have to face temptation. That is so good.

I don't like admitting this, though: part of me is quite anxious about heaven. The Gatlin Brothers used to sing a song about a wino choir: if there was no Mogen David (wine) in heaven, they didn't want to go. I smile at that, but I do understand. Alcohol isn't my problem, but I have some others I'm not ready to leave behind. If I can't be angry in heaven, I'm not sure I want to go. If I can't lust, gossip, or feel self-righteous in heaven, I'm not sure I want to go. If I can't get the praises of people in heaven and it all goes to God instead, I'm not sure I want to go. If I can't be the center of attention in heaven, I'm not sure I want to go.

2. I'm Attracted to the World because of My Stuff

Paul wrote to Timothy, "Those who desire to be rich fall into temptation, into a snare, into many senseless and harmful desires that plunge people into ruin and destruction. For the love of money is a root of all kinds of evils. It is through this craving that some have wandered away from the faith and pierced themselves with many pangs" (1 Timothy 6:9–10).

Money may not be your sin or addiction, but substitute yours for money in that text. Whatever you're attracted to more than Christ is dangerous.

It is said that John Wesley once was being led around a rich man's estate. The man showed Wesley the magnificent formal gardens that surrounded the estate, the stables, and the large mansion with its expensive furnishings and works of art. Wesley

reportedly said, "Ah, these are the things that make it hard for a man to die."

Comfort, sex, alcohol, drugs, religion, self-aggrandizement, someone you worship, a theological position you hold, or almost anything else that attracts you more than Christ is dangerous. It makes it hard to die.

The Jesus Movement of the sixties and seventies was a genuine spiritual awakening in America not altogether different from that of the Great Awakening in the eighteenth century. In the Jesus Movement, the lives of hundreds of thousands of young people were transformed, and we reap its benefits to this day.

At that time I was the pastor of a very formal and established Presbyterian church near Boston. When those freshly converted young people came into our church, everything changed—and it changed for the better. Our Sunday school grew, the congregation almost doubled, and we experienced a new life and vitality I've rarely seen in my ministry since.

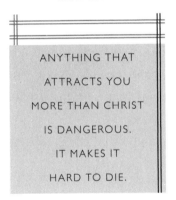

ANYTHING THAT
ATTRACTS YOU
MORE THAN CHRIST
IS DANGEROUS.
IT MAKES IT
HARD TO DIE.

I remember those young people, and even now I think of them with fondness—one young man in particular. Jamie had a ponytail, always wore jeans, and had a smile that would light up the world. He stayed in our church for a couple of years, teaching in the Sunday school, working in evangelism, and serving in any way he could. Then he decided to leave.

"Jamie," I said, "don't leave yet. I need you around here."

Jamie explained that he felt called to Colorado and that God had a place for him there. Nothing I could say would dissuade

him from leaving. I can close my eyes even now and see Jamie walking down the hill from the church with his backpack over his shoulders. I had hugged him and promised to pray for him. I'll never forget what he said.

"You'd like to leave too, wouldn't you?"

I allowed that I was a bit envious.

"But Steve, you can't leave because you can't get everything you have in a backpack. When you can do that, you'll be free."

That was more profound than even he knew. When I can get it all—my reputation, my stuff, my needs, my dreams, my heart—in my backpack, then I'll be free. It doesn't all fit there now, and that's the reason I'm attracted to the world.

I'm getting better. Jesus is still fond of me, and he's helping me deal with my attachments. But I'm not there yet, and sometimes the world is quite attractive because of those attachments.

3. I'm Attracted to the World because Dying Isn't an Altogether Happy Thought for Me

I know, I know. Jesus said that anyone who believed in him would never die (John 11:26). After his death, Jesus got up from a grave—and he said I could do that too. That gives me great hope, and I'm grateful for his promise.

Still, something in me rebels against my own death. While that something may be from God, telling me I wasn't created for death, it still gets to me. When I was younger, I thought death happened to other people, or at least that science would find a cure for death before I got there. I'm a lot older now, and having seen the deaths of so many I love, I've been faced with the awesome and fearful reality that the statistic is one out of one. I'm really not

going to get out of this thing alive. That makes me want to cling to the world for dear life. And that's dangerous.

THE WORLD IS NOT FAIR

I have to brace myself because the world isn't nearly as fair as I thought it was.

The world makes promises that are hard to ignore. Those promises don't sound like the "world" because they're often laced with "God words." But even though they sound religious, they aren't from him. The promises are from those who simply don't know what the Bible says. They say that if you're good, believe and trust in God, and read the Bible and pray, you have nothing to fear. When I was younger, I believed that. I might not have put it quite that way, but essentially, that was a basic philosophy in my life. What was I thinking?

I stopped believing in that when my brother died, my pastor got a divorce, my best friend—the godliest man I knew—was killed in an automobile accident, and a hurricane destroyed my house.

Jesus never lied to me, but the world did. Jesus said, "In the world you will have tribulation" (John 16:33). The world said I could be healthy, wealthy, and wise if I just exercised the right principles, was a good person, and put my faith in God. That's a lie. Oh, the people saying it didn't mean to lie. They wanted it to be true, they really believed it was true, and they taught that it was true. I did too. But it's still not true.

This is what is true: every day the world rolls over on top of a Christian who was just sitting on top of it. As I write this, a woman in our church choir is dying of cancer. They say she won't

make it through the day. She sang in our worship team, she loved God, and we prayed for her. We prayed hard. But she's still dying, and that bothers me.

The world is a dangerous place because it isn't fair. It isn't fair to your unbelieving friends, and it isn't fair for Christians either. As attractive as they are, the promises simply aren't true, and you have to brace yourself against that reality.

There are, of course, promises the world makes that aren't particular to believers. There's the promise of pornography, the promise of wealth, the promise of addictions, the promise of another spouse who better fits your needs, the promise of education, the promise of fame, the promise of health from a gym or a vitamin, the promise of political power. There isn't enough room here to deal with each of these, but all of them promise to deliver very attractive paybacks.

Those are lies too.

THE WORLD IS NOT SAFE

I have to brace myself because the world isn't as safe as I thought it was.

I referred to this fact above, but let's get a bit more specific. We live in a culture that is obsessed with safety. I recently read a report that gave an astonishing statistic about the number of people who die from eating improper foods. The person relating the statistic seemed to suggest that if you eat properly, you won't die. What was that person thinking? Whether or not we eat properly, we're going to die.

I lived in the perfect neighborhood once. We loved it. The whole development had a white picket fence around it, the homes

were all "country," and there was a clubhouse with a pool and all kinds of recreational amenities. A lake in our community gave people a nice place to fish and sail. The telephone and electrical wiring was underground so the beauty of our community wouldn't be marred by the ugliness of utility poles. Our neighbors were nice, our roads were clean and lined with big trees, and our houses and yards were well maintained. The police regularly patrolled our community, and we always felt safe. And the climate was just about perfect. My wife and I often took evening walks, thankful that we lived in that kind of community.

Then a hurricane blew through, and the entire community looked as though someone mowed it down with a gigantic lawnmower—houses, picket fences, clubhouse, trees, and all. Not a single two-story house remained a two-story house. Many of the one-story houses were totally destroyed, and not a single home remained intact.

After my first automobile accident, I found out that the roads weren't as safe as I thought they were. After my brother died, I found out that life wasn't as safe as I thought it was. After my first hurricane, I discovered that the world wasn't as safe as I thought it was either.

Someone sent me a story for my birthday. Let me share it with you:

Once upon a time, in the land of fuzzle-wuzzle, there lived a merry band of teddy bears. All day long they'd laugh and frolic in the fields and valleys. Every evening they'd sit down to a big banquet of honey muffins and oatmeal. After singing a round of silly songs, they'd get all comfy and cozy and

fall asleep beneath the magical lollipop tree. This went on for years and years. . . .

. . . then the battle of Armageddon broke out and they all died. The end.

Hey, do I look like Mother Goose? Deal with it!

Happy Birthday!

No matter what we do to try to protect ourselves and those we love, or the things we love; however effective those efforts are—or are not—it's clear that the world is not a safe place. The question for us is, how will we deal with it?

Perhaps the answer is in how we think about the world. Which brings me to my final point.

THE WORLD IS NOT GOING TO LAST

I have to brace myself because the world isn't going to last the way I thought it would.

The Bible says, "The present form of this world is passing away" (1 Corinthians 7:31). Nothing we can feel, touch, or see right now is going to last. We can dance, rearrange the furniture, enjoy the meals, have parties, and celebrate; but if we're doing it on the *Titanic*, it's all simply an illusion of permanence.

The problem is that there is a conspiracy in which we all participate. We talk as if nothing will change. We build houses and churches, create monuments, establish institutions, and produce wealth . . . all in order to maintain the illusion that all of it, and we ourselves, are permanent. We embalm and dress up the corpse, but it's still a corpse. We paint over and repair our crumbling buildings, but even with our maintenance, in time they will crumble.

Plastic surgery, hair transplants, liposuction, cosmetics, brushed and enhanced photographs, energy pills, and vitamins are all a part of this conspiracy to make us think this all will last. Nothing will. Nothing is permanent.

Jesus told a story about a successful farmer who was hardworking and frugal. He was so successful that he had to tear down his barns and build bigger ones. The farmer sat on his front porch, looking over all that he created, and said to himself, "'You have ample goods laid up for many years; relax, eat, drink, be merry.'

"But God said to him, 'Fool! This night your soul is required of you, and the things you have prepared, whose will they be?'" (Luke 12:19–20).

That is a good question. Whose will they be? Maybe the farmer's goods would be passed along to his children and, when they died, to their children. Eventually, though, those things would be nobody's. Eventually, the Bible says, all those things will fade away into nothingness.

> THOSE WHO SAY JESUS IS ALL THEY NEED NEVER KNOW THAT JESUS IS ALL THEY NEED UNTIL JESUS IS ALL THEY'VE GOT.

I hate change. I hate any kind of change. When I was younger, I could maintain the illusion that things would be permanent. As I grow older, it's not so easy. Someone has said that you know you're getting old when you get down on the floor to retrieve something and ask yourself, *Is there anything else I can do while I'm down here?* Or, you know you're getting old when a pretty girl passes by and your pacemaker opens the garage door. Or, you know you're getting old when hardly anything in your body works, and what does work hurts.

Our humor is often truer than our philosophies. We work hard to maintain the illusion of permanence . . . but our nervous laughter betrays the truth. We know. We try to ignore it, to cover it, and to pretend . . . but we know. Nothing lasts.

That's bad.

No, actually, that's good. If you're still with me after all this doom and gloom, let me give you some good news. If what I've written in this chapter is true (and it is), then why do you care? Even more to the point, why do you believe, and why do you hope? One would think that the facts—once stated and faced—would lead to nothing but hopelessness, meaninglessness, and unbelief. "For men must work, and women must weep, And the sooner it's over, the sooner to sleep."[2]

I don't want this to be just another pious religious cliché, but the older I get, the more real Jesus has become and the less real, or even important, this dangerous world is. Someone has said that those who say Jesus is all they need never know that Jesus is all they need until Jesus is all they've got. When Jesus is all they've got, then they know that Jesus is all they need.

When I find that the world is far more dangerous than I thought it was, something in me says that it isn't supposed to be that way. Something in my genes says that there is a paradise that has been lost, a security that has been shattered, and a reality that is missing. A dangerous and fleeting world makes me look beyond it.

The understanding that the world is dangerous comes with age, with sin, with fear, and with shattered dreams. With all of that, however, comes also a yearning for something more. If this world were less dangerous, less fleeting, and more secure, I may

never have found the only place that is more secure than the world is dangerous.

I just saw a picture of a man wearing a T-shirt that read, "I'm a bomb technician. If you see me running, try to keep up." In other words, a bomb is getting ready to explode, I can't fix it, and I'm running as fast as I can to get away from it. So keep up.

In this world there's only one safe place to run. I told you earlier what Jesus said about tribulation: that in the world—a dangerous world—we will have tribulation. That's a cold, hard fact. Deal with it.

But that wasn't all he said.

What else did Jesus say?

"I have said these things to you, that in me you may have peace. In the world you will have tribulation. But take heart; I have overcome the world" (John 16:33).

The "bomb" has exploded.

But I know where to run.

SOMETIMES PROVIDENCES, LIKE HEBREW
LETTERS, MUST BE READ BACKWARD.

John Flavel

THINGS WILL WORK OUT A LOT BETTER THAN I THOUGHT THEY WOULD

*We know that for those who love God
all things work together for good.*

ROMANS 8:28

WE WON!

Well, that's rather crass. It wasn't really a matter of winning and losing. However, when American ecclesiastical history is written about the twentieth and early twenty-first centuries, one of the great surprises will be the resurgence of evangelicalism. I'm an evangelical, and it did feel like we won.

No one would have expected it.

When I decided to become an evangelical, it wasn't a very popular thing to do.[1] In fact, it was ecclesiastical suicide. My friends thought I had lost my mind, and those who weren't friends said they always knew something was wrong with me. I can remember the pastor of a prominent church in the city where I ministered crossing over to the other side of the street so he wouldn't have to speak to me.

I'm thankful that I made the decision when it wasn't popular. Knowing me, my motivations would have been less pure if I had waited until we "won." When I decided to become an evangelical,

almost all of our churches were small, our seminaries were considered second-rate, and our books and magazines were only read by a small group of "Bible thumpers" who were, as a prominent reporter said, "uneducated and easily led."

I graduated from a mainline "liberal" graduate school of theology, where the words *evangelical* and *scholar* could not be used in the same sentence. In those days we considered evangelicals obscurant, shallow, and unsophisticated.

When *Christianity Today*—a magazine designed to stand for orthodox theology—was founded by Billy Graham and a number of other well-known evangelicals, it was distributed free to pastors and theology students. I remember bound stacks of those magazines left in the seminary lobby. They were never opened and never read. We, of course, read *Christian Century*, the liberal magazine of note, and we sometimes made fun of that "other" magazine.

My decision to become an evangelical was a matter of conscience and need. I was then serving as the student pastor of a small church on Cape Cod. It had become quite apparent that I didn't have much to say of any worth or at least anything that made much difference to people who were sinners—afraid, wounded, and empty. To this day I don't understand how a theological liberal can be a pastor. If you don't believe the doctrines of Scripture, why would you want to be a pastor? That seems insane to me. Anyway, at that time I was, in fact, thinking about leaving.

It's a long story, and the details aren't relevant here, but my move toward evangelicalism involved God's miraculous intervention in my life through the healing of our daughter, some evangelical friends who were intellectuals, and some dear people who loved me and prayed for me.

Bottom line, I joined the "other side."

When I joined the evangelical wing of the church, I knew that I probably would never serve a big church, write books anyone would ever read, or be accepted or liked by those who "mattered" in the American church in general and my denomination in particular. But it didn't matter. Jesus still loved me, and that was enough. He had forgiven, accepted, and called me, and I didn't care where we went or what we did as long as he went with me.

Then a funny thing happened on the way to ecclesiastical oblivion. We won!

To this day I'm not sure what happened. (A number of books have been written on the phenomenal evangelical growth.[2]) Some of it had to do with the Jesus Movement, some of it happened because of the media, and some of it happened because people grew tired of religious platitudes and shallow unbelief cloaked in "God words." But when the history of evangelicalism is written, it will include a great number of faithful Christians who kept "the faith that was once for all delivered to the saints" (Jude 1:3) through some lean years of scorn, rejection, and dismissal.

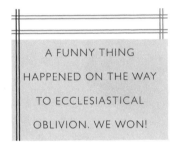

A FUNNY THING HAPPENED ON THE WAY TO ECCLESIASTICAL OBLIVION. WE WON!

I woke up one day to find that evangelical colleges, seminaries, and churches were showing explosive growth. Evangelical books were becoming bestsellers, and *Christianity Today* was the most successful magazine in the history of Christianity. I heard about John Lennon, Bob Dylan, Keith Richards, and Bono announcing they had become Christians.

And all of a sudden I found myself on the "winning side" of the ecclesiastical battle.

I'm not even sure that "winning" was a good thing for the church, but I do know that it was a good thing for me. It meant that what I thought would be a harmful career decision so many years ago, in fact, turned out to be a smart move. I preach in mega-churches, I write books that people read, I have a successful media ministry, and I teach at a prominent seminary—one of the largest in the world. None of that should have happened. For a number of reasons, things really did work out a lot better than I thought they would.

They generally do for believers. No, I haven't lost my mind. I know that things don't always work out well. I know that stuff happens and that this isn't a safe world. I know things often go wrong even when we do right, and some problems have no good solutions. I know about cancer, accidents, and Down syndrome kids. Generally, though, for believers, things do work out better than one might think. Let's look at a few reasons why.

TRUTH

Things work out better because of truth.

Jesus said, "If you abide in my word, you are truly my disciples, and you will know the truth, and the truth will set you free" (John 8:31–32). Paul wrote, "Stand therefore, having fastened on the belt of truth" (Ephesians 6:14). John wrote of Christ's coming that, while Moses brought the Law, "truth came through Jesus Christ" (John 1:17).

Have you noticed some of the silly things some people believe? Some believe that if you get a crystal, join a lot of people on

a mountaintop in Arizona, hold hands, and sound out together, "*Ohmmmmm,*" you'll end world hunger and bring world peace. Others believe that human nature is basically good, so they don't lock their doors. Some think it doesn't matter what you believe as long as you believe something and are sincere about it. I know people who believe you can cure cancer with a spoonful of honey and others who think the world owes them and live their lives as victims. There are even people who call good evil and evil good and who think it doesn't matter what you do as long as you don't hurt anybody.

I'm not that dumb. Well, maybe I am, but God has graciously revealed the truth to me, and it is surprising how often I appear smart and things seem to work out better than I thought they would . . . simply because I know that truth.

I have a friend who, before every important, right, and controversial decision I've made over the last twenty-five years, said to me, "Steve, if you do right, it will come out right." He is, I think, looking at the long view and making the point that ultimately no good deed, no wise decision, and no right action will be lost. He's talking about a God who is sovereign over everything and who will ultimately balance all the books and settle all the accounts.

I understand that, but I also believe things will "come out right" before they come out right in the end. I believe that you usually do receive what you give, that you'll be judged by the same judgment with which you judge others, and that bread cast on waters really does come back to you. I believe that if you exalt yourself, generally you will be humbled, and if you humble yourself, generally you will be exalted. I think that if you do to others

what you would have them do to you—if you go the second mile and are kind—there is a great payback in this life.

Some Christians believe they're called to go through hell in order to get to heaven. They also think unbelievers go through heaven in order to get to hell. In other words, they think things are really hard for them now, but later they will have a dynamite "retirement"—and that those of you who don't believe will have a good time now, but "you'll get yours" one of these days.

That is neurotic. Of course there are hard things about following Christ, and there really is a heaven. But could it be, do you think, that maybe a Christian, because he or she knows the truth, will get a bit of heaven before going there?

If you're reading this book and you aren't a Christian, let me give you some good advice. If you want to be happier, to have things go better, and to be more at peace than you are now, read the Bible and do what it says as best you can. That won't be easy because some of it won't make sense to you, and you may not have a lot of help. But if you're disciplined enough and stay with it, you'll be able to do some of it.

You say, "But I don't believe the Bible." That's OK; I'm not your mother. Just as an experiment, do what I've suggested. You'll be surprised at how much better things work out.

LOVE

Things also work out better because of love.

Jesus said, "As the Father has loved me, so have I loved you. Abide in my love" (John 15:9). Paul said it's the love of Christ that controls us (see 2 Corinthians 5:14) and that nothing will ever be able to separate us from the love of Christ (see Romans 8:38–39).

I already spent time on this subject, and I don't want to overdo it, but I'm always surprised by God's love for me. It's his default position. I'd like to give you a list of my lovable qualities, the ones that attract God to me, but I can't think of any. There really is something unreasonable about God's love for his children.

The man or woman who isn't surprised by the love of God has never experienced the love of God and has no idea how little he or she deserves it. Christ really did die for the ungodly.

I don't know about you, but I'm attracted to people who like me. I hate to admit that, but it's true. God's love does not discriminate, and mine does. I get thousands of letters in my line of work, and many of them are critical and angry, but I get a number of affirming and encouraging ones too. I answer both kinds, but the ones that affirm me receive longer, kinder, more loving answers, because I'm attracted to people who like me.

> THE MAN OR WOMAN WHO ISN'T SURPRISED BY THE LOVE OF GOD HAS NEVER EXPERIENCED THE LOVE OF GOD AND HAS NO IDEA HOW LITTLE HE OR SHE DESERVES IT.

Jesus likes me big time, and my default position is to run to him. I always think he'll be angry, tell me he's had it with me, and tell me to become a Buddhist instead. But that has never happened. And it's always surprising.

Our family has always had German shepherds. Thor is the fifth shepherd in our family. The other four are now in heaven, and if you don't believe that dogs go to heaven, keep your spurious theological views to yourself.

I really do love Thor, but I still haven't gotten over the death

of our last shepherd, Quincy the Wonder Dog. I guess I loved him because, when he was a puppy, they were going to put him down because of his bad hips. The breeder from whom we bought Quincy said she would give us our money back but that it was unconscionable for him to be allowed to breed. So, with the promise that he would be "fixed," we let Quincy live. I guess you could say I saved his life.

To alleviate the hip problem, our veterinarian said Quincy's hips could be removed, and cartilage would grow in their place. He said Quincy would be "almost normal," and he was almost normal for twelve years. The procedure to make Quincy almost normal was extremely painful, and I remember picking him up at the vet's office after the surgery. I had to carry him to the car, and my every movement elicited a whimper from Quincy.

I took him to our family room and laid him on a blanket in the corner. I was sure Quincy would never want anything to do with me again, given that I was the one who had taken him to the vet and thus was responsible for all of his pain. If I could win back Quincy's trust, I was sure it would take a long time.

I sat down in my easy chair and started reading the paper. After about five minutes, I felt something move the paper. I looked down, and it was Quincy. He laid his head on my lap.

I prayed, "Oh God, let me be that way with you. There is so much pain, but let me always come to you and put my head on your lap the way Quincy has just done with me."

One more story about Quincy. (If you aren't a "dog person," you probably just want me to move on, but if you know and love dogs, you'll like this story.)

It was many years later when our vet informed us that Quincy

wouldn't live much longer. We took Quincy home from that appointment, and I was out in the backyard playing with him. Quincy loved chasing and retrieving anything I threw—a Frisbee, a stick, or a ball. So I threw a stick, and as best as he could, Quincy ran to retrieve it. Just as he picked it up, his back went out for the final time. Do you know what he did? He pulled himself with his front elbows across the yard to bring the stick to me.

I prayed, "Oh, God, let me be that way with you."

Quincy loved being with me more than anything else. When I came home, he waited by the door to greet me. When I left, he stood by the door to watch me go. No matter what my mood, he just loved to be around me.

Now, as some of you may know, German shepherds can be pretty scary dogs. We locked the doors in our house to protect the thieves, not our stuff. Our German shepherds always protected our stuff and our family. If you'd met Quincy, you might have been a bit wary, because he was quite a large German shepherd. Quincy looked dangerous, but he wasn't dangerous at all. He was the most gentle and loving dog you would ever meet, and he would run to anybody just to have his ears scratched.

Quincy was a loved dog, and he became a loving dog. When you meet a mean dog, you can almost always assume it has a mean owner. A dog who is loved, however, is a loving dog.

Human beings are like that too. I've walked with God for so long, have run to him so much, and have been loved by him so deeply that I am a far more loving person than I would be if I had never known him. His love has become the defining factor in my life, and he has loved me into becoming a loving person. One can't love until one has been loved—and then only to the degree

to which one has been loved. Jesus said there was no greater love than the love manifested when a man died for his friends.

Then he called me his friend.

I don't think God has called me to discipline, to condemn, or to judge people. I tell them the truth, but I'm not in the business of playing God. He told me to love, and insofar as I allow God to love me, I'm able to love others. The great thing about that is, when you love people, they love you back. They also help you, cover for you, and encourage you to be better. That's why things have worked out a lot better than I thought they would. It's because of love.

GRACE

Things work out better because of grace.

In the first chapter of John cited earlier, John said that the Law came through Moses and that, not only did truth come through Jesus, but grace came through him too (see John 1:17). Paul wrote, "But the free gift is not like the trespass. For if many died through one man's trespass [i.e., Adam's sin], much more have the grace of God and the free gift by the grace of that one man Jesus Christ abounded for many. . . . Where sin increased, grace abounded all the more" (Romans 5:15–20). He wrote in Ephesians 2:8–9, "By grace you have been saved through faith. And this is not your own doing; it is the gift of God, not a result of works, so that no one may boast."

My pastor, Pete Alwinson, has the best definition of grace: "Grace," he says, "is doing good for someone when there is no compelling reason to do so and every reason not to." That's it. That is what God has done and continues to do for me.

Art DeMoss, the founder of the Arthur S. DeMoss foundation, was an acquaintance of mine and one of the most effective evangelists I've ever known. A flight attendant friend of mine met him once on a flight. She told me, "I'm a Christian, but I had the feeling that if I had not already been one, I would have become one before the flight ended." Art loved Christ, he loved people, and he loved life.

Anyway, whenever someone asked Art how he was doing, he answered with his standard response: "I'm doing a lot better than I deserve." That's what grace does. Grace is a gift of a lot more than the recipient deserves.

Groucho Marx once said that he would never join a club that would have him as a member. I sort of feel that way about the church. It's insane, what I do. As I can't but help point out again, I—who ran away from kindergarten—now teach at a graduate school of theology. I struggle with sin as much as anybody I know, and yet I'm a preacher. I graduated fourth from the bottom of a large high school, yet you are now reading a book I wrote. I hate religion as much as anybody I know, and now I'm a religious professional. Not only that. I have enough money to pay

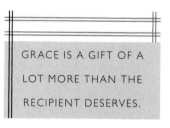

GRACE IS A GIFT OF A LOT MORE THAN THE RECIPIENT DESERVES.

the mortgage, and I have a beautiful wife and wonderful daughters and granddaughters. I drive, as I told you, a brand-new hybrid car, can afford to take my wife to dinner at almost any restaurant, and own the computer at which I am now typing.

Why is that? Is it because I'm smart, good, and wise? No.

God is gracious, and everything I am, do, and have is a gift of his grace. If I received his justice, I'd be dead.

Earlier on, I shared with you a partial quote from my friend Jack Miller. Now let me share with you all of what he said. Jack used to say that the whole Bible can be summed up in two statements: (1) Cheer up: you're a lot worse than you think you are. (2) Cheer up: God's grace is a lot bigger than you think it is.

Grace is the reason things work out a lot better than I thought they would. It's because things work out a lot better than I deserve.

CLOUT IN HIGH PLACES

Things work out better because I have clout in some very high places.

Let me share with you an amazing statement made by Jesus: "Truly, truly, I say to you, whoever believes in me will also do the works that I do; and greater works than these will he do, because I am going to the Father. Whatever you ask in my name, this I will do, that the Father may be glorified in the Son. If you ask me anything in my name, I will do it" (John 14:12–14).

That kind of statement makes us uncomfortable because it speaks to a possibility that doesn't often connect with our experience. But anyone who teaches that text in a way to make Jesus say something other than what he said is wrong.

From an understanding of the whole counsel of God, the Bible, it's obvious that Jesus was not giving us carte blanche to do spiritual magic tricks. But Jesus did tell us that we have a connection to God, enabling us to go to him with any need and any problem. Someone once asked G. Campbell Morgan, the great Bible teacher, if it was OK to go to God with little things. He answered, "Madam, do you know of anything that isn't little to God?"

As I mentioned, I've interviewed best-selling author Anne Lamott on a couple of occasions. While I don't agree with her politics or her theology, I don't think I've ever met anyone more authentic or who loves Jesus more. The first time I interviewed Anne, it was a phone interview taped from a Miami studio. She was late for an appointment, and it was obvious that she didn't want to be interviewed. Anne asked if I could keep it short. I told her that I would do that, but I needed to tell her something before we began.

"Anne," I asked, "do you know those fundamentalist types, the Bible thumpers, the ones who are often condemning?"

Anne said she did, and the way she said it gave me an indication that her experience had not been altogether that positive.

"Well," I confessed, "I'm one of them. But before you jump to conclusions, I want you to know that I loved your book, have given it to all my friends, and have probably sold more copies than you have."

(A smart move. Authors like people who like their books.)

That interview turned out to be a great one—in fact, it went on for some time. I actually had trouble bringing it to a close. Just before our conversation ended, this is what Anne said: "Steve, do you know what we would do if we ever met?"

"No, Anne," I said. "What would we do if we met?"

"We would hold hands and tell each other stories about Jesus."

Earlier I told you about Anne Lamott's three kinds of prayer: "God, help me right now!" "Wow!" and "Thank you, God." Well, there isn't a Christian reading this who can't identify with those words. We've all been in pits so deep that only God could get us out, in sin so bad that no one else would ever forgive, and in

pain so heartbreaking that no doctor could fix. We have all called out to God, "Help me!" And we have all—not all the time, but sometimes—seen God do exactly what we asked. And we've said, "Wow!" and then thanked him.

That is why things will work out a lot better than I thought they would.

HEAVEN

Finally, things work out better because of heaven.

Jesus said, "I am the resurrection and the life. Whoever believes in me, though he die, yet shall he live, and everyone who lives and believes in me shall never die" (John 11:25–26). He promised the thief who died on the cross next to him, "Today you will be with me in Paradise" (Luke 23:43). Paul said that whether we live or die, we're the Lord's (see Romans 14:8). And when we were no longer in our bodies, we will be present before God (see 2 Corinthians 5:8).

In other words, even if things don't work out as well as we thought they would or should, the story isn't over. Things *will* work out fine. A missionary complained that no one cared, because when he came home from the mission field, nobody was there to meet him. "Son," God told him, "you aren't Home yet."

We aren't Home yet, you know. As an old guy beginning to "cram for finals," I've discovered that I really don't have to cram. It has all been done for me, and in the end, I'll be Home. The angels may blush, but they will sing, and I'll be welcomed.

The late Peter Marshall, chaplain to the U.S. Senate, said that when he died, he would stand before God, and all his sins would be read out. Then, just when God was ready to pronounce

judgment, Jesus would put his hand on Marshall's shoulder and say, "It's all right, Father. I took care of Peter's sins on the cross." Then he would be welcomed Home.

During the time I've been writing this chapter, I received an e-mail informing me that the grandmother of one of our former employees, Dawn Givens, had died. It reminded me of the story Dawn told me years ago, when her grandfather died. He'd long been sick, and it had been a difficult time for the family.

Dawn's grandmother, of course, had been devastated by the loss. Some family members arranged to take turns staying with her during the long and lonely nights following her husband's death. One night her great-grandson Jay ("Jay Bird") stayed with her. He was a small boy then, perhaps three or four years old. For purposes of this story, you need to know that Jay called his great-grandmother "Me-Mommy" and his great-grandfather "Paw-Paw."

> "IT'S ALL RIGHT, FATHER. I TOOK CARE OF PETER'S SINS ON THE CROSS."

The night Jay Bird stayed with his great-grandmother, she said prayers with him and then tucked him into bed. "Me-Mommy," Jay said, "do you know what I'm going to do?"

"No, Jay Bird. What are you going to do?"

"I'm going to pray that God will let me dream about Paw-Paw tonight."

"That would be nice," she said, turning off the light.

Jay had only known his great-grandfather when the elderly man was sick. In fact, Jay had never seen his "Paw-Paw" not in a wheelchair.

The next morning Jay's great-grandmother came into his room to find Jay jumping up and down on his bed. She asked him why he was so happy. Jay said that he had dreamed of Paw-Paw. Jay said he had seen Paw-Paw walking and that he (Jay) had run up to him, and his great-grandfather picked him up and hugged him.

"How did he look?" she asked.

"Fine," he said.

"No, Jay," she said, "I mean, did he look sick?"

"No! He didn't look sick. He was new!"

At times I have despaired, doubting that all this—this messy, dangerous, up-and-down life—could ever end well. What was I thinking?

Things are going to work out a lot better than I thought they would.

We're going to be new!

NOTES

CHAPTER 2: Jesus Is a Lot More Radical Than I Thought He Was

1. Albert Schweitzer, *The Quest of the Historical Jesus,* ed. John Bowden (Minneapolis: Augsburg Fortress Press, 2001).

CHAPTER 3: The Holy Spirit Is Working in a Lot More Places Than I Thought He Was

1. Steve Brown, *Follow the Wind* (Grand Rapids: Baker Books, 1999).

2. If you are interested in pursuing some of H. R. Rookmaaker's thoughts on this subject, let me suggest his book *The Creative Gift: Essays on Art and the Christian Life* (Crossway Books, 1981).

3. Henry P. Van Dusen, *Spirit, Son and Father* (New York: Charles Scribner's Sons, 1958), 25.

4. Reggie M. Kidd, *With One Voice: Discovering Christ's Song in Our Worship* (Grand Rapids: Baker Books, 2005).

5. William D. Romanowski, *Eyes Wide Open: Looking for God in Popular Culture* (Grand Rapids: Brazos Press, 2001), 13–14.

6. Leland Ryken, *The Liberated Imagination* (Wheaton, Ill.: Harold Shaw Publishers, 1989), 166.

7. Don Richardson, *Eternity in Their Hearts* (Ventura, Calif.: Regal Books, 1984).

CHAPTER 4: The Bible Reveals a Lot More Than I Thought It Did

1. Émile Cailliet, *Journey into Light* (Grand Rapids: Zondervan Publishers, 1968).

2. Arthur Bennett, ed., *The Valley of Vision: A Collection of Puritan Prayers and Devotions* (Edinburgh: The Banner of Truth, 2002), 150–51.

3. Richard Pratt, *He Gave Us Stories* (Phillipsburg, N.J.: P & R Publishing, 1990).

CHAPTER 5: The Battle Is a Lot More Supernatural Than I Thought It Was

1. John White, *The Fight* (Downers Grove, Ill.: InterVarsity Press, 1978), 12.

2. Anne Lamott, *Traveling Mercies: Some Thoughts on Faith* (New York: Pantheon Books, 1999).

CHAPTER 6: People Are a Lot Worse Than I Thought They Were

1. Deborah Layton, *Seductive Poison: A Jonestown Survivor's Story of Life and Death in the Peoples Temple* (New York: Anchor Books, 1999), 4–5.

2. Brennan Manning, *The Wisdom of Tenderness* (New York: HarperSanFrancisco, 2002), 62.

CHAPTER 7: PEOPLE ARE A LOT BETTER THAN I THOUGHT THEY WERE

1. Richard Pratt, *Designed for Dignity: What God Has Made It Possible for You to Be* (Phillipsburg, N.J.: P & R Publishing, 1993), 50.

2. Spencer Lewerenz and Barbara Nicolosi, eds., *Behind the Screen: Hollywood Insiders on Faith, Film, and Culture* (Grand Rapids: Baker Books, 2005), 8–9.

CHAPTER 8: SELF-RIGHTEOUSNESS IS A LOT MORE DANGEROUS THAN I THOUGHT IT WAS

1. Calvin Miller, *The Singer Trilogy* (Downers Grove, Ill.: InterVarsity Press, 1975), 121.

CHAPTER 9: OBEDIENCE IS A LOT MORE DIFFICULT THAN I THOUGHT IT WAS

1. Martin Luther, quoted by C. F. W. Walther in "The Proper Distinction Between Law and Gospel" (lecture, originally published by Concordia Publishing House, 1929, now in public domain), http://lutherantheology.com/walther/LG/index.html.

2. Martin Luther, quoted in CEP Online, http://cep.anglican.ca/community/viewtopic.php?t=371&highlight=&sid=7c7f4a60ea9cd3de480212805d918d8f.

3. Donald Miller, *Blue Like Jazz: Nonreligious Thoughts on Christian Spirituality* (Nashville: Thomas Nelson Publishers, 2003).

CHAPTER 10: LOVE IS A LOT STRONGER THAN I THOUGHT IT WAS

1. Stephen J. Nichols, *Martin Luther: A Guided Tour of His Life and Thought* (Phillipsburg, N.J.: P & R Publishing, 2002), 50.

2. Ibid.

3. C. S. Lewis, *The Four Loves* (New York: Harvest Books, 1971).

CHAPTER 11: THE WORLD IS A LOT MORE DANGEROUS THAN I THOUGHT IT WAS

1. C. S. Lewis, "Learning in War-Time" (sermon, Oxford, 1939).

2. Charles Kingsley, "The Three Fishers," Representative Poetry Online, University of Toronto, http://rpo.library.utoronto.ca/poem/1164.html.

CHAPTER 12: THINGS WILL WORK OUT A LOT BETTER THAN I THOUGHT THEY WOULD

1. *Evangelical* is from a Latin word taken from Greek. It means "good news." As I use it here, I mean those who have a conservative/orthodox theology. Evangelicals accept the full authority of the Bible and center on the doctrine of salvation by faith in Christ alone. Evangelicals take a variety of theological positions. My particular view is called Reformed, referring to the doctrines of the Protestant Reformation.

2. For example, Dean Kelley's book *Why Conservative Churches Are Growing* (New York: Harper & Row, 1972) and David Shiflett's book *Exodus: Why Americans Are Fleeing Liberal Churches for Conservative Christianity* (New York: Sentinel Publishers, 2005).